Ginn and Company

Oriental Studies

A Selection of the Papers Read before the Oriental Club of Philadelphia 1888-1894

Ginn and Company

Oriental Studies
A Selection of the Papers Read before the Oriental Club of Philadelphia 1888-1894

ISBN/EAN: 9783337277673

Printed in Europe, USA, Canada, Australia, Japan

Cover: Foto ©Suzi / pixelio.de

More available books at **www.hansebooks.com**

Oriental Studies

A SELECTION OF THE PAPERS

READ BEFORE

The Oriental Club of Philadelphia

1888-1894

———

BOSTON
GINN & COMPANY
1894

THE present volume is issued by the Oriental Club of Philadelphia, to mark the successful termination of the first five years of its existence. It contains a selection of the papers prepared by the members for the monthly meetings; and in laying before a larger audience of scholars these results of studies conducted in various fields, the Club hopes to make a modest contribution to Oriental philology and archæology.

The papers are published in the order in which they were received by the Publication Committee.

Each author contributing to this volume assumes the responsibility for his views.

Philadelphia, May, 1894.

(3)

CONTENTS.

(5)

6 CONTENTS.

THE ORIENTAL CLUB OF PHILADELPHIA.

BY THE SECRETARY.

THE Oriental Club, of Philadelphia, was organized April 30th, 1888, at an informal meeting held at the house of Mr. Talcott Williams, in response to a circular letter in which those invited "were requested to co-operate in forming an Oriental Society in Philadelphia, that shall bring together those interested in the several fields of Oriental study, for the interchange of ideas, and the encouragement of Oriental research." This invitation, signed Henry Clay Trumbull, Benjamin Smith Lyman, John P. Peters, Morris Jastrow, Jr., Herman V. Hilprecht, Edward W. Hopkins, Talcott Williams and Stewart Culin, was very generally accepted, the following persons being present at the meeting :

Tatsui Baba,	Stewart Culin,
George Dana Boardman,	Joseph F. Garrison,
M. W. Easton,	Herman V. Hilprecht,
J. Rendel Harris,	Morris Jastrow, Jr.
Edward W. Hopkins,	Benj. Smith Lyman,
Philip H. Law,	Isaac Myer,
E. Y. McCauley,	R. W. Rogers,
John P. Peters,	Mayer Sulzberger,
John Stronach,	Talcott Williams,

Henry Clay Trumbull.

Letters were read from the Rev. Dr. Corcoran, of St. Charles' Seminary, Overbrook, William Goodell and Paul Haupt and Cyrus Adler, expressing an interest in the proposed Society. After a general discussion of the advisability and objects of the proposed Society, a committee was appointed to prepare a form of organization, and to nominate officers.

Upon their report, the following Constitution was agreed upon:

CONSTITUTION.

SECTION 1. The name of this organization shall be the "Oriental Club of Philadelphia," and its object shall be the promotion of Oriental studies by friendly intercourse between students, and such other means as may from time to time be determined.

SEC. 2. The Officers of this Club shall be a President, Secretary and Treasurer, elected annually at the meeting nearest June 1st, who shall constitute an Executive Committee to transact all the business of the Club, including the election of members and the fixing of dues.

At a meeting held at the house of Mr. Lyman on the 14th of the following month, it was agreed that all who attended the first meeting, together with those who accepted the invitation by letter, be regarded as members of the Club. It was ordered that each member shall pay to the Treasurer a sum not exceeding one dollar per year for the current expenses of the Club. It was also agreed that the Council of the Club shall receive all nominations for membership, and after communicating them to the Club, shall in a reasonable time thereafter proceed to pass upon them. At a subsequent meeting, it was decided that the number of members shall not exceed 30, including those who resided outside of the city.

Benj. Smith Lyman, who had been appointed a delegate of the Club to the meeting of the American Oriental Society at Boston, reported that he had had the honor of announcing the formation of the Club to that Society, and that there was a prospect of its holding its next meeting in Philadelphia, in the autumn of the present year.

At a meeting of the Club held on the 18th of October of the same year, the death of Mr. Philip Howard Law was announced as having taken place in Philadelphia on the 22d of May, in the 50th year of his age.

Mr. Talcott Williams called the attention of the Club to the importance of preparing a card catalogue of the Oriental manuscripts and texts in the public and private libraries of this city.

The ninety-sixth regular session of the American Oriental Society was held in Philadelphia on October 31st and November 1st of this year, the members of the Oriental Club generally participating in the meeting. A luncheon was given by the Oriental Club to the members of the Oriental Society, at the Bellevue Hotel on the second day, and in the evening a reception was given by Dr. Henry Clay Trumbull, as President of the Club, to meet the members of the American Oriental Society.

At a meeting of the Club held on the 13th of December, the death of the Rev. John Stronach was announced as having taken place in this city on the 29th of October, and of Mr. Tatsui Baba, also in this city, on the 1st of November, in the 39th year of his age.

At a meeting of the Club held on the 18th of February, 1892, the death of the Rev. Dr. Joseph F. Garrison was announced as having taken place in Camden, N. J., on the 29th of January, in the 70th year of his age. The death of another member, the Rev. Dr. William J. Mann, which took place on June 20th, 1892, was announced at the meeting held November 10th of that year.

At a meeting of the Club held on the 9th of February, 1893, the question of publishing a volume containing papers read before the Club was discussed, a committee on this publication was appointed consisting of Daniel G. Brinton, Morris Jastrow, Jr. and E. W. Hopkins. This committee was subsequently increased by the addition of Stewart Culin. The total membership of the Club during the five years of its existence has been thirty-one; of whom five have died, two removed and two resigned, leaving at present twenty-one members. Forty meetings have been held, comprising one special business meeting and thirty-eight meetings for the reading of papers and discussions. Thirty-six papers have been read before the Club.

OFFICERS.

1888-1889.
President—HENRY CLAY TRUMBULL.
Secretary—STEWART CULIN.
Treasurer—MORTON W. EASTON.

1889-1890.
President—HERMAN V. HILPRECHT
Secretary—STEWART CULIN.
Treasurer—MAYER SULZBERGER.

1890-1891.
President—MAYER SULZBERGER.
Secretary—STEWART CULIN.
Treasurer—BENJ. SMITH LYMAN.

1891-1892.
President—BENJ. SMITH LYMAN.
Secretary—STEWART CULIN.
Treasurer—MORRIS JASTROW, Jr.

1892-1893.
President—TALCOTT WILLIAMS.
Secretary—STEWART CULIN.
Treasurer—MORRIS JASTROW, Jr.

1893-1894.
President—EDWARD W. HOPKINS.
Secretary—STEWART CULIN.
Treasurer—BENJ. SMITH LYMAN.

(11)

LIST OF MEMBERS.

CYRUS ADLER, PH.D. Founder.
Librarian of the Smithsonian Institution, Washington, D. C.

TATSUI BABA. Founder. Died November 1, 1888.

G. A. BARTON, PH.D. Elected December 17, 1891.
Associate in Biblical Literature and Semitic Languages, Bryn Mawr College, Bryn Mawr, Penna.

GEORGE DANA BOARDMAN, D. D., LL.D. Founder. Resigned December 12, 1889.

DANIEL G. BRINTON, M. D., LL.D., Sc.D. Elected October 18, 1888.
Professor of American Archæology and Linguistics, University of Pennsylvania, Philadelphia.

HERMANN COLLITZ, PH.D. Elected December 13, 1888.
Associate Professor of German and Teutonic Philology, Bryn Mawr College, Bryn Mawr, Penna.

STEWART CULIN. Founder.
Director of the Museum of Archæology and Palaeontology, University of Pennsylvania.

MORTON W. EASTON, PH.D. Founder.
Professor of English and Comparative Philology, University of Pennsylvania.

JOSEPH F. GARRISON, D. D., LL.D. Founder. Died January 29, 1892.

WILLIAM GOODELL. Founder. Resigned November 13, 1890.

J. RENDELL HARRIS, A. M. Founder. Removed.

HERMAN V. HILPRECHT, PH.D. Founder.
Professor of Assyrian, University of Pennsylvania.

PAUL HAUPT, PH.D. Founder.
Professor of Semitic Languages, Johns Hopkins University, Baltimore.

EDWARD WASHBURN HOPKINS, PH.D. Founder.
Professor of Greek, Sanskrit and Comparative Philology, Bryn Mawr College, Bryn Mawr, Penna.

MARCUS JASTROW, PH.D. Founder.
Germantown, Philadelphia.

MORRIS JASTROW, JR., PH.D. Founder.
Professor of Semitic Languages, University of Pennsylvania, Philadelphia.

PHILIP HOWARD LAW. Founder. Died May 22, 1888.

J. PETER LESLEY, LL.D. Elected October 18, 1888.
1008 Clinton Street, Philadelphia.

BENJ. SMITH LYMAN, M. E. Founder.
708 South Washington Square.

WILLIAM J. MANN, D. D. Elected December 13, 1888. Died June 20, 1892.

ADMIRAL E. Y. McCAULEY, U. S. N. Founder.
334 South 9th Street, Philadelphia.

W. MAX MÜLLER, PH.D. Elected December 11, 1890.
4543 Chestnut Street, Philadelphia.

ISAAC MYER. Founder.
21 East 60th Street, New York City.

JOHN P. PETERS, PH.D. Founder.
225 West 99th Street, New York City.

ROBERT W. ROGERS, PH.D. Founder.
Drew Theological Seminary, Madison, N. J.

JOHN STRONACH, D. D. Founder. Died October 29, 1888.

MRS. CORNELIUS STEVENSON. Elected January 15, 1891.
Hon. Curator Egyptian Section, Museum of Archæology, University of Pennsylvania.

MAYER SULZBERGER, M. A. Founder.
1303 Girard Avenue, Philadelphia.

SWAMEE BHASKARA NAND SARASWATEE. Elected February 13, 1890. Removed.

HENRY CLAY TRUMBULL, D. D. Founder.
1031 Walnut Street, Philadelphia.

LOUIS VOSSION. Founder.
Consul de France, Philadelphia.

TALCOTT WILLIAMS, M. A. Founder.
331 South Sixteenth Street, Philadelphia.

LIST OF MEETINGS AND PAPERS.

The papers marked with a * are published in the present volume of the Oriental Club.

1888.

April 30. Organization.

May 14. Organization. Discussion opened by John P. Peters of the plans for the proposed University of Pennsylvania Expedition to Babylonia.

Dec. 13. Paper by Morris Jastrow, Jr. : "Fragment of Brick with Cuneiform Inscription, from the Library of Asurbanapal."[1]

1889.

Jan. 17. Paper by Morton W. Easton : "Primitive Conditions."

March 14. Paper by Stewart Culin : "Chinese Games with Dice."[2]

April 25. Paper by Marcus Jastrow : "Gladiators in the Talmud."[3]

May 28. Exhibition of Arabic MS., with Comments, by Dr. Trumbull.

Nov. 26. Accounts were given by Daniel G. Brinton of his recent visit among the Kabyles; by Herman V. Hilprecht, of his personal experiences as a member of the Babylonian Expedition of the University of Pennsylvania; and by Talcott Williams, of a trip to Fez and Mequinez.

Dec. 12. Paper by Daniel G. Brinton : "The Cradle of the Semites."[4]

1890.

Jan. 9. Discussion of the preceding paper, by Morris Jastrow, Jr.

Feb. 13. Continuation of discussion by Morris Jastrow, Jr.[4]

March 13. Paper by Talcott Williams : "The Historical Survivals of Morocco."[5]

[1] Published in the University of Pennsylvania Series in Philology, Literature and Archæology, under the title, "A Fragment of the Dibbarra Epic." 1891.

[2] Privately printed. Philadelphia, 1889.

[3] Published in the Sunday-School Times, May —, 1889.

[4] Published under the title, "The Cradle of the Semites." Two papers, etc , by D. G. Brinton and Morris Jastrow, Jr.

[5] Published in the "Papers of the American Historical Association " for 1892.

April 10. Paper by Edward W. Hopkins: "The Garden of Paradise and the Deluge."

May 15. Paper by Morton W. Easton: "The Terrace at Perse-polis."[1]

Nov. 13. Paper by Morris Jastrow, Jr.: "The Text Books of the Babylonians and Assyrians."[2]

1891.

Jan. 15. Address by John P. Peters: "Itinerary to the Site of Explorations in Babylonia."

Feb. 12. Address by William N. Chambers: "Civil Polity of the Armenian Church"; and by W. R. Abbott, on "Adventures in Madagascar."

March 19. Paper by M. W. Müller: "The Relations between the Egyptian and Semitic Languages."

April 25. Paper by Paul Haupt:[*] "The Book of Ecclesiastes."

Nov. 19. Paper by Morris Jastrow, Jr.: "Letters from Palestine";[3] "Notes on Psalms 120-122," by Paul Haupt.

Dec. 17. Paper by Dr. Jaunaris: "The Mohammedan Household."

1892.

Jan. 15. Paper by Stewart Culin: "Popular Literature of the Chinese in the United States."[*]

Feb. 18. Paper by Mrs. Cornelius Stevenson: "Early Forms of Religious Symbolism, the Stone Axe and the Flying Sun Disc."[*]

March 17. Extemporaneous Account of his Recent Travels in the East in the Interest of the Columbian Exposition, by Cyrus Adler.

April 14. Paper by Marcus Jastrow: "Psalms 24th, 73d, and 90th."[*]

May 12. Paper by Morris Jastrow, Jr.: "Babylonian Contract Tablet in the Collection of Mayer Sulzberger."[*]

Nov. 10. Paper by G. A. Barton: "Some Features of the Semitic Ishtar Cults."

Dec. 8. Paper by Talcott Williams: "Music and Musical Instruments of North Morocco."

[1] Published in the University of Pennsylvania Series in Philology, Literature and Archæology. Vol. II. 1892.

[2] Published in Extract in the Proceedings of the American Oriental Society. October, 1890.

[3] Published in Hebraica, Vol. VIII., under title, "The Letters of Abdiheba."

1893.

Jan.   12.   Paper by Morton W. Easton : " The Physical Geography of India." *

Feb.   9.   Paper by Daniel G. Brinton : " Alphabets of the Berbers."*

March 16.   Paper by Dr. Max Ohnefalsch-Richter : " Explorations in Cyprus."

April 13.   Paper by Herman V. Hilprecht : " Sargon I. and the Oldest Semitic Rulers of Babylon." [1]

May   11.   Paper by Dr. W. Max Müller : "Asiatic Nations as Recorded in the Egyptian Monuments." [2]

Nov.   9.   Paper by W. Max Müller : " Who Were the Ancient Egyptians ? " *

Dec. 14.   Paper by G. A. Barton: " Some Israelitish Deities ; "* Communication by Herman V. Hilprecht on " A New Numerical Fragment."*

1894.

Jan.   11.   Paper by E. W. Hopkins : " Holy Numbers of the Rig Veda." *

Feb.   22.   Papers by Benj. Smith Lyman on " The Change from Surd to Sonant in Japanese Compounds ; "* by Daniel G. Brinton on " The Origin of Holy Numbers ; " and by Herman Collitz* on " The Aryan Name of the Tongue."

March 22.   Paper by Herman V. Hilprecht : " The Boss of Tarkondemos."

April 12.   Paper by Paul Haupt on " The Rivers of Paradise."

May   10.   Paper by Morris Jastrow, Jr., on "The Element $b\check{\imath}t$ in Hebrew Proper Names;" and by Stewart Culin, "On Mancala."

[1] Embodied in Vol. I. of Hilprecht's " Old Babylonian Texts."

[2] Embodied in Müller's work, " Asien und Europa nach Altaegyptischen Denkmaelen."

THE PHYSICAL GEOGRAPHY OF INDIA.

BY MORTON W. EASTON.

THE territory drained by the Ganges, the Brahmaputra, the San-po and the Indus, with their adjuncts, and the peninsula stretching from the Vindhyas to Cape Comorin, do not, in all their aspects, form one connected whole. Peninsular India, in its geologic history, its ethnology, and its philology, is almost another world ; in the remote past it was an island, and in some respects it has always preserved its insular character. Yet the climatic conditions are such that, especially to the meteorologist, all these lands form one single district, and one distinctly marked off from the rest of Asia.

Its extreme length is about 1,900 miles, its extreme breadth about the same, and its total area is nearly as great as that of the continent of Europe west of Russia.

Considered in its relation to the Asiatic continent, its orography and its coast line, it has often been compared to Italy, and for certain purposes this comparison is a good one ; it serves as a good starting point for the study of the mountain systems and the principal hydrographical basin, although every farther step taken in the study of the two lands and peoples only brings their differences into stronger contrast. Italy is naturally adapted to be the seat of one empire.

Like Italy, India is isolated on the north by the main mountain system of the continent to which it belongs;

2 (17)

south of these mountains, each country has a 'quadrangular plain, drained by a great delta river flowing to the east, and both countries alike have narrower peninsulas stretching towards the south.

The northern mountains of India consist in part of the broken rim of the vast central plateau of Asia, above which their average elevation is by no means great ;* in part of systems of spurs running southwards and bounding the Indo-Gangetic quadrilateral on the east and west. The rim of the plateau is made up of a number of imperfectly known mountain systems, among which the Himalaya proper is but one, and perhaps by no means the loftiest. But at present, it is not possible to determine the precise limitations under which the name Himalaya should be used—some geographers consider that it should be applied only to the long line of eternal snows seen from the Gangetic plain—yet, whatever be the nature of the rocks, it does not seem far wrong to use the term of the whole series of elevations extending from Attock† on the Indus to the sacred gorge of the Brahmaputra, at the head of the Assam valley on the east. Throughout the whole of this tract, extending 1,400 miles from east to west, there is no break through which any important part of the drainage of the Tibetan plateau can find its way. The Indus and the San-po, now considered as the upper stream of the Brahmaputra, rise close together at the north and flow, in opposite directions, around its ends. The average height of the whole mass is 19,000 feet, and when it is remembered

* 2,000–3,000 feet.

† Attock has only 1,000 feet of elevation ; therefore a marked demarcation point.

that the table land behind it is rarely less than 16,000 feet above the sea, much of it higher still, the serious character of the barrier in this direction needs no comment.

The structural features of the region are as yet imperfectly known; political conditions render part of it inaccessible; but, apart from certain lower ranges on its southern border, it may be regarded as consisting of a pair of parallel lines of elevation, often close together, sometimes separated by broad but comparatively speaking shallow valleys.* Whether there is one, or more anticlinal and synclinal axes is unknown. The northern line forms a continuous watershed, but the southern is greatly broken up by watercourses flowing to the south, so that the resulting surface contour resembles a vast number of parallel ridges, running transverse to the general east and west strike of the whole, but joining at the north to form the continuous watershed described above. At the southern ends of these short ridges stand the highest peaks in partial and impressive isolation. One hundred and twenty of these peaks attain a height of over 20,000 feet; fifty-seven are over 23,000; Mt. Everest and Kinchinjinga attain respectively an altitude of 29,000 and 28,000 feet. It is not worth while to attempt to determine precisely the precise summits named by the Hindoo authors of antiquity.

The site of the range was once a trough of the sea: later, but still in the remote geologic past, when it was much lower than now, it was washed by the sea all along its southern base; then came a period of great lateral compression, pushing up the whole mass of the

* Never less than 15,000 feet above the sea.

central Asian plateau and its mountain masses, while a
great plain emerged on the south, occupying the site of
the present Ganges and the lower Indus.   Across the
east of the plain ran a ridge connecting the Assam and
the Rajmahal hills at a point not far from the head of
the present delta ; the plain sloped westward and was
drained by a great river, which attained the sea at a
point north of the head of the present Arabian Sea.

In late tertiary times, a low ridge appeared, dividing
the plain into two portions, while the hills which had
filled the gap between the Assam and the Rajmahal
ranges sank down hundreds of feet below the Bay of
Bengal.   West of the new ridge, the country was tra-
versed by the Indus; on its east appeared the Ganges,
flowing in a direction just the reverse of that of the old
river, crossing the sunken crest of the connecting hills,
and carrying, in its delta, the new coast line far to the
east.   The waters of the Arabian gulf receded, and the
plains about the lower Indus arose.

The watershed dividing the Indus from the Ganges
has attained no great elevation, only 924 feet above the
sea, and its slopes are so gentle that its existence cannot
be detected by the unassisted eye.   Thus there is not the
slightest natural barrier between the plain of the Ganges
and the district of the Punjaub, and the ignorance, if
real, on the part of the Vedic Indians concerning the
great stream and the fauna farther east must have been
due to other than topographical conditions.

The Indus plain and its adjuncts are of such interest
to Sanscrit students that I shall speak of it at length
further on.   The Ganges districts lie so low, and are so
well watered in parts, that, when the latitude is considered, one would expect to find it a tropical paradise.

But travelers dwell but little on the character of its scenery; for most of them, it may be presumed that it is not their first introduction to the tropical world, while the dead level everywhere may perhaps lack certain picturesque elements.   We hear, however, of the "clumps of waving and delicate bamboo, the tamarinds, the huge banyans and the slender palms; of the cottages half hidden by the large-leaved gourds, and overshadowed by the gigantic glossy leaves of the plantain, all alive with vast flocks of the most brilliant birds."   With these scant hints, it is easy to imagine the prevailing conditions, and these are perhaps intensified in the Assam extension of the Gangetic plain.   It is densely populated, containing three times as many inhabitants to the square mile as France; every ounce of nutriment in good seasons is consumed, and yet the people are underfed, so that the failure of the rains infallibly brings on destructive famines.

Yet even along the Ganges plain one who goes from Calcutta to Delhi sees much desolate land.   The rapid torrents from the steep gradients on the north cover large areas with unproductive detritus; the Ganges itself often changes its course and leaves great marshes where the malaria is deadly to human life.

The scenery among the Himalayas, on the contrary, should be the most sublime scenery to be found on the globe.   Of certain views this is true, but on the whole, the records of travelers sound a note of disappointment. The main ridges rise from bases so high that the effect of the great elevation is partly lost, while they are also screened by the hills consisting of or connected with the foot ranges.   One observer says that the finest view of Everest is to be obtained from a point ninety miles away,

and even from this only 8,000 feet of its mass is visible!
From Simla, the ridge seems "only a long, serrate,
white line, hardly higher than your own level, every
separate peak dwarfed by its multitudinous neighbors."
On the whole, Sikkim affords the best views; there the
observer stands but 2,000 feet above the sea and sees the
whole cone of Kinchinjinga towering 26,000 feet above
him.

On the upper Indus is what has been described as the
most magnificent snow view on the globe. "Below the
observer is a precipice falling sheer 16,000 feet. Before
him lie the Nangaparbat mountains; a mass of glaciers,
snow-fields, ice-cliffs and jagged needles of bare rock,
visible for its whole 24,000 feet of vertical measurement." Figures such as these are not vulgar; they
alone can give a conception of the aerial effect which
totally separates such scenery from any on a much
smaller scale.

Yet, in general, the impression won everywhere seems
to be that of monotony. That the visible vertical measurements do not often exceed those seen in Switzerland
is perhaps not at all to the point; but the grace and
variety, and above all the charming lake scenery of the
Swiss Alps, is everywhere wanting.

Turning now to other parts of the northern circle of
mountains, we may pass briefly over the region on the
north-east, beyond the Assam range. It is a wild and
broken mountain tract, but the density of the jungle,
rather than the character of the gradients, serves as a
barrier, and one very difficult to surmount. On the
east coast of the Bay of Bengal, most maps show an
apparently broad strip of level country, but the route is
practically closed up by mountain spurs running from
the water-shed of the Irrawaddy to the sea.

On the north-west of India, and over Kafiristan, is a region of central importance in connection with the physical geography of Asia considered as a whole. So far as concerns India in particular, it needs only to be remarked that the obstructions in this direction are no less formidable, to say the least, than those existing eastward in the Himalayas proper.

Southward from this, west of the Indus depression, runs a spur of the great central plateau, but very much lower in mean level. Cabul, at 6396 feet elevation, may be taken as the general height of the country; but it is crossed in every direction by great interlacing mountain ridges, in which lie long narrow levels, as fair and under irrigation as fertile as Italy, the land of Afghanistan. North of Cabul the summits are free from snow during eight months of the year, and present no formidable obstacle to the movements even of modern artillery. This was the route of the early Chinese pilgrims to Buddhistic India ; Alexander and Genghis Khan came this way, and it, if any, is the future road of a Russian army.

The valley of the Cabul river is bounded on the south by the Sufid Koh, and running east and west, never falling below 12,500 feet. The trade route to India from Cabul, for many centuries, led directly over its crest. The road by the renowned Khaibar pass, directly down the river, and over a short spur through a deep gorge, is in itself easy, but difficult where an armed force is in the way. The Sufid Koh abuts with many spurs on the Indus, rendering a long stretch of its shore impracticable. Southward from the Sufid Koh run the Sulimani mountains. They resemble, in surface contour at least, the Himalayas ; there is a twin ridge, with

an uninterrupted water-shed, between which and the
Indus is a broken line, in which, as in the Himalayas,
are the highest summits. Their loftiest peak, the
Takht-i-Sulimani (throne of Solomon), is over 11,000 feet
in height. It and the jagged line of crests of which it
is the chief, rather than the far higher Himalayas or the
peaks above Kafiristan, may have been the mighty
mountains of the Vedic poet. This higher axis of the
Sulimani ends in a great promontory, once perhaps a
bold headland over the eocene ocean. But the westward lying axis, the true watershed, keeps on, gradually diminishing in height to Cape Monze on the Arabian Sea.

Throughout this whole chain of mountains, south of
the Cabul river, the passes are almost innumerable.
Many of them while "not precisely easy," present nothing to hinder any properly equipped force from debouch-
ing at many points upon the plain of the Indus. But
along the lower Indus and to the eastward, the desert
renders the march difficult, and the proper road for an
invading army lies through a narrow, fertile strip lying
along the base of the Himalayas. The reason for the
existence of this and of the desert will be given further
on. At present I may note that it is to these strategic
considerations that Delhi owes its existence. But the
fertile belt is cut across by many streams, the "seven
rivers" of the Hindoos, and among these a force might
keep invaders in check, if the defenders were resolute.
But any one who weighs the circumstances well and re-
members how much more inviting were the basins of the
Euphrates, the Tigris and the Nile, must feel that the
Ganges valley was always secluded rather than defended.
Like Germany in Roman times, it probably owed its

safety to the neglect of the Western powers, a conclusion not invalidated, in either case, by the adverse issue
of single campaigns.

In peninsular India, the geological history and the
structure of the country are very different from the conditions north of the Vindhyas.   "There[*] is not in the
Peninsula a single great range with a definite axis of
elevation; not one, with the possible exception of the
Arvali, is along an anticlinal or synclinal line.   It is a
table land, denuded by subaerial agencies, and the
mountain chains are merely dividing lines left unde-
nuded between the different drainage areas.   All the
principal elevations are plateaux, not ridges."

We should picture to ourselves the whole peninsula
as a vast truncated pyramid,[†] sloping to the east and
deeply scored by watercourses, the principal ones rising
on its extreme western rim, which find their way
through an intricate tangle of irregular ridges into the
Bay of Bengal.   Along the eastern side of this pyramid
lies a broad flat plain, over which the streams have
raised for themselves dykes, along the summits of which
they flow to finally end in a succession of deltas.

Over one part of the surface of the pyramid covering an area about as large as the whole of France and
to a depth of six thousand feet, has flowed a sheet of
eruptive rock.   This has settled into a uniform level,
and its surface has become extremely porous, so that
much of the rainfall over the interior, insufficient at
best, sinks deep into the thirsty soil and is lost.   In
consequence, the traveler finds, to his surprise, bare arid

---

[*] Medlicott and Blandford.

[†] 300–3,000 feet of elevation.

plains where he had expected to see a country rich in tropical vegetation.

The north side of the pyramid is constituted by the Vindhyas (using the term in its widest sense), a confused jumble "of forests, ridges, peaks, cultivated valleys and broad high plains," nowhere of great elevation, yet from the dense vegetation, and still more from the deadly miasm prevailing along their northern slopes, serving as a complete barrier to intercourse with the regions on the north.

Most of the districts south of the Vindhyas are shut in, on the remaining two sides, by the Ghats.   The Western Ghats, bordering on the Arabian Sea, are the higher,* and are clad with impenetrable forests, nourished by one of the heaviest rainfalls known.   Along their feet runs a narrow belt of level land, fringed with a beach of bright yellow sand, and covered with endless groves of the coco-palm, out of which jut here and there bright red cliffs of eruptive rock washed down from above.   Over the forest-clad slopes hang precipices of peculiar form, not unlike great circular bastions.   It is under these natural bastions that the steep defiles run by which alone access can be gained from the west coast to the interior, and a small force posted above can hold an army in check.   The scenery along all this coast resembles that of certain of the high islands of Polynesia, and is perhaps the only instance of such scenery on a continental scale.

The Eastern Ghats, facing the Bay of Bengal, cannot be said to form a continuous range, and there are many

* Averaging 4,000 feet, but the mountains attain 8,400 in the Neilgherry hills; the Eastern Ghats rarely rise above 1,500.

gates by which the interior, in parts, can be reached, so that Calcutta, rather than Bombay or Goa, is the key to the peninsula. Yet there are many river defiles, and many tracts forming natural fortresses, impregnable to any arm which the native rulers could command. Travelers testify that it is in these defiles that the most picturesque scenery to be found in India is to be seen.

The comprehension, in outline at least, of the relation to the lowlands of the various mountain systems of both the Indo-Gangetic plains and peninsular India, is indispensable, not only in order to understand the various degrees of isolation under which the various peoples live, with relation to the rest of Asia and to each other, but also to comprehend the distribution of the rains, a subject of special interest to the student of the whole of India.

The year is divided into a hot season, lasting from April to November, during which the southwest monsoon, the rain-bringing wind for the greater part of the country prevails, and a colder season, the period of the northeast monsoon.

The origin of the southwest monsoon may be said to be still a subject of debate. Under conditions which also are as yet imperfectly understood, it is deflected from its normal course so as to blow as a more or less east or west wind directly over the land. The part of it which traverses the Arabian Sea turns over the peninsula. From the Bengal Bay branch of the monsoon, a westwardly directed current blows up the long trough lying between the Himalayas and the system of the Vindhyas, followed a few weeks later, in a reverse course, by the northern part of the branch coming from the Arabian Sea.

Both branches let fall an excess of rain on their first encounter with the land. Two to three hundred inches of rain per year, sometimes more than twice as much, fall on the Assam hills and the Ganges delta, and two hundred and fifty inches on the west slope of the Western Ghats. But the Bengal Bay branch lets fall less and less rain as it advances up the Ganges, and brings but very little to the region lying west of the divide between the Ganges and Indus basins ; for the other branch about seventy-five inches are registered at Bombay, thirty-five over the Ganges, and almost none in the interior of the peninsula; at Madras it becomes a hot dry wind.

Along the slopes of the Himalayas, the precipitation from both branches of the southwest monsoon is very great, and, indeed, but little moisture from these sources reaches the central plateau beyond. In consequence the phenomena of snow, glacier and avalanche, are on the grandest scale, far exceeding anything known elsewhere in the world in the temperate or the tropical zones, and not surpassed in the display of active, moving forces by anything in the Arctic regions, excepting in the icebergs of Melville Bay, or those in the Antarctic Seas.

Denudation goes on at a rate paralleled nowhere else. During the height of the monsoon some of the mountain torrents are little else than streams of mud, and the vast delta formed by the united Ganges and the Brahmaputra testifies to the destructive agency of the feeders of these streams, which bring down five times as much sediment as our Mississippi.

The detailed statistics of the rainfall in various parts of the land are exceedingly interesting, but cannot be given in full here ; no doubt the figures given above will prove sufficiently suggestive. It may be noted, however, that the winds blowing at this season over the lower Indus seem to come not from the sea, but from over the arid regions on the west ; and in this part of its course the river flows through a desert ; no rainfalls occur.

The northeast monsoon becomes saturated in crossing the Bay of Bengal, and is the source of the rainfall over the east coast, and the interior of the peninsula. In the latter region, the amount of precipitation (above thirty-five inches) about equals that registered in the northeastern parts of the United States. but this is, in India, considered a very insufficient supply, especially in the districts covered with the porous eruptive rock described above. However, by an interesting arrangement of compensation, the principal water-courses have their sources on the summits of the Western Ghats, and so both of the monsoons contribute to swell their volume while irrigation on a stupendous scales goes far towards supplying the deficiencies of the rainfall.

Over the lower Indus, as I have already said, there is practically no rain at all. Some years are exceptional, and a few inches may fall, from what source is not clear; meteorologists talk vaguely of upper currents in the atmosphere. At the junction of the Indus and the stream formed by the combination of the five rivers, the annual precipitation attains about six inches; but this is totally inadequate for the support of a permanent, succulent vegetation. So also between the five rivers in their lower courses, the land is everywhere barren, except along the borders of the canals which have been dug for the purposes of irrigation. Even the torrents which at certain seasons come down from the outer mountain slopes soon sink into the thirsty soil and disappear.

The Indus, the five rivers, and the Sarasvati make up the well-known "seven streams." All of these except the Sarasvati derive their supply from the melting snows, a perennially flowing fount, and the rains of the highest crests of the Himalayas; the Sarasvati depends entirely upon the low outer hills and the periodical rains, so that at times it is only a feeble stream and never reaches the sea.

In former times the conditions seem to have been different; there seems to have been a much greater precipitation, and at that time this river must have held its own throughout the year; at the same period, the belt of fertility along the base of the mountains extended much farther to the south.

The country about the lower Indus is thus simply a continuation of the great desert lying west. To the east lies the desert of Thar, where there is not a single stream for hundreds of miles. It is covered with great numbers of sand dunes, some of them nearly four hundred feet in height, so arranged that they seem to require the assumption of the past prevalence of a different system of winds from that now existing. During the greater part of the year they show a scanty growth of long-rooted almost leafless plants; after some slight fall of rain, and for a brief space of time, they afford pasturage for herds of cattle driven in by a temporary immigrant population, which is compelled to wage incessant war with great numbers of fierce wolves, just as little permanent occupants of the soil as themselves. A few wretched Bhils manage to find subsistence there all the year through.

Between the desert and the sea is the strange Runn*

* Solitude.

of Cutch, stretching about 150 miles to the eastward, and, in some places, sixty miles to the northward. Its history is too'well known to need recounting here, and affords valuable evidence as to the manner in which the levels farther north may have been produced through the agency of earthquakes. It is almost perfectly flat, excepting a slight convexity at the centre, and the southwest monsoon drives the sea over the entire plain, covering it with three feet of water, slightly increasing in depth at the depressed rim. In the drier season it is incrusted with salt, but after a period of scanty rains, it is covered here and there with little lakes, blowing about from place to place. Only a few tamarisks grow on its surface, and the only noticeable animal life consists of herds of wild asses, which feed on its margin at night, and take refuge in its centre during the day.

It is crossed at all seasons by caravans, toiling over the hot, salty plain, or, during the monsoon, wading through an apparently boundless sea. But mirages, due to the unequal circulation, and violent tornadoes, caused by the fierce heat of its saline incrustation, make it an uncanny and a dangerous land.

The subject of the physical geography of a country is inseparable from the consideration of its flora and fauna, and above all in the case of an association, such as is ours, which is chiefly interested in anthropology and philology. But in the time allotted me, it is impossible to touch upon these points. Even were I to confine myself to the treatment of the characteristics of the various native peoples, a single paper which should attempt to cover the whole of India could do no more than to recount, in bare outline, facts perfectly well known to all. It is a subject imperatively demanding abundant detail.

In the choice of the details given in the foregoing pages, I have, however, constantly borne in mind, and attempted, sub silentio, to cast some light upon the peculiar problems that are presented in India by the marked preservation of such great and infinite diversity in races, forms of speech, and institutions, trusting that the simple presentation of the very interesting physical conditions will at once connect itself with these well known characteristics of the various peoples.

I speak of the preservation, not of the origin of these characteristics; the sum of these could not be accounted for by any description of the climate and topography of India, however extended it might be; the Indo-Germanic native peoples ran through no small part of their course of development in a different land: the whole range of the Himalayas is occupied by the Mongolian stock, and so on. Nor is it indeed easy to believe that the physical geography of any land can ever afford the solution of such problems, unless the question is as simple as that relating to the connection between the defective nourishment of a people and its palpable consequences on their physical conformation.

Indeed, it is necessary to lay special emphasis on the limited territorial district from which certain national characters may have radiated. The Roman type, for instance, was not Italic: it spread from one city, and perhaps originated from a very few families in this. Above all, this may be true of religious conceptions when assuming any well-defined form. Buddhism, even though we give no credence to its childish legends, has all the aspects of a creed originally emanating from one individual; and why appeal to Himalayan torrents, miasmatic swamps, and the "hot-house atmosphere of the Gangetic plain," when one single favoring spot might—if we knew where 'to find it—account for his pessimism, and certain social conditions for the eager reception of his teachings.   ·

Only those who have paid some attention to the unwarrantably discredited study of genealogies and pedigrees, know to what an extent the blood of a few individuals is diffused among, for instance, the English speaking peoples of Great Britain and America.   I am not advancing the hypothesis of the origin from single pairs, either for the present or for any period of the past—the analogies of evolution are all against such an assumption—but there is good reason for believing that in course of time the blood of a single pair may come to permeate a whole tribe or people and bring with it identity of at least physical characteristics. .

Botanists recognize certain species of plants having "stations" of very limited area, perhaps one particular pool, or the bank of one particular stream, with specific characters which may be due to certain very exceptional combinations of soil, water-supply, altitude and exposure to wind and sun.   So it is quite as possible as anything else that the physical surroundings in some little valley, hardly large enough for a homestead—*ubi fons placuit*—may have been the cause of the special character of some single family, which is afterwards to become not indeed the whole ancestry, but one of the progenitors of every individual in the nation; and still more possible that exceptional social surroundings—for instance, accidental opportunity to command its neighbors—may have had more to do with its mental endowments than any obvious physical environment.   A people's history is the resultant of the physical geography of the coun-

3

try, and their original environments.   In this light the study of the physical geography of the country is of the last degree of utility, but it contributes little to the solution of the question of origins.

AN INTERPRETATION OF TWO PSALMS.

PSALM LXXIII.

BY MARCUS JASTROW.

AND yet there is a boon for Israel,
A God for those pure in heart.
But I—my feet had well nigh wavered,
It lacked but little and my steps had slipped.
For I envied the merry-makers,
When I beheld the peace of the wicked;
For there are no fetters for their ilk,
And their nature is strong.
In the trouble of man, they share not,
And with mankind are they not afflicted.
Indeed, their necklace is haughtiness,
Violence their fine embroidered cloak.
Their scheme has left the fat of their reins,
The carvings of their heart have gone forth.
Mockingly they speak of the evil ;
".It is a wrong from on high," they say.
They set their mouth against the heavens,
And their speech travels quickly over the land :
    " Truly, let his people turn hither,
And waters of fulness shall be quaffed by them,
And let them say, ' How does God know,
Or is there knowledge in the Most High ?
Here are the villains,
And the prosperous men of the world—
They increase in wealth.
Verily, in vain have I cleansed my heart,
And washed my hands in innocency;
Yet have I been plagued all the day long,
And my chastisement was renewed with every morning.' "

(35)

If I said, " Thus will I speak,"
Behold, here is the generation of thy children
To whom I should be faithless.
But thinking, I came to know this:
A trouble is this in my eyes,
Until I shall enter the sanctuaries of God,
When I shall get an insight into their destined end.
Verily, on slippery ground hast thou made a foundation
        for them,
Thou castest them down into ruins.
How are they turned into desolation in a moment !
They are gone, they have ceased from terrifying,
As a dream disappears on awakening ;
O Lord, at the awakening
Thou makest contemptible their image.—
When my heart was fermenting,
And in my reins I was stung,
I was foolish and knew not
That animal-like I was with thee.
But I will always be with thee ;
Thou seizest me by my right hand,
Thou shalt guide me with thy counsel,
Until at last thou takest me away in glory.
Whom have I in the heavens?
And besides thee I want none on earth.
My flesh and my heart are consumed :
The rock of my heart and my portion
Is God forever.
For behold those far from thee
Shall perish ; thou silencest
Every one that strayeth away from thee.
But I—the nearness of God is my boon.
I place in the Lord God my trust,
To proclaim all thy messages.

There are in the above translation only a few deviations from the accepted version, which need a justification. _L'molham_, in verse four, is translated in the King
James' version and others "in their death" (from _ma-_

veth). Mr. Leeser has "for them", taking *l'motham* as a poetic form for *l'mohem* or *lamo*. In Talmudic Hebrew we have *k'mothi* for *kamothi*, *k'motho* for *kamohu*, etc. *L'motham* might therefore be translated by "for those people," "people of that ilk."

The usual translation of *yasa meheleb enemo* "their eyes stand out with (or from) fatness," apart from its harshness of expression, is physiologically incorrect. It is the eyes of haggard persons that stand forth. We take *'ayin* to be *scheme, plan*, (cf. Job, xi. 20 and xxxvi. 7) and *heleb* to be a poetic expression for *kilyah, kidney*, with which *heleb* is frequently associated (cf. Lev. iii. 4, 10, and the expression "fat of kidneys of wheat," Deut. xxxii. 14). The kidneys are to the Hebrew the seat of deliberation and counsel; the heart, the seat of thought and speculation. In our poem, the heart is compared to a quarry or workshop in which the marble is hewn and shaped into *maskiyoth*. The figure of speech gains additional significance by reference to Leviticus xxvi. 1, where *eben maskith* is shown, by the context, to mean a carved stone used as an idol.

When the work is finished, it leaves the workshop to be exhibited to public gaze. So have the carvings of those wicked men left the workshop—the heart—just as their schemes have gone forth from the kidneys in which they were planned. To this figure of speech corresponds "image," (*selem*) in verse twenty, where it says, "Thou despisest"—*i. e.* showest the contemptibility of—"their image."

Of minor deviations from the accepted version, I shall mention only *ya'atof shith* in verse six. The union of these words (by means of the Makkef) proves that *ya'atof* is here meant to be a noun. As a proper noun *Yaakob* is formed from '*akab:* so a noun, *ya'átòf,* is formed from '*átaf,* the construct being *ya'átòf,* a *wrap.* The last word of our psalm, *malákhothekha,* usually translated "thy works," has been taken in the sense of *malákkuth* (Haggai, i. 13), "message."

As a parallel to our psalm, as well as in illustration of it, let us read the utterances of that prophet, who, both in style and temperament, approaches most nearly to a mean between the two divisions of Israel's religious poetry—the prophetic and the psalmodic :

"Righteous art thou, O Lord, when I plead with thee : yet let me talk with thee of thy judgments : Wherefore doth the way of the wicked prosper? wherefore are all they happy that deal treacherously?

"Thou hast planted them, yea, they have taken root : they grow, yea, they bring forth fruit : thou art near in their mouth and far from their reins. But thou, O Lord, knowest me : thou hast seen me and tried mine heart, toward thee : pull them out like sheep for the slaughter, and prepare them for the day of slaughter.

"How long shall the land mourn, and the herbs of every field wither, for the wickedness of them that dwell therein? The beasts are consumed and the birds ; because they said, He shall not see our last end." (Jeremiah xii. 1–4.)

Both the prophet and the psalmist of whom we speak lived in one of those epochs of human history when despair threatens to seize noble and sympathetic souls. I would call them the "might-makes-right" periods.

Power, in self-glorification, occupies the throne ; her minions surround her, covering all defects with flattery's gorgeous cloak; her self-seeking servants greedily seize the morsels of spoils which are thrown out from

the tents of tyranny. Festivity in the palaces, weeping
in the huts ; revelry among the upper thousands, star-
vation among the oppressed ; wealth and abundance the
portion of the cruel, poverty and toil the lot of the pure
in heart. And where, during all this time, is the ever-
living, the ever-wise, ever-beneficent, all-ruling God
whom Israel's teachers proclaim ? to spread whose name
among the nations, Israel was commissioned at Sinai's
foot ? "Come, ye foolish ones, ye who still keep aloof
from the seat of tyrannical power, who prefer bearing
the weight of oppression to ranking among the oppres-
sors! Don't you see, the world is a fish-pond ; the large
fish swallow the small ! Come with us, kneel down before the throne of might, and partake of the crumbs of
plenty that fall to our share from the table of despot-
ism !" This is the theme : numberless are the varia-
tions upon it in all such periods when "might makes
right." The noble-hearted hear this proclamation of
the rule of material force, and sigh and ponder, and ask
question after question. No response comes to them,
and their faith is shaken to its very foundations. A
moment of such deep despair gave birth to our psalm.
It begins with a protest against the singer's own doubts.
"And yet Israel possesses a boon, the pure-hearted
have a God," of whom no ill fate can rob them. His
own feet came very near going astray, his steps had well
nigh slipped. "I envied," says he, "the merry-makers,
when I saw the prosperity of the wicked. They have
no fetters to restrain them, they have a strong constitution." The conscientious find restrictions at every
turn. "Conscience doth make cowards," says Hamlet,
the pessimist. Where the thoughtless man rushes forward, trusting in his strength, the pure-hearted asks, Is

it right? and hesitates, while those who recognize no power but material force have reached the goal ere he has yet made a start. "Happy are the merry-makers," says he, "for in the misery of humanity they share not, and when men suffer they feel no pain." To the psalmist, in his despairing mood, sympathy with suffering humanity is a source of misery and distress: happy are those whose hearts beat not for others. Even more, "haughtiness is their necklace, violence their fine embroidered cloak." There are periods in the history of a nation when the crafty despoilers of the people no longer find it necessary to hide their wicked schemes, but rather boast of them openly.

So says the poet. They boast of their wrongs, "their schemes have gone forth, have left the fat of their reins." As we said before, by the ancients, the kidneys were held to be the seat of counsel, of scheming—"the carvings of their hearts have left their workshop"—they are on exhibition, a psalmist of our day would say. Furthermore, they speak scornfully, they talk of oppression as an evil. "It comes from on high," they say mockingly. "They set their mouth against heaven, and their speech travels quickly over the land." "It is *your* God," say they to the suffering believers in divine justice. "Therefore, let his people come hither, and let them quaff water in full draughts." What boots it to suffer for an idea? It is time to cast off the yoke of useless martyrdom in order to drain freely the cup of earthly pleasure. "Let his people come over to us and say, 'How does God know? How can I say there is a Providence? Here are those whom I call wicked constantly increasing in prosperity, while I am sorely afflicted, and misery is my portion.'"

The mockery here placed in the mouths of the wicked seems even more striking to us when contrasted with the prophecy of Isaiah. He foretells the time when the nations will recognize that Israel has suffered for their good, when they will say: "He was despised and shunned by men, a man of pains and acquainted with disease; but only our diseases did he bear himself, while we considered him stricken, smitten of God and afflicted." In our psalm just the reverse is expressed. The enemy says, "Let the faithful of God's people come over to us, and admit that all martyrdom was in vain."

For a moment our poet wavers. He thinks, "Suppose I speak in the same vein, suppose I dissemble, and pretend to give up my mission, suppose I surrender"— but he looks at the young, the growing generation, and feels that he would be faithless to them, to Israel's future, were he, though but in appearance, to join the ranks of the persecutors.

But how is the problem to be solved? Why is the way of the wicked successful? Why do the faithless prosper? "And in my reflection," says he, "I learnt this: the wrong and the misery that I see about me are such in my eyes only while I am here on earth, until I enter the sanctuary whence God directs the world, until I shall be able to look beyond the narrow present, and see the vast future unrolled before me. Wrong is a castle built on slippery ground, a rock on an inclined plane —one shock, and the stronghold is shattered! What appeared so frightful in the dark, the spectre that imagination conjured up in the twilight, disappears when the sun rises, and we laugh at our fears. The morning comes, the dream is fled, and when the hour of awaking arrives, the Lord shows the schemes of the wicked in their true, contemptible light.

And now our psalmist turns from the sufferings of his people to the condition of his own soul. Was he right to murmur against divine dispensations? Was not his very doubt a departure from God? "No," says he, "when my heart was troubled, when I felt the stinging in my reins, I was indeed ignorant, for I knew not that even unconsciously I was with thee." Is not indignation at the sight of wrong a manifestation of the deep-seated sense of right in the heart of the noble? As a discord offends the finely attuned ear of the musician, so the true man's heart is torn with emotion when he sees the weak oppressed and the strong haughty. This bitterness of heart is in itself an instinctive worship of the all-just God. "But," continues the psalmist, "I will always be with thee; thou seizest me by my right hand, thou wilt lead me by *thy* counsel, until at last thou takest me away to glory." In the religious poetry of the Scriptures, death is a "being taken away." This short span of life will soon be ended, and a morning of glory will rise for me.

"Whom have I in heaven but thee? and on earth, too, I desire none but thee. I will yield to no power but thine. My flesh and my heart will perish, but the rock of my heart, my portion, is God forevermore. For behold those who are far from thee shall be lost, thou annihilatest all that stray away from thee." Here and in the life beyond, the day of reckoning will come.

"But as for me, the nearness of God is my boon. I place in the Lord my God my trust, to proclaim all thy messages."

Thus the poet closes with the confirmation of the protest with which he began: "And yet Israel has a boon there *is* a God for those pure of heart!"

PSALM XC.

BY MARCUS JASTROW.

A Prayer of Moses, the Man of God.

O Lord! thou hast been our Providence in all generations.
Before yet the mountains were brought forth,
And the earth and the world began their course,
Even from everlasting to everlasting,
Thou art God.
Thou sentest man back to the dust,
When thou saidst, Return, ye children of man.
Indeed, a thousand years in thy sight
Are but as yesterday when it is passed,
And as a watch in the night.
Thou pourest them out—they are a sleep.
In the morning, the grass-like glistens,
In the morning, he blooms and glistens;
In the evening, he is cut down, he is withered.
Truly, we perish in thine anger,
And by thy wrath are we carried away.
Thou hast set our iniquities in thy presence, .
What we would hide—before the light of thy countenance.
Indeed, all our days pass away in thy wrath,
We finish our lives like a flash of thought.
The days of our lives—at times seventy years,
And if by strength—eighty years,
And their pride—toil and vanity;
For the wind strikes,
And we are blown away.
Who understands the strength of thine anger?
And that like the fear of thee is thy wrath?
Make known a basis for the days allotted to us,
That we may carry off a wise heart.
Return, O Lord, unto my people,
And bethink thyself of thy servants!
Satisfy us in the morning with thy grace,
And we shall sing and rejoice throughout all our days.

Give us joy according to the days,
When thou didst afflict us,
The years wherein we saw evil.
Let thy doing be visible to thy servants,
Let thy glory shine upon their children,
And let the beauty of the Lord our God be upon us,
And what our hands undertake, confirm thou for us;
And what our hands accomplish, give permanence to it.

"A Prayer of Moses, the man of God." The designation of Moses as the man of God clearly indicates to us that the poet will not have us look upon Moses as the author of the poem; at the outset he wishes to convey to us the idea that he is placing himself in the position and frame of mind of Moses, that he would pray as Moses might have prayed in the troublous times to which the song refers.

Were a modern poet to introduce a poem with the words, *A Prayer of Moses*, no one would fail to understand that he had selected some important situation in the life of Moses as his theme in order to give poetic expression to Mosaic thoughts. Are we not justified in attributing to this unknown author the same feelings and impulses that have at all times called|into activity the best powers of the poetical imagination?

What situation in the life of Moses has been selected by our poet can be determined only by an examination of the poem itself, and by a comparison between it and certain scenes depicted for us in the Pentateuch.

The poem speaks of the sin of the people and of the punishment following thereupon. (V. 7–9).

Does one not immediately think of the erection of the golden calf and of the subsequent plague? (Exodus xxxii. 35, cf. Ps. cvi. 19–23).

Our poet likewise has in mind the prayer of Moses, on
the same occasion, that Israel may be forgiven, and that
the majesty of the Lord may again dwell in its midst, as
well as the expression of the ardent desire of the great
prophet to know the ways of God.   In a few verses, ex-
quisite in their poetry, he combines all this material in
his "prayer," in which we find some of the very words
and phrases of the source of his inspiration.

"Return from thy fierce wrath and bethink thee of
the evil of thy people," says Moses (Exodus xxxii. 12b).
"Return, O Lord, unto my people and bethink thyself
of thy servants," says our poet.

Even though the translation here offered for *mathay*,
be set aside as unwarranted, and the customary "how
long yet" be substituted in its place, nevertheless the
two passages quoted agree sufficiently to justify the
assumption of a studied connection between them.   It is
not a matter of chance that the parallelism in each case
depends upon the words *shub* and *hinnahem*.

We find the phrase '*ad mathay* used thus abruptly in
only one other instance, Psalm vi. 4, in which the in-
tense excitement of the poet not only justifies the un-
finished exclamation, but is most vividly brought before
our minds by this most artistic and dramatic device.   In
the poem under consideration, however, the prevailing
tone is calmly speculative.   We have before us the
prayer of a philosopher, and the phrase "how long
yet" would detract from the beauty of the poem rather
than heighten its effect.

If, however, we derive *mathay* from *m'thim*, the verse
acquires new force.   We have *m'thayikh* and *m'thav*,
why not also *m'thay* becoming *mathay* in pause?   The
exigencies of the rhythm could in all probability account for the change from *me* to *ma*.

The validity of these assumptions granted, the poem displays a delicacy and beauty that have hitherto escaped us entirely.

In the Talmudic literature our attention is directed to the fact that God says to Moses: "Get thee down, for *thy* people, which thou hast brought up out of the land of Egypt, is corrupt" (Exodus xxxii. 7), while Moses prays: "Why should thy wrath wax hot against *thy* people that thou hast brought forth out of the land of Egypt?" (v. 11) and again, "Consider that this nation is *thy* people" (xxxiii. 13).

Our poet, recalling these verses, combines the two points of view, exclaiming, "Return, O Lord, to *my* people, and bethink thee of *thy* servants."

There is but one more essential departure from the accepted interpretation of the text of this poem to be considered before proceeding to an analysis of its meaning.

The word *kēn* in verse 12, if looked upon as a particle, stands entirely without connection in the sentence; in addition, the phrase *hod'a limnoth yamenu* (teach to number our days) is, to say the least, harsh in construction. We should expect *hodi'enu (ekh) limnoth yamenu.* I take *ken* and *m'noth* to be substantives, the first meaning basis, reality, permanence or true existence, and translate *m'noth yamenu* "our allotted span of life," just as *m'nath kosi* means my allotted portion.

"Make known to us the principle of the life-time allotted to us," *i. e.* teach us the true meaning and purpose of life, especially of the life of the Israelitish nation, "that our hearts may gain in wisdom, that we may learn to know thy Providence." This idea is in complete accord with the prayer of the prophet, "Make me know thy way that I may know thee, in order that I may find

grace in thy eyes" (Ex. xxxiii. 13), the parallel to which
we find further on in the chapter, in the words, "Let
me see thy glory." (V. 18.)

After these preliminary remarks, we may turn to the
elucidation of the meaning of the poem.

The poet reflects how God has ruled from the beginning of all things, how he has ever been the guide and
the teacher of mankind.

He selects the term *ma'on* to express the idea of
Providence. Just as *makom* from *kum* signifies place
and also that which gives permanence (hence in post-
biblical Hebrew it is used to indicate God), so does
ma'on mean *glance* (*vide* 1 Sam. ii. 32, *sar ma'on*, with
envious glance), *provision* (*ib.* v. 29, *asher sivvithi ma'on*,
the offerings which I have commanded as a provision
for the priests), and personified, *Providence.* The sig-
nification, *dwelling-place*, must be traced to a different
association of ideas, an investigation of which lies outside the limits of this essay.

God's providence, says the poet, is eternal and un-
changing. He ruled before the earth was brought forth,
and his existence will ever continue, from everlasting
unto everlasting. This reflection leads the poet to think
of the first man, of death decreed as a punishment for his
sin. At that time God said to him, "Dust thou wast,
to dust thou shalt return," for Adam had been warned,
"On the day that thou eatest therefrom, thou shalt
surely die."

Our poet uses the term *dakka* (crumbs), instead of
'afar (dust), and he sings, "Thou sentest man back
to the dust when thou saidst, Return, ye children of
men." (Gen. ii. 17, and iii. 19.)

Adam, it is true, attained the age of nearly one thousand years; but in comparison with God's eternity, a thousand years are but as yesterday when it is past, etc.

God pours out a thousand years like rain, and when past, they are but as a night's sleep, a ·dream, a vision.

Man's life is even as the life of a flower; he, too, lives but for a day, a morning and an evening; he, too, blooms and fades away. The comparison of the life of man to the life of a flower (Is. xl. 6–8 ; li. 12; Ps. cii. 12 ; ciii. 15 ; cxxix. 6, *et al.*) is so frequent in biblical diction that the poet could employ *kehasir*, "the grasslike" as a designation for man.

After this general observation, the poet turns his attention to the existing situation.

He sees the human flowers rearing their heads proudly aloft in the morning, and at evening withered and cut down. A plague works havoc among the people against whom the anger of the Lord burns fiercely; and his wrath is just, for their sin ascends before the judgment-seat of the Lord to accuse them, even though the offending object has been removed from the eyes of men. Man seeks to conceal his fault, hence the poet uses *'alumenu* as a parallel to *'avonothenu*.

If God will not, in his mercy, cry a halt to the devastating plague, the nation whose existence has but just begun must perish from the earth, like a thought that is forgotten when scarcely conceived.

And what is the length of man's life, his day of existence? Seventy years, at most eighty years (about the age of Moses, which he looks upon as a special favor of Providence,) and its boast is but pride and vanity. A wind passes over the flowers, and they are blown away. The abstract term *hish* (haste) is used for the concrete *ruah* (wind) (vide Ps. ciii. 16), just as *dakka* was used for *'afar*.

" Who understands the strength of thine anger, and
that like the fear of thee is thy wrath ?"

Kimchi has explained this difficult passage correctly
by a reference to Lev. x. 3 ("on those who are near
unto me will I be sanctified," etc.) Both Bible and
Talmud again and again express the thought that he
who is destined for high purposes, he from whom great
things are expected, bears a heavier weight of responsibility than the ordinary human being, and must suffer
more severe punishment for his sins. It is unnecessary
to cite particular instances. Such is the idea here expressed by our poet. It is true that the very violence
of divine wrath against Israel is a proof of its high
mission, that the Lord's indignation is in proportion
to the reverence for him expected from Israel and
promised by it: but who can understand the law of
God's rulership? Whose is the wisdom rightly to comprehend and appreciate these divine dispensations?
Therefore he prays that God may reveal to him the
true principle of (Israel's) existence, in order that man
may gain wisdom from the trials of life. In the same
spirit Moses exclaims, "Let me know thy ways that I
may comprehend thee," or "Let me behold thy
glory."

He prays that the majesty of the Lord may return to
Israel's camp, that God may again become reconciled
to his chosen servants, that thereby may be made manifest the principle underlying life. If the Lord's mercy
were shown them in abundance now in the morning of
their existence, happy would be the consequences
throughout the life of the people, joy would brighten
their entire career. "We will sing (the praise of the
Lord), we will rejoice all our days."

4

It would surprise us greatly not to find in this poem any reference to the sufferings in Egypt, since the passage, in Exodus referred to speak so frequently and with such emphasis of the deliverance from slavery. And indeed, the reference in verse 15 is more than a mere allusion. In a truly poetic spirit, the bard makes use of the fact that the sinning people has but just risen from the degradation of slavery to the heights of national existence.

"Give us joy even as the days of our sufferings, the years wherein we knew evil." After centuries of oppression and slavery, may not a people justly lay claim to the happiness which the Lord, in his mercy, can bestow upon them? Therefore, let the present generation clearly *behold* God's mercy, let its reflection brighten the path of all posterity.

What is the *visible* sign of God's return to his peoples of his forgiveness?

"For wherein shall it be known, in any wise," says Moses, "that I have found grace in thy eyes, I with thy people? Is it not in that thou goest with us? So shall we be distinguished, I and thy people, from all the people that are upon the face of the earth."

The erection of a portable dwelling in which God resided in Israel's midst when Israel halted, and which journeyed with it when it went on its way, the building of the tabernacle and the divine worship connected with it, form this visible sign.

The Midrash, with delicate insight, connects the end of our poem with the completion of the tabernacle. (Num. Rabbah, 12).

In this particular, too, the psalm stands in close relation to the Pentateuchal text. The elevation, the sub-

limity of this prayer that God may firmly establish
and sanctify the work of man, dispels the gloomy
and depressing air surrounding this poem, which
has so frequently led to the misinterpretation of our
psalm as a pessimistic reflection on the vanity of human
life.   M.

POPULAR LITERATURE OF THE CHINESE LABORERS IN THE UNITED STATES.

BY STEWART CULIN.

ROMANCES, dramas and song books constitute the greater part of the Chinese literature current among the Chinese laborers in the United States. There exists, however, a remainder, covering a wide range of subjects and consisting of selections from the *folk literature* of Southern China, as opposed to the national classics. It is to this, the practical part of the popular literature of our Chinese, that I shall refer in this paper. In it both moral treatises and philosophical writings are conspicuously absent, and the canonical books that are well known at least by reputation in the West are not represented. A spirit of respect for antiquity and for what is right and proper prevades it, as indeed they pervade almost the entire field of Chinese literature, yet there are few books of a distinctively religious character, either Confucian, Taoistic or Buddhistic, among it, nor is the slightest reference to Christianity to be found in the contents of the thin volumes that are piled on the shelves in our Chinese shops. The absence of devotional literature, it should be explained, is probably due to the lack of demand on the part of the Chinese here, as such publications hold a prominent place in the literature of the millions in China. Tracts are, in fact, frequently placed for dis-

(52)

tribution in the Chinese shops in New York city, and recently a thin pamphlet entitled "*Kwán Tai ming shing king;* or, The Enlightened Holiness Classic of the God of War," was thus offered in the shop of the "Wo Ke" Company in that city.

Like the novels, the books to be described are, with two exceptions, printed on brown Chinese paper from wooden blocks. No indication of the use of movable types is to be observed in them, nor of foreign influence in their manufacture.

Their title pages are usually printed on yellow paper and bear the full name of the book and usually its date, with place and name of its publisher. The name of the writer, when it occurs, is usually appended to the pre-. face or introduction.

First among them, at least in point of variety, if not in intrinsic worth, are the almanacs which are annually received from China. They are so varied, so curious and full of interest, that I shall leave them for a more extended notice than I can give them here, and proceed at once to the subject of divination, upon which several popular treatises are found. An hereditary descent is claimed for works on divination from the *Yik King*, or "Book of the Changes," and when an attempt is made to obtain information concerning the subject from the Chinese here, they always refer the inquirer to this highly unintelligible book. The most voluminous of these works found on our booksellers' shelves is entitled *Tsang shan puk yik*, or "Casting Lots, Revised and Corrected," by *Li cho tsz*. This book, in 12 duodecimo volumes, describes a method of divination by means of 64 cards, or slips of bamboo, called *kwá ts'im*, of which a set is exhibited in the collection of objects used in fortune telling in the Museum of the University of Pennsylvania. This system of divination, which is very complicated, is highly esteemed by the Chinese, and it is said by the Chinese here to have been invented by *Man Wong*, and is hence known as *Man Wong Kwâ*. *Man Wong* is the name by which *Ch'êung*, Duke of *Chau* (B. C. 1231–1135), was canonized. It is said that during two years he passed in prison he devoted his leisure to composing an arrangement of the *Yik King*, or "Book of Changes."

Another treatise, in a single volume, is entitled *Ngâ p'âi shan shò t'ò chü ts'êung kái*, or, "Illustrated Complete Explanation of the Divine Numbers of Dominoes," and is, as its name implies, an explanation of a method of fortune telling with dominoes.

Lau Chòng Shan Seung ts'im pin, the "Complete Book of Lau Chong's Divine Introspection" is a treatise on physiognomy and palmistry. *Kwán tai ling ts'im*, or "*Kwán Tai*, divining lots" is a collection of verses with commentaries, used when the divining sticks are thrown before the god *Kwán*. The pages of this book are numbered from 1 to 100, and correspond with the divining sticks which bear the same numbers. It is found in use in many shops and laundries, and is oftener referred to than any other work used in fortune-telling.

The step from divination to gambling seems a comparatively short one, and yet, while the latter subject is tabooed, both in letters and polite conversation, a handbook for calculating the prices of tickets and the resulting prizes for the literary lottery called the "White Pigeon Ticket" is sold here. This book is lithographed on thick white paper, and bears no imprint, at least in the writer's copy, but is said to have been made in San Francisco. There seem to be at least two editions, the writer's being entitled *Shang ts'oi tsit king*, or "A Quick Way to Get Rich." A translation or explanation of this book was published in San Francisco in 1891 by "Pun Wen." This practically anonymous treatise is entitled "The Chinese Lottery Exposed, containing a brief description of the manner by which the Chinese count, combine and establish the different tickets in the Chinese lottery, accompanied by their tables and system of computing in general." The calculations are intricate, and appear to be determined by experiment, none of the methods known to Western mathematicians for shortening such work being employed. This so-called "exposure" is something of a literary curiosity. It can be understood only by one very well versed in mathematics, and is interesting as an illustration of Chinese arithmetical processes.

ARITHMETIC.

The Chinese were by no means deficient in their mathematical knowledge in the early time compared with other nations, and in the seventeenth century they became acquainted, through the Jesuit missionaries, with the science as it was then understood in the West. More recently the Protestant missionaries have translated European text-books, so that facilities for acquiring an advanced knowledge of the subject are now open to them. The only works on arithmetic, however, that are sold here are small manuals for the use of the abacus. One of these in the writer's collection is entitled *K'án yik sün fát kwai ch'u ts'üt iü*, or "The important part of a summary of easy mathematical rules of multipli-

cation and division." The first of the two small volumes is illustrated with a picture of a schoolmaster
with a *sün p'ún*, or abacus, on the table before him, and
a seated pupil who bends over his book.

MEDICINE.

It is not surprising to find the Chinese here well
equipped with books on the subject of medicine, as they
are frequently beyond the reach of their physicians, and
have to rely upon self-prescribed remedies. The shops
sell a book entitled *I Tsung Kam Kám*, or "The
Golden Mirror of the Physician's Temple," which Dr.
Wylie pronounces one of the best Chinese works of
modern times for general medical information. It was
composed in compliance with an imperial order issued
in 1739, in ninety books, and consists of several treatises,
two of which date back to the Han dynasty (202 B. C.–
220 A. D), and were written, according to Dr. Wylie,
by the earliest Chinese medical writer, who gives pre-
scriptions in addition to theory. The work, as sold
here, is incomplete, containing only 40 books, ten of
which are devoted to *ngoi fo*, or "external practice,"
and 30 to *noi fo*, or "internal practice," the former corresponding somewhat with our surgery. A treatise
on *materia medica* is also sold here, the *Pun ts' ò kong*
muk, or the Chinese herbal. The great work of this
name was compiled by *Li Shi-chan*, of the Ming
dynasty, and comprised an account of 1892 different
medicaments. The one used here, an abridgment of
the famous original, was published in 1773. It is contained in 12 duodecimo volumes, and describes 520 rem-
edial agents. The first volume has 477 rude wood-cuts,
representing different plants and animal and mineral

substances, which are described in the work. It is not unusual to find Chinese here who are well acquainted with this and the book on medical practice.

HISTORY.

It has been stated that the historical novels are the only channel through which a large part of the Chinese people obtain their knowledge of history, but there are several popular historical works sold in the shops here. One of these, in two octavo volumes, is entitled *Ku Sz' K'ing Lam*, or "Coral Forest of Ancient Matters." It is prefaced with rude maps of the constellations and of the country of China, which are followed by a picture of the unicorn (*Lun*) that is said to have announced the birth of Confucius, and opposite to it a picture of the sage himself. After this there is a series of rude woodcuts representing the legendary heroes of China, commencing with Pw'ánku, the first man, and succeeded by pictures of the first sovereign of each dynasty down to the present. In the space left for the last there is no picture, but instead the inscription *Shing tai mán mán sui;* literally, 'Supreme Ruler, ten thousand, ten thousand years;" that is, "O King, live forever !"

SCHOOL BOOKS.

Although there are few Chinese children here, and no Chinese school or school-masters who practice their profession, I found several elementary school-books for sale in one of the shops in New York city. They consisted of the first, second and fourth books, as described by Dr. Williams, that are placed in the hands of Chinese children. They are long, narrow pamphlets, of white paper, with red paper covers, and printed in large characters of the kind called *Sung*, of great beauty. It is the custom for pupils to cover these books with an envelope of semi-transparent paper, upon which they copy with a brush the characters beneath. The first book is entitled the *Sâm Tsz' King*, or "Trimetrial Classic," written in the Sung dynasty (A. D. 1050). It begins with a sentence, the first which a Chinese learns at school, and which, according to Dr. Williams, contains one of the most disputed doctrines of the ancient heathen world :

> Men at their birth are by nature radically good ;
> Though alike in this, in practice they widely diverge.
> If not educated the natural character grows worse ;
> A course of education is made valuable by close attention.
>
> *   *   *   *   *
>
> As gems unwrought serve no useful end,
> So men untaught will never know what right conduct is.

The next book of the three, although according to Dr. Williams, another called the *Pâk-kâ-sing*, or "Century of Surnames," intervenes, is the *Tin tsz' man*, or "Thousand Character Classic," which is composed of just 1,000 characters, no two of which are alike in form or meaning. It is attributed to the sixth century of our era, and treats of man in the various relations of life, interspersed with numerous historical illustrations. The third book, entitled *Yau hok shi*, or "Odes for Children," is written in rhymed pentameters, and according to Dr. Williams contains a brief description and praise of literary life, and allusion to the changes of the season and the beauties of nature.

DICTIONARIES.

The Chinese, according to Dr. Wylie, have bestowed much labor upon the compilation of dictionaries, in or-

der to preserve the purity of the language to after ages.
These books may be ranged, on his authority, in the
following three divisions, according to the plan of their
construction: First, those in which the words are
arranged in various categories fixed upon with regard to
affinity of subjects. Next, those arranged according to
the radical part of the character, the first work of this
kind having been published A. D. 100; and thirdly,
those which are arranged in accordance with the tones
and final sounds of the characters. It is to this last class
to which the native dictionaries used by the Chinese
laborers in the United States belong. The book most
frequently consulted by them is a thin octavo volume,
entitled *Tung yam tsz' lui*, "Collection of characters
agreeing in sound." It contains 10,025 characters,
arranged in thirty-six divisions, under as many final
sounds. These are indicated by well-known characters,
placed at the head of each division. This book is thus.
as its name implies, a rhyming dictionary. Its chief
use is to enable a writer to select the correct character
from among those having the same sound, short defini-
tions under each enabling him to determine the one
with the desired meaning. It is inadequate in many
ways. Thus, there are fifty-three finals or rhymes in
the Canton dialect, while all the characters in this *tsz'
lui*, as such books are familiarly called, are arranged
under thirty-six final sounds. The person, too, who
uses it is supposed to know the sound of the character
he wants, as Dr. Williams justly remarks concerning
the next described volume. This book, which is sold
in the Chinese shops here, is entitled *Kong-ú ch'ik-tuk,
Fan-wan ts'üt-iü hóp tsáp*, or, as it has been translated
by a distinguished scholar of this city, "River and

Lake (i. e., universal) letter-model rhyme distinguishing selected, important gathered collection." It may
be observed that many translations from the Chinese
lose much of the force and conciseness of the original
in an attempt to bring them into accord with the
English idiom. This work, which, according to Dr.
Williams, is the standard of pronunciation for the Canton dialect, is in the form of a small dudecimo handbook. The edition sold here is in four volumes, bound
in two, and contains 7327 characters.

The latter are arranged under the thirty-three finals
of the first three upper tones. Their sounds are represented, as in the *tsz' lui*, by standard and well known
characters, the remaining twenty finals in the fourth
tone, which end in *k*, *p* and *t*, being included under
them. The unwritten sounds or colloquial words used
by the people of Canton, according to Dr. Williams, are
nearly all omitted, which is one of its greatest defects,
and renders it far less useful to the foreigner, who is
learning the dialect, than the superior local vocabularies
of Amoy and Funchan.

CHINESE AND ENGLISH.

The Chinese and English dictionaries used by the
Chinese in the United States have the words arranged
in categories, according to the affinity of subjects, a
method of arrangement generally adopted in the compilation of Chinese dictionaries in foreign languages. The
one work highly esteemed is entitled *Ying ü Tsáp Tsün*,
"English words collected completely," by *T'ong Ting
Kü*. The copy in the writer's collection, a gift from Mr.
Simon Stern, who obtained it at San Francisco, is in
six octavo volumes, printed on white paper and protected

by two board covers, between which it is secured by
tapes.   In its externals it presents a good specimen of
high-class Chinese book-making.

The author, in a modest English preface, states that it
was written by him, "a native of Canton, in the Canton
dialect, chiefly to suit the taste of Canton people who
have transactions or are connected with foreigners.   The
words are first given in Chinese; then the pronunciation
of such words, written in English; then the meaning of
those words in the English language; and lastly, the
pronunciation of the English words written in Chinese,
so that the book is not only useful for Chinese to learn
English, but at the same time it will enable foreigners
to learn Chinese."   The preface bears the date of April
21st, 1862.   The English characters are written fairly
and distinctly in script, and the Chinese characters are
of great beauty.   The book is, in fact, a perfect *fac
simile* of the author's manuscript, which was pasted,
sheet by sheet, upon the engraver's wooden blocks, as is
the custom with "copy" furnished to the printer in
China.   This work is most highly esteemed by the Chinese as the one best adapted for its purpose, and is celebrated for the perfection of its English text.   Its author,
who is living, has since written a book of travels in
foreign countries, and obtained a distinguished official
position in China.

It is or was the custom in San Francisco for several
Chinese to club together and buy one of these books
and hire a teacher to instruct them in the English language.   The original edition is so expensive there that
it has been reproduced by a Chinese firm in that city.
This pirated edition is lithographed on thick paper and
bound in one volume.   Neither the Chinese nor the

American edition of this work is sold in the Chinese
shops I have described here, but it is said to be the
source of the Chinese and English hand-books that are
found in their collections. The one in common use is
in two small octavo volumes entitled *Fä ying t'ung ü*
or "Chinese and English dictionary." It contains
about 2,000 English words, with a number of English
phrases, all arranged in categories according to the subject. The words are those used in trade, shipping and
domestic service. It is printed on brown paper in the
ordinary Chinese manner. The words and phrases are
written in ruled spaces in English script, with the corresponding Chinese text above them, and the English
pronunciation written phonetically in Chinese characters
below. It bears the date 1872, but, from references to
an earlier date in the business forms in the text, was
probably written some years before that time. This
vocabulary is too limited and restricted for more than
the most elementary instruction in English, and many
Chinese use the dictionary by Kwong Ki Chiu, which
was published in Hong Kong in 1875.

THE ALPHABETS OF THE BERBERS.

BY D. G. BRINTON.

THE Berber tribes are called by some writers, collectively Hamites, and by others Proto-Semites. From the dawn of history they have occupied most of the area between the Nile Valley and the Atlantic Ocean north of the Soudan. They have also linguistic kinsfolk in Abyssinia and in adjacent parts of East Africa. The ancient Ethiopians or Cushites were of their lineage; Timbuctoo was founded by one of their chieftians, and the extinct Guanches of the Canary Islands were members of their stock. To them belonged the classical Libyans, Numidians, Mauritanians, and Getulians, and in later times petty tribes innumerable, the most prominent of which to-day are 'the Rifians of Morocco, the Kabyles of Algeria, the Touaregs or Tamachek of the Sahara, the Mzabis, etc. They extended into Palestine and Syria, and it is probable that the ancient Amorites, Canaanites and their relatives were of Hamitic blood.

The physical type of the pure Hamite is that of the blonde, with gray or blue eyes, yellowish or reddish hair, tall in stature and dolichocephalic.

During two short visits to North Africa in the years 1888 and 1889, I became much interested in the ethnology of this stock, which offers many most interesting problems. ·The one to which I shall confine myself at present is its methods of writing.

The Berber hordes of to-day, with one exception, employ the Arabic alphabet, though it fails to render some of the sounds with precision. The exception is that of the Touaregs of the Sahara. They employ an alphabet of their own, of great antiquity and disputed origin. They call it *tifinar*, which is a plural from the singular *tafinek*. As in the Berber dialects, the radicals are single or small groups of consonants, invariable, and inflected by vowel changes: we have in *tafinek* the quadriliteral radical *t-f-n-k*, as is held by Rinn; or, if the initial *t* be regarded as a neuter prefix, there will be the triliteral root *f-n-k*. The primitive meaning of this root is a sign, mark, or token by which a place or thing is recognized. Peculiarly-shaped stones or ridges, which serve as landmarks, are called *efinagha* (Barth).

Strictly speaking, the word *tifinar* applies only to those letters of the alphabet which can be represented by straight lines; while a number of others, expressed by dots, receive the name *tiddebakin* (Rinn). All letters, whether simple or compound, can be and usually are written by one or other of these methods, straight lines or dots, as is shown by the alphabet presented, from Hanoteau's Grammaire Tamachek. The cursive script, however, permits the use of curved variants in some cases, all of which are shown on the alphabet I submit.

The Touareg alphabet is far from systematic. The order in which the letters are arranged is purely arbitrary; there is considerable difference in the forms of letters in different tribes; there are no vowel-points like those in modern Hebrew, and no accessory signs to represent pure vowels. What is worse, there is no rule as to whether the script should be read from left to right or from right to left, from above downward or from below upward. The assertions made to the contrary by

Hanoteau and Halévy are disproved by the documents published by Rinn, which I show. They were written by native Touaregs to native Touaregs. The writer sometimes begins at a corner of the page, and proceeds from right to left or from left to right as he pleases; arrived at the further margin, he turns his sheet, so as to go perpendicularly or in any other way that suits him. As the words are frequently not separated, as punctuation and capital letters are unknown, and as the sequence of the lines is not fixed, it is no easy matter to decipher a Touareg manuscript. When a native undertakes the task, he begins by spelling the consonants aloud, in a chanting voice, applying to them successively the various vowels, until he finds the words which make sense (Hanoteau).

Imperfect as the alphabet seems, it is in very extensive use among the Touaregs, both men and women. Barth found that his young camel-driver could read it with ease. Captain Bissuel writes: "A de trés rares exceptions prés, tous les Touaregs de l'ouest, hommes et femmes, savent lire et ecrire." Duveyrier makes a similar statement of the Touaregs of the north.

Most writers, one following the other, have traced the Touareg alphabet back to the Carthaginians, and have sought to identify its letters with those of the Punic writing.

Its history, however, is by no means so easy to unravel. That certain of its letters are identical with the Semitic alphabets is unquestioned ; but some of them are not ; and those that are alike, may they not be mere loans, or even independent derivatives, from some one common source?

The material to solve these problems must be drawn

5

from ancient inscriptions. These are by no means lacking, and prove that an old Berber alphabet was in use
in Northern Africa long before the Christian era; yes,
in the opinion of some archæologists, as Collignon and
Rinn, long before the founding of Carthage.

These inscriptions are of two classes, the one carved
on dressed stones, such as grave and memorial tablets;
the other on native rocks, *in situ*, where a smooth surface offered a favorable exposure.

A large number of the former were copied and published by General Faidherbe, and have been studied by
Professor Halévy. The latter explains most of the letters by the Punic alphabet, and presents transliterations
and renderings of the epitaphs. His identifications,
however, have not satisfied later students. I find, for
instance, that while Halévy's "Essai d'Epigraphie
Libyque" was published in 1875, Réné Basset, probably
the most thorough Berber scholar living, writes in 1887
in his "Grammaire Kabyle:" "Le déchiffrement de ces
inscriptions est encore aujour d'hui sujet à contestation,
au moins pour le valeur de plusieurs lettres." In a similar strain, M. Philippe Berger in his "Histoire de
l'Ecriture" (Paris, 1891) rejects nearly all Halévy's renderings as incomplete and improbable.

This difficulty very much increases when we come to
the other class of inscriptions—those engraved on the
living rocks. The mortuary epitaphs collected by
Faidherbe may be referred with probability to a period
two or three centuries before Christ; but the rupestrian
writing is of much more uncertain age. Some of it has
the patine and other attributes of high antiquity; in
other instances it is evidently recent. Examples of it
are found in abundance on both slopes of the Atlas

range from Morocco to the Libyan Plateau. Unquestionable instances have been reported from the Canary Islands by Dr. Verneau; Barth found them south of Fezzan; Captain Bernard copied some in southern Algiers; last year M. Flamand described a number of stations in southern Oran; Dr. Hamy has made an instructive study of them; and a number of other travellers have added to our knowledge about them. They are often carefully and cleanly cut into the faces of hard rocks, and are thus calculated to resist the elements for many generations.

What is noteworthy about the oldest types of these rock-writings is this: that while they contain some letters which are common to the Touareg, Libyan, and Punic alphabets, they also present a certain number which are not, and which cannot be explained by them. Thus, in the most recent article on the subject, published last year in *L'Anthropologic*, M. Flamand writes that these glyphs show "bien characterisées, des lettres Libyco-Berberes, et aussi des signes qu'il a été jusqu'ici impossible de comparer avec aucun de ces alphabets." The copies of these inscriptions which I show will give an idea of some of these unknown signs. They are three in number, and fair examples of hundreds to be seen in the localities referred to. One was copied by Barth at a place southwest of Fezzan; the second by Captain Bernard, near Laghouat; the third by Captain Boucher, near Figuig. While each presents letters identical with some in the Touareg alphabet, or in the Numidian mortuary inscriptions, the majority of the letters belong to neither class.

Very noteworthy is the resemblance which certain elements in some of the oldest of these rupestrian in-

scriptions bear to the alphabetiform signs cut into the
surface of the dolmens and menhirs of Western France
and Northern Spain. This resemblance has been
forcibly brought out and abundantly illustrated very
recently by M. Ch. Letourneau before the Anthropologi-
cal Society of Paris. His studies and comparisons have
led him to the conclusion that these inscribed figures
on the megalithic remains are in many features identical with those on the rocks in Tunisia and the Sahara,
and that they represent the rudiments of an alphabet
more ancient than the Punic or perhaps the Phenician,
one independently derived by the ancestors of the Berbers, and carried through their influence far into the
area of continental Europe.

The probability that in some of these megalithic inscriptions of France we may find traces of some of the
ancient Berber alphabets is increased by the undoubted
resemblance of some of the Celtiberic characters to those
of the Libyan inscriptions. This resemblance is com-
mented on in positive terms by M. Berger in his work
above quoted, and he considers that it demands for its
explanation "an invasion, or at least a penetration, of
the African element into the Iberic peninsula" (Hist.
de l'Eciture, p. 339). We know that some forms of the
Celtiberic alphabet are extremely ancient; and that they
had some other origin than from the Phenician is the
more likely, as not a single Phenician, Punic, or other
ancient Semitic inscription has ever been found in the
Iberic peninsula (Berger, ibid., p. 333). If the opinion
of Letourneau, above quoted, is well-founded, we may
reasonably believe that the primitive Celtiberians par-
took in culture, as it is likely they did in blood, with
the builders of the Megalithic monuments, though

whether they were "Celtic" or not, may remain an open question.

It is the opinion of some careful students, therefore, and it seems evident, that for a portion of the ancient Libyan alphabet we must look elsewhere than to a Semitic source. The question is a new one; but there can scarcely be more than one answer to it. We must look directly to Egypt, whither the Semitic alphabets themselves must finally trace their origin. Nor does such an answer present the least historic difficulty. Earlier than the twelfth century B.C., there were direct and much-traveled caravan routes from the heart of the Berber country into Egypt. "I have not the slightest doubt," writes Barth, "that the Imoshagh (Touaregs) are represented in the ancient sculptures of Egypt as the Tamhu and the Mashawash."

We are well aware that thousands of Berber soldiers were enlisted in the Egyptian armies in the Ramesside epoch. The high culture they possessed is attested by the catalogue of spoils in the inscription of Merenptah I. These included gold and silver drinking vases, swords and armor of hardened copper, razors, etc., indicating a developed condition of the arts. The signal defeat they encountered in the decisive battle at Per-erschepset did not break the power of the Libyan kings. We know that they recovered themselves, and in the reign of Merenptah II., grandson of the first of the name, possessed themselves of the whole of the western delta; nor was it until their defeat by the powerful Rameses III., that their destructive inroads ceased (Erman, *Ægypten*, Bd. I., §§ 77–80).

Unquestionably, during this long intercourse in peace and war, a knowledge of some of the Egyptian methods of writing must have extended among the Berbers. As M. Berger remarks—"There is too great a lacuna between the Punic and the Libyan alphabets for us to admit that they were derived the one from the other." (ibid, p. 332). Doubtless they were related in origin, and at a later date stood geographically side by side and exerted some influence on each other; but there is no necessity any longer of accepting the popular theory that the old Libyans and Numidians were ignorant of writing until Dido founded her famous city.

In his latest work, Mr. Flinders Petrie maintains that the letters of the Phenician alphabet were derived directly from Egypt; it is quite likely that one or more of the earliest Berber alphabets were also derived directly from the same venerable seat of culture, adopting, in part signs identical, in part diverse from the multiform Phenician alphabets of the earliest epochs. Intercourse with the Semitic traders and colonists led to a greater or less unification of the methods of writing, as has occurred in so many other instances; so that the Libyan alphabet of the third century B. C. was easily enough mistaken for a daughter, instead of a sister, of that in use by the Carthaginians. But they never reached a complete identity, and as the farther we go back the greater seems the diversity, the theory of an independent origin appears to be alone that which will satisfy the facts in the case; and this theory has in itself a high historic probability.

The principal works to be consulted, copies of all of which from my own library I lay before you, are the following:

Faidherbe, "Collection Compléte des Inscriptions Numidiques."

Hanoteau, "Essai de Grammaire Kabyle."

Hanoteau, "Essai de Grammaire de la Langue Tamachek."

Halévy, "Essai d'Epigraphe Libyque."

Bissuel, "Les Touaregs de l'Ouest."

Basset, "Notes de Lexicographie Berbère."

Rinn, "Les Origines Berbères."

Numerous articles on the rupestrian inscriptions are scattered through the *Revue d'Ethnographie, L'Anthropologie*, etc. As the subject is one, I believe, entirely new to American Orientalists, and as it may possibly prove of considerable significance to the history of the development of Mediterranean civilization, this brief presentation of it will, I trust, lead to further researches.

WHO WERE THE ANCIENT ETHIOPIANS?

BY W. MAX MÜLLER.

WE no longer believe as some Greeks supposed, that
the ancient Ethiopians, i. e., the inhabitants of Napata
and Meroe, possessed a wonderful self-created civilization, that was the source of Egypt's culture, and therefore the earliest culture of the world. Since Lepsius
explored the ruins of their capitals, we know that these
famous Ethiopians were only feeble imitators of the
Egyptians, civilized by them at a comparatively modern date, and independent only since about 1100 B. C.
Their culture, however, is still interesting, being unique
in ancient Africa, and attested to by remarkable monuments. The part played in the world's history by the
kings of Meroe after 750 B. C. is no insignificant one.
Nevertheless the question, "who were these people?"
has never been thoroughly discussed. Most scholars
seem to be content with the idea that they were indigenous Africans, no matter whether jet-black or blackish,
brown or yellow. But everybody acquainted with the
knotty problems of African linguistics will acknowledge
both the importance and the difficulty of an exact determination. No part of the world except the Caucasus
shows such a medley of the most heterogeneous languages as Central Africa. At least three of the six
principal African races* live in the old territory of the

---

*Dwarf-tribes, Hottentots, Negroes, Bantu, "Nubas" and Hamites.

Meroitic kingdom at present, so that even the race cannot be determined easily.

To a large extent the classical writers are responsible
for our uncertainty. The Greeks, who were poorly
gifted for linguistic and ethnographic observations,
were able indeed to distinguish the Egyptians and the
Libyans, marked too conspicuously by their white skin.
But all the rest were "Aithiopes," *i. e.*, dark people. If
we were dependent entirely on classical writers, most
likely we should not be able to recognize the existence
even of the great Hamitic branch of nations, not to
mention darker races.* The ancient Egyptians it appears were not much better. See my book, Asien &
Europa (Leipzig, 1893), p. 112–113, on the deplorable
fact that their expression *nḥsi* (pronounce with vowels
nḥése?) is not restricted to "Negro," but is used to include all East-Africans, black, brown and brownish,
exactly like that vague term "Aithiopes." In view
of these difficulties it is best to determine first of all
the race of the Meroites, leaving the far more difficult
question as to their language aside until we shall have
more linguistic material.

I keep the fifth race, notwithstanding its inappropriate name—the
Nubas themselves most likely do not belong to it—to designate the
mixed zone north from the Bantu territory. It is true, F. Müller's
(Grundriss der Sprachwissenschaft, III.) list of seven "Nuba" languages contains five which possibly belong to other branches, but we
need some repository for doubtful languages of this kind. I suppose after our material has been increased a "Sub-Bantu" family
will have to be established, while most other "Nuba" languages will
be added to the northern families.

* The attempts to distinguish the (Hamitic) tribes on the coast, the
Troglodytes and Ichthyophagi, from the proper "Ethiopians" are
unfortunate.

The Egyptians nowhere have given an indication about the race of the Meroites which could be of any use to modern ethnographers and linguists. If King Amen-hotpe III. calls the people around Napata *nhsi* (Amada, Lepsius, Denkmaeler III., 65a), just as, 1000 years before, the tribes near the second cataract were styled (L. D. III., 136 h. i.), this does not prove that they were negroes. (See above on the vague expression *nhsi*.) Even the nearest Hamitic relations of the Egyptians, the red Punti, bore the same designation (Asien & Europa, 112). Therefore, I do not deny that there is some significance in the name officially accepted by the Meroitic kingdom, *Ptompanhêse*,* "Negroland," but it offers only a weak and doubtful argument.

The latter observation has escaped the attention of Lepsius, who, in his Nuba-Grammar, developed bold theories, based only upon the designation *nhêse* and its alleged meaning—"negro." It would have upset his whole theory on the Meroites.

Lepsius and Brugsch are the only Egyptologists who pronounced a distinct opinion on the ethnologic position of the Meroites. The first declared them to have been Hamites, identical with the modern Bisharin or Bedjas, the latter looked at the modern Nubas (Barabras) as direct descendants of the Meroites. During Lepsius' lifetime, the Nuba theory stood in the background; lately it has found some adherents.

I think the hypothesis of Lepsius † (Briefe aus Aegyp-

---

* *P-ta-nhs* Mon. div. 1, 11; 5, 12, L. D. V, 52, VI. demot. Nr. 8 (p-ta-n-nhs), the same as Ptoemphaneis Ptolemy 4, 7, 34, Ptoemphae (sic!) Pliny 6, 192.

† The only attempt of a proof is found Nuba-Grammar, p. cxxvi. Arabic writers speak (*very positively!*) of an old alphabet of the

ten 181, 266, Nuba-Grammatik cxxiv.) is based merely upon the wide-spread prejudice against the negro-race. The negro is considered too inferior a creature to produce any civilization, and a state like that of Meroe can be due, they say, only to the white Mediterranean race. Now, the first prejudice is not quite unjust, although it must not be exaggerated. But, at least, so much is certain, that our Hamitic relatives do not deserve the favorable prejudice. The negro everywhere leads a settled, agricultural life, the Kushitic Hamite, where he has not been mixed with Semites (the Agaü tribes) or Negroes (the Gallas), has the most expressedly nomadic and pastoral customs. The negro builds towns and even large fortified cities, but where is a real Bishari city? The negro forms states, and his despotic monarchs sometimes rule enormous territories; the Kushite never has advanced beyond the formation of clans and tribes like those of Bedawees, therefore, he has only chiefs, no kings. The negro is mostly peaceable, our Kushitic relatives are more inclined to war and robbery.

All negro tribes have shown some ability as smiths, potters, etc.; of the Kushitic nations hardly anything of that kind is known. Certainly, the negro is not able

---

Nubas, and, at the same time, assert that (*in their time!*), the Nubas being Christians, used (only?) Greek, Syriac (!) and Coptic writing. Lepsius is right that the Meroitic writing is mistaken here for Nubian. The Kitab-el-fihrist speaks of a national writing of the Bedjas (yet the author of that book confesses that he never saw a specimen of it!). Therefore, Lepsius argues, the only known Ethiopic alphabet, that of Meroe, is that of the Bedja-Bisharin, and these must be the Meroites themselves. Who will admit that this strange logic is "sufficiently convincing" (Lepsius)?—The alleged Bedja writing must have consisted in some remainders of Meroitic writing, which was given up sooner by the Nubians because they were earlier Christianized.

to develop a higher culture by himself, and his cultured states mostly depend upon foreign influence; however, we see he is docile and imitates with some success. The Bishari and Somali is nowadays almost on the same level of culture as 3000, maybe 5000, years ago. In brief, the Kushitic nations east of Meroe seem perfectly unable to have formed that great empire. The Nile valley is too narrow for shepherds, and would not have allowed any other dense population in and around the great cities except an agricultural one. Such a population could not consist of Hamites, and least of all, of Bisharin. On the other hand, no population would fulfil all the conditions better than negroes with an Egyptian aristocracy and hierarchy.*

Lepsius regarded the ancient Nubas as negroes, and therefore, owing to his prejudice, opposed Brugsch's view; Brugsch on the other hand asserted that, according to the monuments, the Meroites were a red-brown race like the modern Nubas,† therefore apparently identical with them. Yet it seems that Lepsius did not examine the Meroitic sculptures at all, and that Brugsch did not study them carefully enough.

The monuments of the Egyptians do not furnish much material. The Egyptian painters liked to caricature the hostile nations of the "vile Kôsh," and to exaggerate the immixture of negro-blood, common to all Africans, and perceptible to a certain extent even in the

---

* Kaufmann, Central Africa (Brixen, 1862), p. 203: "We find (among the negroes on the White Nile) all elements of culture . . . if only they would put on clothing, one would not call them savages." P. 204 he states their superiority over the Islamitic Nubians and Arabs in the Soudan.

† Compare Duemichen, Ä. Z., 87, 93. Lepsius, Letters, 230.

Egyptians. But when in the tomb of Huy (Lepsius, Denkm. III., 117), we see the princes of northern Nubia represented as negroes of monstrous ugliness, we must not overlook that they appear mixed with brown and red figures. Similar varieties of color appear in all representations of negro tribes, prove the fact that the upper Nile valley had a mixed population almost everywhere. But the contempt shown in the pictures and the neglect of names and countries of the "miserable nhêse," makes it impossible to determine the percentage of negro-blood in each one of the numerous tribes reaching from Assuan to Khartum and even more southward, who suffered in the wars (or slave-huntings) of the Pharaohs. The accounts neglect to give even geographical details. I also rather think Naville is wrong in saying: if Assarhaddon represents his enemy Taharqa on the stela of Sindjirli (now in Berlin) as a negro, we must believe him (Rec. trav., 15, 101). Such pictures always are caricatures, and the Assyrian sculptor could not show his loyalty better than by disfiguring the wretched enemy. We have to consider this low esteem of the negro also in Napata and Meroe, where we must expect negro-descendence to have been concealed. Besides, the portraits of the Meroitic kings have the common conventional style of later Egyptian art, in which the Ethiopian Taharqa, the Persian Darius, the Greek Ptolemy and the Roman Augustus, show the same traditional face. Therefore, only a very close and critical examination will discover any ethnologic details in the Meroitic sculptures.* The results are the following:

   1. *The color* of the Ethiopic kings is, of course, the

---

* In later time and in the extreme south (Ben Naga and Es-Sofra) the fetters of Egyptian conventionalism relaxed considerably.

conventional red, prescribed for every artist from 3000 B. C. If they appear red, like Darius, Ptolemy and Augustus, this is no indication of their real color. But while the yellow color is prescribed for women, we find Lepsius Denkmaeler V., 5, the wife of Taharqa red like her husband, which is quite unusual (compib. 19). This unique realistic boldness points to a brown color for the Meroites. Unfortunately, we can not determine what tint of brown.*

2. Before the Roman time not even common people are represented with a face different from the conventional type (23?). But then we find protruding lips, indications of prognathism, 63, 72, 73, etc.

3. The conventional style of representation requires the artificial beard tied to the chin even for the Roman emperors. But the Theban artists (Lepsius V., 3, 5, etc.), and even those of Napata (8, etc.), avoided that beard so conspicuously (exceptions 18 and only later 49, 51, 60–66; the artificial character is shown in the case of a queen, 64, 66!), that we must conclude they thought it absurd with Ethiopians. They were a beardless nation.

4. The curled hair, 20, 21, 27, 44, 50, 57, 59, 62, does not prove much, as the wig with innumerable small curls, dating from the time of pyramids, is a part of the conventional representation. But the hair is, everywhere, kept so short (comp. e. g., 75,) that we cannot doubt its crisp nature.†

* Passages as Herodotus 7, 70 (Nubians north of Napata?), Agatharchides 1, 16, etc., on dark "Ethiopians" lack geographical precision and are worthless, if we compare Herodotus' (2, 104) exaggeration of "black (melanchroes) and woolly-haired Egyptians."

† The golden head-dress of the kings, looking like a golden cap ornamented with small bosses or ornaments of curled form, is worthy of examination. I consider it an imitation of the old barbarous hair-dress, but furnishing no argument for the time of the sculptures.

5. A well known characteristic of the negro race is the ill-shaped breast of the women. See for this, 23, 41, 48, 49.* A feeble attempt to flatter noble women and to distinguish them from the common people, 48, but the queen herself, 50, 66, 67 b, d, 68 a, c, 70 b, c, is represented in such an ugly manner that one is tempted to take it for a caricature (figure 1).

6. All women belonging to the aristocracy are ugly, fat monsters, of a fatness which would stir up the envy of any royal harem in Uganda and the surrounding countries. All Orientals, ancient and modern, appreciate fat beauties, but only the black race reaches that perfection in the accumulation of fat which we find with all Meroitic queens (figure 2). Besides, in these we can observe something which does not seem to have been treated as a characteristic of some negroes: I mean the enormous accumulation of fat called by anatomists "steatopygy." It has been known as a peculiarity of the Hottentot race, but Schweinfurth (Heart of Africa, I., 296; II., 121,) mentions it as common among the Bongo negroes. I add to it the two well known instances of fat women from Punt, i. e., most likely the Somali coast,† inhabited 1500 B. C. not yet by Somalis, but by near relations of the Gallas‡ mixed with negroes. The same phenomenon in Meroe furnishes a new argument. It is greatly to be desired that this question be advanced

---

* L. D., III., 117, 119, with negroes.

† See my book Asien & Europa, p. 110. I must, however, express some doubt whether the artist is right in representing the steatopygy so marked in Punt. The pure Hamitic type of the Punti does not agree with it. I suppose he had in mind rather a well known characteristic of the Nilotic tribes. [See our figure 3.]

‡ See Schleicher's Somaligrammatik, p. x.

by illustrations from other tribes. Certainly the steatopygy is not common to all negroes. The Bongo live at
present 11 degrees southwest of Meroe, too far off to
warrant comparison.

7. The figures of the women show also a most decided
characteristic of the negro,* the oblique pelvis and the
seeming protrudance of the upper part of the body before
the lower. The figures of the men are too conventional ;
nevertheless 50A, the figure of an old, fat priest, de-
serves attention (figure 4). Female figures, 33, 34, 35,
37, 40, 41, 64B, confirm the observation.

I think there can be no longer any doubt that the
Meroites, probably a few families of the aristocracy ex-
cepted, were negroes, or at least so strongly mixed with
negroes that their type did not differ much from these.
Lepsius' theory about the Meroites may be dismissed
completely. Brugsch's theory, on the other hand, becomes more probable, only, however, on the condition
that we do not compare the modern Nubas, but assume
their forefathers to have been pure negroes as Lepsius
assumed. Brugsch has tried to decipher a few lines of
the Meroitic language (Zeitschr. f. Aeg. Sprache, 1887),
written in wretched hieroglyphics, and promised to do
so also with the cursive inscriptions. Owing to the
miserable material, his results are very doubtful. In
some places they deserve attention,† but it is better to
leave them aside until they are confirmed by new evidence. In the meantime we have to treat the Nuba
theory with the utmost caution. Its defenders do not

* Emphasized by Lepsius, Nuba Grammar, ix. (cf. L. D., III., 120,
etc.)

† E. g., his supposed form (i)*mipul,* "beloved" (p. 30), is explained
very ingeniously.

Fig.1

Fig.2

Fig.3.

Fig.4.

seem to have observed that it is contradicted by classical writers. The points may be summed up as follows :

Eratosthenes (ca. 200 B. C.) states (in Strabo, 786): "On the left side of the Nile live the Nubae, in Libya, a great nation, beginning from Meroe to the curves, *not subject to the Ethiopians*, but under several kings of their own" (while all nations between Egypt, Meroe and the Red Sea are more or less subject to the Meroites and, therefore, are confounded with them).* Note the important distinction between Meroites and Nubae. Also, the rest of the note has not yet been explained. "The curves" must mean the great curve beginning at Korusko, not that of Abu-Hamed, or even Ed-Dabe. No "great nation" could live in the steppe Bayûda. The Meroites possessed the caravan road to the north, ending at Korusko and the lower borders of the Nile. There, indeed, we find Meroitic kings as builders, while they have left no traces later than Persian time between Korusko and the two other curves. This strange political condition is, therefore, not improbable. The exist-ence of Nubae north of Meroe, hinted at also by Strabo, 819, is confirmed already for the time of Eratosthenes by the fact that he knows only Nuba names for the three rivers, Asta-boras, Asta-pus (Astape, Pomp. Mela, 1, 50), Asta-soba, compounded with *asta*,† "water." An Egyp-tian inscription, 100 years later, calls a region of north-ern Nubia (containing silver mines,‡ therefore probably

---

* The statement about continual wars between the inhabitants of the two banks of the Nile, Strabo, 822, refers to Nubae and Blemmyans by Lepsius. But it seems to apply to the tribes on the Bahr-el-Abiad.

† Now *essi* in Nuba (for *esti*), in the kindred dialects of Kordofan (Lepsius lxxviii.) *otu* (for *ottu*). Mediæval Arabs mention a Nuba city, *Astenun*, near the second cataract. Note the old form *Aste*.

‡ Edrisi mentions silver in the well-known gold mines of Allaqi, Olaqi.

under 27° lat.) *Ast-rnn* (or *-lnn*).* On *Astemuras*, see below.

The classical reports on Nubae or Nobades on the frontier of Egypt in Roman time are familiar. It seems that they inhabited the western and parts of the eastern bank of the Nile, including the district formerly subject to the Meroites and abandoned by them, as we may conclude from the absence of monuments, after the expedition of Petronius (in Augustus' reign, *cf.* Strabo, 820). On the southern Nobades, we do not find any distinct mention,† and it is largely hypothetical to assume, according to their present seats, the mountains of Kordofan as the original home of the Nuba-people. Thence they extended only northward, entering the Nile valley near Napata. Even if they touched the White Nile east of Kordofan, the distinction between Nubae and Meroites remains in force.

---

* Duemichen, Ä. Z., 87, 93. Determinative : mineral or color. The Nuba-names of minerals have, unfortunately, been replaced by the Arabic words.

† Pliny gives a note 6, 192, from Aristocreon, "from the island in the Nile obeying the queen of the Semberritae (Senaar or Meroe itself?) the Nubei Aethiopes are 8 days journey distant." The suspicion that the direction towards the south is a mistake, is strengthened by the remark, "oppidum eorum Nilo impositum Tenupsis." Is this not *Pnupsis* (*Pnups*, Ptolem.), Hierosycaminus, *i. e.*, Maharaqa near Korusko, so that the northern Nubae are meant? Also, the following division of the country into *To-nobari* (read *-nobadi*, "Nuba-country"?) and Ptoenphae (! "Negro-country," see above, both Egyptian names) does not look like the banks of the White Nile. Ptol., 4, 7, 31, the remark after the Nubae, "west of the Aualites," is, possibly, based upon Eratosthenes in Strabo, 786. The Nyngbenitae Aethiopes, 4, 7, 35, are doubtful. So are the Nubae in the eastern Soudan, 4, 6, 16, 21, connected it seems, with a "lake Nuba" (or Nutha?) 13 (18?) of impossible situation and dto. mountains (16). Who will solve this confusion ?

Yet one could advance the theory that the distinction between Nubas and Meroites indicates only a political division. So much is certain that we find the Nuba-word *asta* "water" on Meroitic inscriptions. If we read that king Nestosenen (L. D. V., 16, l. 17), went to the city of *Asdemur(a)sa*, certainly the Astaboras * is meant; not the river itself, however, but a city at the junction of Nile and Atbara, not far from the modern Berber. But, what if that city, although belonging to the Meroitic kingdom, had a Nuba population? More forcible is the fact, not observed by Brugsch (Ae. Z., 87, 12), that the titles of the Nile-god L. D. V., 66, begin with *a-t* or *o-t*, which recalls the modern Kordofan-pronunciation for the word *asta*, "river, water." But if the Nubae lived opposite Meroe and held such a vast territory, should we not expect Nuba elements in the language of Meroe, especially in the time of its decline in the second century A. D. or later? Let us beware of forming a hasty conclusion from one word.

When the Meroitic inscriptions are deciphered, must we expect to find one uniform language in them? Certainly, those Egyptologists are wrong who speak of one single Ethiopic nation and think any name from the Upper Nile is Ethiopic, *i. e.*, Meroitic. Krall (Studien IV, in Sitzungsberichte, Wien, 1890), has pointed out the great difference in the phonetic system of the geographical names, and observed that the absence

---

* Change between m and w, b also in the name Meroe, written in earlier time Beruwa, later with m. If the Geez (Dillmann, Grammar, p. 52), has received the same peculiarity from the ancient Agaü dialects, I do not deny the possibility that some languages of Eastern Africa, quite different in structure, may have been influenced by a common foreign element in their pronunciation.

of the Semitic letter *cheth* (*kheth*) in modern Nuba
(which lacks even *h*) and in the ancient names of northern Nubia (p. 38) contrasts with its occurrence in the
names of Meroitic kings, and also in names of countries
raided by these (L. D. V., 16, rev. 29, etc.). The latter
fact is strange, because the Nilotic negro-languages down
to the Equator do not possess that sound, common to
the Semites and (earlier) Hamites, and avoid even the
sound of *h*, just as the Nuba does. Those hostile countries may have been influenced by Hamitic pronunciation.

It is, of course, quite impossible to determine anything beyond our conclusion that the Meroites were a
negro-tribe. They were similar in appearance to the
ancient Nubas before their strong admixture with Hamitic and Arabic blood. To the Nubas, I refer the passages on black Ethiopians * quoted p. 78. The language of the famous Ethiopians may have had a very
limited sphere, at least in Roman time; it may not have
comprised more than the Nile valley between Napata
and Khartum. Earlier extension to the North is not
impossible, but this would belong to the period before
Alexander, at least. We may well assume that, also
at that time, the Meroites were only one small tribe
ruling over the most heterogeneous nations. Especially
in the south, they seem to have been surrounded by the
same linguistic chaos as is found to-day south of Khartum; in the north and west they were shut in by Nubas,
from the east by Hamites. Though the evidence be
decisive that the ruling warriors of Napata were different from both, the possibility is not to be denied of a

---

* Undoubtedly Ptolemy, 1, 9, 9, refers to them.

connection either with the more distant relations of the Nubas, *e. g.*, the black Kunama and Barea, or, perhaps, with an even more remote dialect of the Nuba. Let us trust that the decipherment of the inscriptions will soon permit us to operate with more positive material, and to determine the character of that remarkable nation, doubly remarkable now as the only member of the black race which ever made its appearance upon the stage of the world's history.

NATIVE ISRAELITISH DEITIES.

BY GEORGE A. BARTON.

THE following paper is not by any means an exhaustive study of the subject which it touches. It is rather an attempt to set forth in a tentative and suggestive manner a few facts and seemingly reasonable theories with reference to the native polytheism of primitive Israel.

YAHWE.

In treating of native Israelitish deities, it is but fitting to begin with Yahwe, by far the most important of them. We must in the first place try to determine the most primitive character in which Yahwe was known to his worshippers. This is by no means an easy task, as it makes it necessary to enter that shadowy region before the beginnings of history, where we are compelled from indirect hints afforded by a later literature to guess at the outline of every character. Such hints give us some ground for the belief that in the first place Yahwe was known as a storm-god. He is in the theophanies usually represented as coming in a storm. This is the case in Psalm xviii., Ezekiel i., Habakkuk iii., Isa. xix. 1, and Job xxxviii. 1. In Exodus xiii. and xiv., Yahwe leads his people as a cloud, and in Exodus xix. and 1 Kings viii. 10, 11, Yahwe appears on Mount Sinai and in the temple as a cloud. Indeed, in Exodus, Leviticus, Numbers, and Deuteronomy, the

(86)

"cloud" is spoken of as a token of Yahwe's presence more than forty times. For other indications of the connection of Yahwe with storms, see Ps. civ. 13, 14, and Ps. cxlvii. 8, 16–18.

These indications are strengthened by the only satisfactory etymology one is able to suggest for the name Yahwe. The etymology of Ex. iii. 14, is a folk etymology, and fails to meet the facts of the case. The root *hâyâ* would give *Yahye*, and not *Yahwe*, as the divine name. The derivation of the name by Professor Frederic Delitzsch, in his "*Wo Lag das Paradies*," pp. 158–164, from the name of the Babylonian Ea, is also exceedingly improbable, if not impossible.

It is not probable that a long form like Yahwe, was derived from a short form like Ea or Ya. The original form must have been a word which would cover the form *Yahwe*, and also account for the contractions *yâ*, *yô*, and *yehô*, in such proper names as *Yonathan* and *Yᵉhoshaphat*. The form *Yahwe* is the only one which will, in accordance with the well-known tendency of words to wear away rather than to expand as time goes on, account for all the other forms.

It would seem a more probable etymology to derive *Yahwe* from *hâwâ*, which is used in Job xxxvii. 6, of the falling of snow and rain upon the earth. In Arabic, *hawa* means "to fall," and this word in Job is probably connected with it. Yahwe would then mean, "he who causes [rain or snow] to fall," a name exactly suited to the indications of his character which we have already noticed. Neither the literary indications nor the etymology constitute an absolute proof, but they open our eyes to a new vista of possibilities.*

* Since the text was in the hands of the printer, Dr. W. Max Mül-

The original home of Yahwe was Horeb. It was there that the name was said to have been revealed to Moses (Ex. iii. 14 and vi. 3). Yahwe was said to come from Horeb, for the help of his people (Deut. xxxiii. 2; Hab. iii. 1; Jud. v. 5; Ps. lxviii. 5). Moses meets Yahwe in Horeb, and Elijah retires there for the same purpose. Perhaps, originally, Yahwe was the god of some tribe near Horeb—a tribe which possibly the Israelites absorbed. At all events, Israel as a whole seems to have become acquainted with him there, and to have adopted his worship. To this conclusion the facts that

ler's learned work *Asien und Europa nach Altägyptischen Denkmä-lern* has come to hand. Dr. Müller is very sure that he has found traces of Yahwe-worship in Palestine in the reign of Thothmes III., in the sixteenth century B. C. Cf. Op. Cit., pp. 239, 312. His evidence for this is the occurrence of *Bai-ti-y-'-â* as the name of a Palestinian city. Dr. Müller feels sure that this name is but the Egyptian transliteration of *Bêth-ya*, and that it gives us evidence not only of the presence of Yahwe-worship in Palestine at the date mentioned, but that the shorter form of that name already existed.

This opinion of Dr. Müller's has prompted a re-examination of some names I had noticed in the El-Amarna tablets. If we may assume with Dr. Müller the shorter form *Ya* of the divine name, some of these names will reveal to us their meaning. *Ḫa-ya* (Winckler und Abel's *Thoutafelfund von El Amarna*, 57; 14, 20) spelled once *Ḫa-a-ya* (144, 8) would mean "My life is Yahwe." *Tu-u-ya* (92 Rev. 24) would mean "Gazelle of Yahwe." *Li-i-ya* (92 Rev. 25) would mean "Bull of Yahwe," while *Pa-a-lu-ya* (33, 9) would mean "Yahwe has made." I have also noticed two similar names for which I am as yet unable to offer any probable explanation. They are *Pi-id-ya* (119, 5, 122, 3) and *Ma-a-ya* (147, 26, 158, 27). It is true that in the case of these names it is not certain that *Ya* is the name of a deity. The determinative *ilu* does not occur before it. This determinative is, however, often omitted in these tablets. In the name *Arad-A-ši-ir-ta*, which occurs in these tablets more than twenty-five times, and in which *A-ši-ir-ta* is certainly a goddess, identical with the Hebrew *Ashera*, the determinative *ilu* is written before *A-ši-ir-ta* but twice. (Cf. *Journal of Biblical Literature*, Vol. X., p. 82). It is therefore the home of Yahwe was Horeb, that Moses is said to have received the revelation of the name Yahwe and the law there, and that there Israel entered into covenant to serve him, all point. This theory is also supported by the statement of Exodus vi. 2, 3, that the name Yahwe was not known to the fathers. This adoption of Yahwe-worship appears to have been general among the Israelites before the conquest of Canaan, and seems to have been the work of Moses, aided perhaps by Jethro.

That the relation of Yahwe to his people was a cove-

perfectly possible in accordance with the usage of these tablets that *Ya* may be a divine name, although not specifically so designated.

If Müller is right and the explanation of these names terminating in *Ya*, here suggested, is right, there was a *Ya* cult in Palestine before the Israelitish occupation.

If this be true there are three possibilities. 1. *Ya* was in this early period connected with the Babylonian Ea, but distinct from Yahwe and only identified with him at a later period. This is simply supposable; we have no evidence to support it. The identification of *Ya* and *Yahwe* in the Old Testament would tend to negative such a supposition. 2. *Ya* is the original of *Yahwe*, and the view of Delitzsch which I have rejected in the text is after all right. *Ya* is identical with *Ea*, and Yahwe is a lengthened form, invented to make the name sound more honorable and glorious. This supposition has in its favor the fact that nearly all the great Semitic deities appear in some form in more than one Semitic nation; thus Baal, Ashtoreth, Melek, Shamash, etc., are found almost everywhere. It may with some reason therefore be urged that a deity so prominent and important as Yahwe would probably be represented in more than one family of the Semitic peoples. The principle, however, in order to be convincing, should be in the Semitic world of universal application. There are though other important exceptions. Nabu, *e. g.*, appears to be confined to the closely related Assyrians and Babylonians of the Mesopotamian Valley. If he could originate there, why not Yahwe in Palestine? The difficulty of deriving a long form like Yahwe from a short one like Ya, which I have already expressed in the text, seems not to be met, notwithstanding the facts here brought out. The anal-

nant relation, and not a relation of kinship, was a fact
of the greatest significance in the prophetic period, as
it enabled the prophets to differentiate his worship from
the nature cults about them, and establish religion on
an ethical basis. It was thus apparently that Yahwe
became the national God of Israel. This he remained
all through the Old Testament period. The religious
leaders were persistently antagonistic to foreign deities.
For proof of this, see Judges vi. 25, xi. 24; 1 Sam.

ogy of language is all in favor of shortening rather than of lengthening words, and until this difficulty is overcome by the presentation of
analogies, in which it shall be clearly proven that words under similar
circumstances have been deliberately lengthened, this objection will
render such lengthening in the name of Yahwe uncertain. While
therefore the existence of the name *Ya* in Canaan in the sixteenth and
fifteenth centuries B. C. affords some arguments in favor of Delitzsch's
view, the case for that view is as yet, I think, not clearly made out.
3. We may still suppose that *Yahwe* is the original and that *Ya* is
an abbreviation of it. Our pre-Israelitish evidence all comes at present from proper names, and in the Old Testament *Ya* is the regular
form in proper names. It is quite as possible that *Yahwe* was the
ordinary form of the divine name in the reigns of Thothmes III.,
Amenophis III., and Amenophis IV., but that *Ya* was used in proper
names, as that such should be the case in the Old Testament. We
can trace the usage in the Old Testament, but we may not be able to
trace it in this earlier period, simply because the full name *Yahwe* did
not have the good fortune to be embalmed in any literary monument
which has survived till our times. These considerations lead me still
to hold to the view of the origin of the name Yahwe, which is expressed in the text.

If Yahwe were already known in Palestine before the conquest, he
may have been worshipped by one of the clans which was absorbed
afterwards into the Hebrew nation. That clans appear in the El-
Amarna tablets which again appear at a later time as parts of Israel,
Professor Jastrow has already shown. (Cf. *Journal of Bibl. Lit.*, Vol.
XI., p. 95 ff., and Vol. XII., p. 61 ff). It may be therefore that the
worship of one of these clans, through the agencies suggested in the
text, became the germ of Hebrew monotheism.

xxvi. 19; 1 Kings xii. 28 (perhaps also xv. 13), xviii.
21; Amos iii. 1, 2; Hosea xi. (cf. Ch. iii.); Isa. viii.
12, 13; Jer. ii. 1-12; Ezek. xvi. 8, etc.

As a national God, Yahwe had national limitations.
1. He could be approached only on Israelitish soil.
See 1 Sam. xxvi. 19; 2 Kings v. 17, and Zech. xiv. 16.
2. Through a great part of the Old Testament, Yahwe
stands apparently on a par with other national gods, as
one of many deities, c. g., see Ex. xx. 3; Deut. v. 7,
vi. 14; 2 Kings xvii. 35; Jer. xxv. 6, xxxv. 15, and
Micah iv.· 5.   3. Yahwe is often represented as caring
especially for his own people.   See Hosea xi., Isa. x.,
and Ps. xxxiii. 12.   These national limitations, however, did not prevent a practical recognition of Yahwe's
omnipotence and omniscience.   He could do whatever
needed to be done, and knew what his enemies were
doing.   The prevalent conception of him though was
ethically defective.   With the mass of the people, the
worship of Yahwe was performed along with the worship of other gods down to the period of the prophets.
These deities were the Teraphim, Baal, Ashtoreth, etc.,
etc.   It was only as the national consciousness grew by
the unifying of the nation under the monarchy, the
teaching of the prophets, and the national disasters,
that Yahwe assumed the place of the sole recipient of
Israel's homage.   By the time of Elijah, the national
consciousness was sufficiently developed to enable him
to begin war on foreign deities.   This war was carried
on by successive prophets, and continued down to the
exile, and it increased at each successive stage the
aloneness of Yahwe among the people.   At last, the
exile practically eliminated the worshippers of all gods
but Yahwe from the part of the nation resident in Pal-

estine, as few but monotheists returned from Babylon.   Soon after the exile, the prophets of Yahwe were
sufficiently strong to root out the last sporadic traces of
such native cults as those of Gad and Meni (cf. Isa.
lxv. and lxvi.), and Yahwe, the God of the nation,
henceforth received the nation's undivided homage.

While this is in general the history of Yahwe among
the people, among the prophets and national leaders
Yahwe was, from Amos down, practically the only
God.   No prophet describes Yahwe's supremacy in
higher terms than Amos.   See Amos iv. 13 and v. 1–
10.   All the prophets from Amos on recognize the
aloneness of Yahwe, and hold a unitary view of the
world, *i. e.*, the prophets are practical monotheists.
That this was reached only gradually in Israel by
means of struggle and development, is indicated by the
long continuance of idolatry among the people already
noted, and by a wavering in the matter of monotheistic statement, where we should least expect it, *e. g.*,
in the decalogue.   See Ex. xx. 1; Deut. v. 7; also
Deut. xxxii. 8 (where with the lxx. we read *b'nê
Elôhim*); Deut. xxxii. 12; Micah iv. 5, vii. 18, and Ps.
lxxxii. 1.

After the exile, however, when the nation had been
sifted and only the monotheistic remnant returned, not
only the prophets, but men, women and children, identified Yahwe with the one supreme God, and the rescued
Israel became a nation of monotheists.   Thus a nation
was prepared in which there was a basis for the fuller
revelation of God made by Jesus Christ.   Through the
ministry of Christ, the Yahwe of the Old Testament
became the God of the New.   His national limitations
and ethical defects were eliminated, and His worship

was henceforth destined to become the universal religion of mankind.*

Many, no doubt, will entertain theological objections to the above hypothesis, and will be ready to brand it as materialistic. But to the writer it seems free from the charge of materialism. It does not attempt to evolve God by a process of development, but simply to study the method by which He has unfolded the knowledge of Himself to mankind. All will agree that this has been accomplished by a gradual process; and should it appear that He had led men's thoughts steadily onward from the conception of a tribal storm-god to that of the universal and absolute deity, it should but make His ways seem to us the more wonderful, in that He has called us from such darkness into such marvellous light.†

DEITIES IN PROPER NAMES.

Before proceeding to the discussion of other Israelitish deities, it will be found exceedingly helpful to note a few facts with reference to old Semitic proper names.

1. These names when given in childhood (*i. e.*, when not nick-names) are usually brief sentences, as *Assurahi-iddina* = "Assur has added to the brothers." *Abi-Melek* = "My father is Melek." *Abi-Baal* = "My

---

* The development here outlined is not a theory, original with the present writer. It was suggested to him partly by his teacher, Professor C. H. Toy, upon various occasions, and partly by a paper read some four years since by Mr. R. E. Blount, before the Semitic Seminary at Harvard. It is also substantially the theory of Stade. It is incorporated into the present paper for the sake of completeness.

† Cf. 1 Pet. ii. 9.

father is Baal," and *Abd-ul-Melek* = "The servant of Melek."

2. One element of these names is that of a god, as *Arad-Marduk* = "Servant of Marduk." *Bel-ahi-iddin* = "Bel has added to the brothers." *Nabu-nadin-ahi* = "Nabu has added to the brothers." *Itti-Šamaš-balatu* = "With Shamash is life." *Mi-ka-el* = "Who is like El?" *Abi-yahû* = "My father is Yahwe." *Baal-yittên* = "Baal has given." *Bod-Melkart* = "Servant of Melkart." *Amat-Aštoreth* = "Maid of Ashtoreth." *Abd-ul-'Uzza* = "Servant of Al Uzza."

3. Many Hebrew and Phœnician names come from a time when the god was a member of the clan, and assert the kinship of the clansman to the deity, *e. g.*, *Abi-el* = "My father is El," *Abi-Melek* = "My father is Melek," *Abi-Baal* = "My father is Baal," *Abi-yahu* = "My father is Yahwe," *Akhi-ya* = "My brother is Yahwe," *Akhi-Melek* = "My brother is Melek."

4. Growing out of this habit of asserting that the deity was a father or brother, we have a number of names in which the words *Ab* and *Akh* are made to stand for some deity who is not more definitely described, and the name asserts something concerning him, *e. g.*, *Abi-dan* = "My father is judge," *Abi-da'* probably for Abi-yada' = "My father knows," *Abi-khail* = "My father is strong," *Abi-tôb* = "My father is good," *Abi-Nadab* = "My father is noble," *Abi-no'am* = "My father is pleasant," *Abi-'ezer* = "My father is help," *Akhi-tôb* = "My brother is good," *Akhi-no'am* = "My brother is pleasant," *Akhi-'ezer* = "My brother is help," etc. By bearing these facts in mind we shall be greatly aided in determining many of the points which will come before us in the subsequent pages.

ELÔAH AND ELÔHÎM.

Elôhîm is apparently the plural of *Elôah*. Both are used in the Old Testament as "God," though *Elôhîm* also frequently means "gods." There are three inquiries necessary in connection with these names. 1. Was *Elôah* ever the proper name of a special deity in Israel? 2. Was *Elôhîm* ever the proper name of a special deity? 3. And should both these inquiries receive affirmative answers, which was the earlier of the two?

1. With reference to the first inquiry, it must be said that we have not much evidence. *Elôah* has never, so far as I know, been found in a theophorous proper name. It is used chiefly in poetry, occurring more than forty times in Job, and several times in the Psalms. We have, however, one noteworthy pre-exilian use. In Deut. xxxii. 15, we read, "He forsook *Elôah* who made him." In this passage *Elôah* is apparently used of Yahwe, and is almost equivalent to a proper name. We cannot be sure, however, that in ancient Israelitish heathenism there was ever a deity *Elôah*, as the word may be like the Assyrian *ilu*, simply the generic name. When monotheism became established in Israel, and Yahwe was identified with the supreme God, this generic name was applied to him, becoming a synonym of Yahwe. That it was such a generic name we learn from its use in the Balaam poetry. Cf. Num. xxiii. 21.

2. As to the word *Elôhîm*, we have reason from the El-Amarna tablets to think that it was used by the Canaanites as a singular in the 15th century B. C., before the Israelitish conquest, and that this usage extended to Phœnicia.* We shall, perhaps, not be far

* Cf. My article in the *Proc. Am. Oriental Soc.* for 1892.

wrong, if we suppose that anterior to that there was a
time when it was simply the plural of *Elôah* and meant
"gods." *

In Amos iv. 11, we have evidence that it had been
adopted in Israel as a name of Yahwe:—"As when
Elôhîm overthrew Sodom and Gomorrah." On the
lips of Amos such an expression could refer to none but
Yahwe. From the whole tenor of his prophecy, we
could not conceive of his using it otherwise.

As to how the application of the plural to a single
deity came about, we are left largely to conjecture. In
the time of the El-Amarna tablets, *Elôhîm* seems to
have been used as a generic term like the Assyrian *ilu*.
We have traces of such a use in the Old Testament.
In 1 Sam. ii. 25, *Elôhîm* seems to be used in the sense
of "divine powers," while in 1 Sam. xiv. 15, we have
an adjectival use of *Elôhîm* which could only have been
produced by a long anterior use of the word in the general sense of "divine powers." These together with
the expression *benê Elôhîm*, which occurs so often in the
Old Testament, would indicate that the Hebrews
adopted from the Canaanites the use of *Elôhîm* in the
generic sense at least, as early, and probably before they
appropriated it as one of the designations of Yahwe.
With this generic use we should compare "*ilâni rabûti*"
in Assyrian, which is often used as though the gods in
a mass were thought of almost as though they were one
individual. In Assyrian, however, outside the El-
Amarna tablets, *ilâni* was seldom if ever used as a real
singular.† We must suppose, however, that in ancient
Canaanitish a similar use of *Elôhîm* existed, and that

* Cf. Smith's *Rel. of the Sem.*, p. 426.

† See the *Proc. Am. Oriental Soc.* above referred to.

before the 15th century B. C. it had further developed so
that the plural conception was partly lost from the word
and in the generic sense it was used as a real singular.
It would seem that such a use of *Elôhim* was adopted in
Israel, before the literary period, and if so the term
would naturally be applied to Yahwe by those in whose
minds the conception of Yahwe as the only God first
took shape.

3. *Elôah* and *Elôhim* seem, then, neither of them to
have been used as proper names in any historic period
until they became, in a measure, names of Yahwe.
We may, however, still inquire which of them was thus
applied to Yahwe first. So far as we can trace this in
the literature, *Elôah* is, even if we accept the critical
date of Deuteronomy, used at least as early as *Elôhim*,
the former appearing in Amos, and the latter in Deut.
xxxii. for the first time.*

If the use of *Elôhim* came about as we have supposed
above, it might naturally be used of Yahwe as early as
Elôah would be. But as has been already noted, the
use of *Elôah* is largely poetical, and as poetry is everywhere so fond of archaic forms, one may conjecture that
this use of *Elôah* is older than that of *Elôhim*.

EL.

El, which is etymologically connected with the Assyrian *ilu*, "god," unlike the two names last considered, was evidently once the name of a special deity.
This is indicated by the fact that we find it as a com-
ponent part of so many proper names as *Nethan-el*,
Yisra-el, etc. It is, however, distinctly shown by the
name *Eli-el* (= "My god is El,") which occurs in 1

---

* Deut. xxxii. appears to be older than JE. Cf. Driver's *Intro.*, p. 89.

Chron. xi. 46, 47; xii. 11, etc. *Pěnû-el* and *Bêth-el* seem to have been especial sanctuaries of this deity as their names evince, though *El* was at an early time identified with Yahwe, and these places became centres about which the sacred traditions of Yahwe revolved. (See Genesis xxviii. and xxxii). At some very early time, perhaps through the similarity of its sound to *Elôah*, it came to be used for "god" in general, and then was identified with Yahwe. This identification had taken place as early as the reign of Jeroboam II., as *El* is used with the evident meaning of Yahwe in the Balaam poems, which critics refer to that reign.

One might infer from the fact that *Bêth-el* and *Pěnû-el* were evidently sanctuaries of *El*, that the god was native among the Canaanites and was adopted by the Israelites after the conquest. If so, *El* soon became so thoroughly naturalized in Israel, (as the many proper names of which it forms a part show), as to be practically a native Israelitish deity. His original characteristics as an individual deity are hopelessly lost to us.

In form *El* is identical with the Assyrian *ilu*. *Ilu*, however, seems never to have been used of a specific deity so far as we can tell from the literature, but always as a generic term. On the other hand it would seem that in Canaan, in the most ancient times known to us, *El* was a specific deity and *Elôah* the generic term, this latter developing in course of time into *Elôhîm*. In Old Testament times, as already stated, *El* became a generic term, and also appears as such in several Phœnician inscriptions of rather late date.*

* See C. I. S., 119, 2; 257, 4; 258, 4–5; 259, 3; 377, 4, 6; 378, 3.

ELYÔN.

This word occurs in Genesis xiv. 18, as an epithet of
El, in Ps. vii. 18, as an epithet of Yahwe, and in Ps.
lvii. 3, as an epithet of *Elôhîm*. It also occurs alone as
a name for God or Yahwe in Ps. ix. 3 and xxi. 8. The
word seems to be from the root '*alâ*, "high," and we
should be inclined to regard it merely as an epithet did
not Philo of Biblos mention a deity Elyôn. ('Ελιοῦν Καλόυ-
μενος "Υψιστος. See Eusebius, *Praep. Evang.*, I., 10, 14).
This may be sufficient evidence that in Phœnicia in
later times there was a god *Elyôn*. This opens before
us two alternatives, either of which are possible. *Elyôn*
may have been in ancient times merely an epithet, freely
applied to various deities, and developed in Phœnicia at
a later period into a separate god, or it may have been
an old deity among both Hebrews and Phœnicians, and
have been so early identified by the Hebrews with
Yahwe, that in the literary period the name survived
merely as an epithet. The absence, however, of proper
names among either Israelites or Phœnicians in which
Elyôn is one element, seems to incline the scale rather
to the side of the former alternative, viz., that 'Ελιοῦν
among the Phœnicians arose from the deification of
what originally was a mere epithet.

SHADDAI.

Shaddai, usually rendered "Almighty," is an old
Hebrew divine name. It occurs frequently alone, as in
Num. xxiv. 4, frequently as an epithet of *El*, as in Gen.
xlviii. 4, and in Old Testament times was identified
with Yahwe as is shown in Gen. xvii. 1. The occurrence of *Shaddai* as an element in proper names, as in

*Ammi-shaddai** ("My kindred is Shaddai"), *Ṣuri-shaddai*† ("My rock is Shaddai"), and *Shedê-ûr*‡ ("Shaddai is light"), would seem to be evidence that there was once a time when Shaddai was a separate deity. *Shaddai* occurs alone as a divine name in the blessing of Jacob (Gen. xlix. 25) one of the oldest of the extant Israelitish poems, and in Exodus vi. 3, the fathers are said to have worshipped Yahwe under the name *El Shaddai.* Further proof of the antiquity of the name is found in Job, where it occurs as a divine name more than thirty times. Although the book of Job dates probably from the exile or a time just subsequent, nevertheless as poetry prefers archaic forms, its use of *Shaddai* is evidence of the early date at which that name became current in Israel.

To determine the character of *Shaddai* as a separate deity is a difficult matter. Some help might be expected from the etymology of the word, but unfortunately that is at present undetermined. It used to be connected with the Arabic root *shadda*, "strong," but in 1883, Professor Fred. Delitzsch, in his *Hebrew Language*, p. 48, n.,§ connected it with the Assyrian *šadu*, which he thought was defined in V. R. 28, 82, as *šaku*, "to be high." This is very doubtful as the reading is as Jensen has pointed out, *šaku*, and not *šaku*. Halevy, (*Z. K.*, II., 105–107), Jensen (*Z. A.*, Vol. I., p. 251), and Nöldehe (*Z. D. M. G.*, Vol. XL., p. 735 sq.), unite in declaring Delitzsch's verb stem *šadu* impossible, though neither of them has a more satisfactory etymology to offer. Notwithstanding this there is, as my friend Professor Hilprecht suggests to me, much to be said in favor

---

*Num. i. 12; ii. 25.   †Num. i. 6; ii. 12.   ‡Num. i. 5; ii. 10.
§Cf. also his *Prologomena*, p. 96.

of such a stem. K and k are constantly expressed in
Assyrian by the same sign, as every Assyriologist knows.
The preposition *šud*,* which occurs frequently in such
expressions as *ilâni šu-ud šami irṣitim* (*e. g.*, V. R., I.,
86), and in such words as *šudšaku* seems to be best
explained from this root. The word *šadu*, mountain,
would also seem to demand such a root for its explanation. Should we admit, however, that a verbal root
šadu is not yet absolutely established, the fact remains
that *Shaddai* seems to be connected with the Assyrian
šadu, "mountain."

Halevy conjectures (*Recherches Bibliques*, p. 52), that
Shaddai may be an archaic form for *shadè = šadu*,
"mountain," and that our form may mean "dweller
on the mountain." This conjecture probably points in
the right direction, even if we admit Delitzsch's verb
stem *šadu*. The "inhabitant of the mountain" would
easily become "the mighty one" or "the almighty
one," in consequence of the fixedness of the mountain and the impregnable character of the sanctuary.
To this conjecture the name *Ṣuri-shaddai* ("my rock
is Shaddai"), as well as the later use of *ṣuri* as an
epithet of Yahwe in Ps. xviii. 2, xxxi. 3, and 2 Sam.
xxii. 2, would add strength. It may be then that *Shaddai* was originally a mountain deity, worshipped on the
top of Carmel or some other mountain, as Livy says
Poeninus was worshipped on the summit of one of the
Alps. (See Bk. xxi., ch. xxxviii.).

The frequency of the combination *El Shaddai* in the
Old Testament would indicate that *Shaddai* was first
identified with *El*, and then both with Yahwe.

---

* Cf. Delitzsch in *Zeitschrift für Keilschriftforschung*, II., 289.

If our conjecture as to the origin of *Shaddai* be correct, not only the necessities of a rapidly growing monotheism, and the appropriateness of the term "Almighty" to a god who now stood alone, but the very nature of *Shaddai*, would facilitate the identification with Yahwe. Yahwe too originally had his home in a mountain—Horeb, as we have already seen—so that the two may have been really kindred. This hypothesis cannot be proved at present, but does not from what is now known seem improbable.

BA'AL.

Ba'al was in ancient times in Israel an epithet of Yahwe. This is proved by the fact that Gideon was called Yerubba'al, and that Saul and David, each a faithful Yahwe worshipper, named sons Ish-ba'al, "Ba'al's man," Meriba'al, "Ba'al's warrior," and Be'elyada', "Ba'al knows." Indeed, as Wellhausen has pointed out, Yerubba'al, by all Semitic analogy, must have been Gideon's original name,* while Gideon, "the tree-feller," a designation for a warrior like our "Ironsides," must have been given him later in life. Further proof is found in the fact that Hosea in ch. ii. 16, speaking in the name of Yahwe, forbids in future the application of the name *Ba'al* to him.†

As *ba'al*, means simply "owner," "possessor," or "lord," one can see how naturally it would be applied to Yahwe as the giver of Israel's land and the recipient of Israel's first fruits. So offensive, however, did the Canaanitish *ba'alim* become to the pure moralists of prophetic times, and so excellent were the opportunities

---

* Cf. *History of Israel*, p. 238 sq.

† Cf. Hosea ii. 16. Cf. *Journal of Bibl. Literature*, Vol. X., p. 84 sq.

when Yahwe was called a *ba'al* for the introduction of impure rites into his worship, that from the days of Hosea onward the name was suppressed as an epithet of Yahwe, and became exceedingly offensive to the later Jews. *Ba'al*, then, was never a native Israelitish deity, except in the sense that in the early centuries of the national history, Yahwe was a *ba'al*.

ADÔN.

Adôn, so far as I can find, never was a separate deity in Israel. It seems to have been a synonym of *ba'al*, meaning "owner," "possessor," "lord," etc., and is an epithet of Yahwe from Amos (See ch. i. 8) down to the latest times. As is well known, it displaced the name of Yahwe itself.

In Phœnician, the only other Semitic language in which it is extensively used, the name in early times was simply an epithet, and perhaps to the Phœnicians themselves always continued to be. It was, however, in later times an especial epithet of Tammuz, and among the Greeks as Ἀδωνις it became the proper name of that god.*

The only thing analogous to this among the Israelites, was the displacement of the name Yahwe by *Adôn* in post-Biblical Hebrew.

MELEK.

Melek appears as a divine name in Israel in such names as *Abi-melek*, "my father is Melek," the name of a son of Gideon, and *Akhi-melek*, "my brother is Melek," the name of a priest at Nob in the time of David. Two explanations are in this case possible.

* See Lucian's *Die Syria Dea, passim.*

One, that in ancient Israel before Yahwe worship became supreme, there was a god Melek, and that such
names as those just cited are survivals from that time.
In favor of this view the fact may be urged that the
chief deity of the Ammonites was Moloch (or Molok) a
god identical with Melek in name.   There is evidence
also in the tablets from El-Amarna that the Canaanitish
inhabitants of Palestine, in the 15th century B. C., worshipped a god Melek.   The names *Mil-ki-ilu*, "Melek is
god," * *A-bi-mil-ki*, "My father is Melek," † and *A-bi-
šarru*, ‡ a translation of the latter into Assyrian, occur.
In common then with their Canaanitish neighbors and
the Ammonites, all kindred peoples, it is probable, it
may be urged, that the Israelites too had a god Melek,
especially as we find his name used as an element in
proper names by the Israelites themselves.

The other explanation is that Melek, "king," was
only an epithet of Yahwe, and that *Abi-melek* was only
another way of saying, "My father is Yahwe."   As we
have already seen (supra, p. 94) *abi* and *akhi* are used in
proper names to denote the name of a deity not otherwise mentioned, *e. g.*, *Abi-tûb*, "My father is good,"
and *Abi-khail*, "My father is strong."

This explanation is somewhat supported by the fact
that Gideon was a faithful servant of Yahwe and could
hardly have named his son, it may be said, for another
god, and that Akhimelek likewise was a priest of
Yahwe.   Against this last consideration, however, it
may be urged that a study of Assyrian proper names

* See Winckler & Abel's *Thontofelfund von El Amarna*, No. 103,
29; 105, 11 ; 106, 6.

† Ibid., No. 98, 2.

‡ Ibid., No. 99, 2.

abundantly proves that in a polytheitsic community a devotee of one deity might name his son from another.

The scale then seems to be pretty evenly balanced between these two theories, though in my opinion it is slightly inclined towards the latter.

If Melek then was an epithet of Yahwe, it disappeared at a comparatively early period, its identity with Moloch making it, no doubt, very offensive to the faithful disciples of Yahwe.

YAHWE ṢᴱBAÔTH.

This peculiar and oft-recurring combination of names was formerly the source of much perplexity, it being doubted whether Ṣᵉbaôth, which evidently meant "hosts," referred to the heavenly hosts or stars, or to earthly armies. It now seems tolerably clear that it was the latter. In Assyrian, ṣâbu is the ordinary word for soldier, and it would seem that Yahwe Ṣᵉbaôth, was the "Yahwe of war hosts." This view is strengthened by the fact that we have a trace in Num. xxi., of a "book of the wars of Yahwe." During the conquest of Canaan it was Yahwe who gave victory to the armies of Israel, as Assur was thought by the Assyrians to give victory to their armies. In the subsequent wars the devout Israelites felt none the less sure that the issue of battle was in the hands of Yahwe, and regarded Israel's armies as his armies. No wonder then that Yahwe Ṣᵉbaôth became a very common name of Yahwe, and one which peculiarly expressed his might and sovereign power. Thus this designation came to have a striking significance. One might compare with this the development of Ishtar in Assyria, where the goddess of love became the supreme goddess, and having as such to

take a peculiar interest in the national wars, in course
of time became differentiated, Ishtar of Nineveh being
the patroness of love, and Ishtar of Arbela, the patroness of war.   In Israel no such marked change occurred.
The opportune development of monotheism made this
impossible.   But none the less did this epithet Ṣᵉbaôth,
represent the warlike might, unconquerable power,
majesty, and sovereign character of Yahwe.   It occurs
most often in Isaiah, Jeremiah and Zechariah, and it
would seem, was intended to remind the Israelite of all
those qualities in his God, the recognition of which
would strengthen his heart to endure when enemies invaded and oppressed, and would assure him that Yahwe
must ultimately be victorious.

TERAPHIM.

The Teraphim seem to have been household gods
among the Hebrews, like the Lares and Penates among
the Romans.   Sometimes the word has a plural meaning, as in Genesis xxxi. 19, and sometimes, though
plural in form, the meaning is not plural, as in 1 Sam.
xix. 13, 16.   From this latter passage it is evident,
since David's wife could pass one off for David himself,
that the Teraphim were made in the human form, and
that those in David's house were as large as a man.
They were not always so large, however, as Rachel
could hide her father's in a camel's saddle.   See Gen.
xxxi. 34.

Gesenius, I think, first suggested that the root of Teraphim was the same as the Arabic root *tarifa*, "to live
in abundance," and with this the late Professor Delitzsch * and Davies agree, though Dillmann declares

---

* *Commentar über Genesis, ed. 1887,* p. 395.

that a satisfactory etymology has never been found.*
If this be the origin of the name, the Teraphim would
be deities of household plenty. That they really were
deities is shown by Genesis xxxi. 30, where *Elôhim* is
used for them. Delitzsch compares them to the Latin
Penates, who were gods of the *penes*, the storehouse of
family supplies and the inner sanctuary. All this seems
probable, and the Ethiopic root, *tarfa*, which has the
general meaning of abundance, would coincide with
this view.

While the Teraphim seem to have been household
gods, they were also used for purposes of divination.
See 1 Sam. xv. 23, 2 Kings xxiii. 24, and Ezekiel xxi.
21. Just what this use was and how accomplished we
have no means of knowing. Castelle compares the
name with the Syriac *t'raph*, "to inquire," but it would
seem more likely that this is a denominative verb derived in consequence of the practice of divination by
Teraphim, than that Teraphim is derived from it. If
it be objected that we do not know that the Aramæans
had Teraphim, it may be rejoined that according to
Ezekiel xxi. 21, they were a Babylonian institution,
and as they existed on both sides of the Aramæans, the
presence of such a word as *t'raph* in an Aramaic language makes the presumption very strong that they had
Teraphim too.

In the days of the Judges, the Teraphim were worshipped along with Yahwe, as is shown by the description of Micah's temple in Judges xvii. and xviii. This
state of things continued down through the days of
Hosea, who (ch. iii. 4), mentions the Teraphim as a
legitimate means of worship.

* Dillmann's *Genesis, ed. 1886,* p. 345.

When the reform of Josiah came, however, all this
was changed, and the Teraphim along with other idola-
trous symbols were expelled from the temple of Yahwe.
See 2 Kings xxiii. 24.

GAD.

In Isa. lxv. 11, the prophet speaks of "preparing a
table for Gad." From the context it is evident that
the word contains a reference to some deity other than
Yahwe. Gad then was a god, perhaps holding a relation to the tribe of Gad similar to that which the god
Edom held to the Edomites.*

Reasoning from what we know of primitive Semitic
tribes, we should say that Gad was the old tribal god of
the tribe of the same name. When that tribe became
a part of the united nation, and Yahwe had become the
national god, Gad would lose some of his general characteristics and would become the god of some special
sphere of human life. That this was in general his
history, we infer from the fact that there was a proper
name *Ba'al-Gad*, showing that there was a time when it
could be said "Baal is Gad," or "Gad is lord," and
from the fact that the name Gad came later to mean
"fortune." In Genesis xxx. 11, *bāgād*† means "fortunately!" Thus Gad became, by the development of
monotheism, the god of fortune, and then was banished
altogether.

This would seem in general to be his history, as
nearly as we can reconstruct it from the few data that

---

* That Edom was a god the name Obed-Edom, "Servant of Edom,"
shows. 2 Sam. vi. 10, 11, 12. Cf. Smith's *Religion of the Semites*,
p. 43.

† The lxx. renders this ἐν τύχῃ.

remain, although the root GD had similarly the meaning
"fortune" or "fortunate" in other Semitic languages.
Cf. the Arabic *gaddun*, and the Syriac *gada'*.

Of the actual worship of Gad among the Hebrews, I
have found no trace except in Isa. lxv.

MENI.

Along with the Gad cult just considered, mention is
made in Isa. lxv. 11, of "mingling wine unto Mᶜni."
Again we have evident mention of a deity.   As the LXX.
renders the word by τύχη, it is also evident that the deity
was at least in later times a god of fortune.   The same
root means "fortune" in Arabic, as is manifest from the
use of *manûn*, *e. g.*, Koran lii. 30.   Connected with
this root is the name of the Arabic goddess Manāt, who
is generally acknowledged to have been a goddess of
fortune.*   From a comparison of the Arabic and the
connection with Gad in Isa. lxv. 11, we are tempted to
conjecture that Mᶜni was a goddess—the female counterpart of Gad.   Against this, however, is the fact that
the form of the name is in Hebrew masculine.   If Mᶜni
were a goddess, this would be our one trace of a native,
female, Israelitish deity.†   This cult does not appear
elsewhere in the Old Testament.   The Phœnicians
would seem to have had the same deity, as the name
Ebed-meni occurs in an inscription from Citium (Cf.
Gesenius' *Scrip. Ling. Phon.*, *Pl. 3*, Tab. 12, No. 12).
Perhaps we should also compare the name '*Akal-meni.
Neop. Ins.*, 33.

* Cf. Wellhausen's *Reste Arab Heidentum*, p. 35.

† Ashera of Jud. iii. 7 and 1 Kings xv. 13, was probably borrowed.

ṢEDEK.

There are two Old Testament proper names, which afford evidence of the existence of a god Ṣedek. They are *Melchisedek* (Gen. xiv. 18), and *Adonisedek* (Josh. x. 1, 3). These names, "my king is Sedek" and "my lord is Ṣedek," are proof that Ṣedek was a deity. This is confirmed by Philo of Byblos, who mentions among the Phœnician gods a Συδύκ,* evidently identical with the Ṣedek of our proper names. It will be noticed that the Old Testament represents the above proper names as belonging, not to native Israelites, but to men of the old Canaanitish stock. It is therefore probable that the god Ṣedek was not native among the Israelites, but that they knew him only through their Canaanitish neighbors. Of the characteristics of Ṣedek we know nothing. The root ṢDK means "just" or "true" in all the Semitic languages which have it, and this would indicate that Ṣedek was a god of justice, but we cannot attach much weight to this as the divine name Ṣedek may have had nothing to do with this meaning. The Συδύκ of Philo sounds certainly very different from the Hebrew *Ṣĕdĕk*.

MAUTH.

Through Hebrew proper names we are led to believe that the Israelites had a god Mauth. These names are, as now printed in our Bibles, *Akhi-môth* (1 Chr. vi. 10 [25] and *'Az-maweth* (2 Sam. xxiii. 31; 1 Chr. xxvii. 25). As it is absurd to think that a Semitic father would name his child "my brother is death," or "death is strong," if he thought of death in the abstract, we cannot escape

---

* See Eusebius, *Praep. Evang.*, I., 10, 13.

the conclusion that these names are analogous to other
Semitic theophorous proper names, and are to be rendered "my brother is Mauth" and "Mauth is strong."
This conclusion is strengthened by the statement of
Philo of Byblos, that the Phœnicians had a god Μώτ,[*]
evidently identical with the Mauth of these proper names.
As to the character of this deity either among Hebrews
or Phœnicians, we are left solely to conjecture, but he
was probably simply a personification of death.

AB.[†]

That Ab was also an old Hebrew deity, is indicated
by the name *Eli-ab*, "my god is Ab," 1 Chr. xxv. 4.
This name does not seem to be like *Eli-athâ* or *Eli-dad*,
in which an action or a quality is asserted of "my god,"
but seems to be more like *Eli-ja*, "my god is Yahwe."
Some additional probability that Ab was a deity arises
from the fact that *abu* was one of the epithets of Sin,
the Moon-god at Ur,[‡] from which place Abraham is said
to have migrated. This epithet would very naturally
arise in a patriarchal state of society. That Palestinian
society was organized on the patriarchial basis, in early
times, both Genesis and the El-Amarna tablets would

---

* Eusebius, *Praep. Evang.*, I., 10, 2.

† Since the above text was written, Professor Jastrow has kindly
called my attention to De Jong's "*Over de Met Ab, Ach enz. Zamen-
gestelde Hebreeuwsche Eigennamen,*" which had not come to my notice. As will be seen, my conclusions differ in the main quite radically
from his. My fourth statement with reference to the usage in proper
names (supra p. 94) recognizes a fact which seems to me to invalidate
many of De Jong's conclusions. I confess that the name *Eli-ab* is a
precarious basis on which to build the theory of a god *Ab*, and I put
forward the suggestion with much reserve.

‡ Cf. I. R., 69, Col. I., l. 17.

lead us to believe. We may therefore conjecture that this epithet, which possibly originated in Babylonia, was in Palestine gradually developed into a separate'deity. Analogous to this is the fact that in Assyria *bil*, in the early literature an epithet of Assur, and *bilit*, an epithet of Ishtar, became in later times separate deities.*

SAKKUT AND KAIWAN.

In Amos v. 26, occurs a difficult passage, which all Hebrew scholars will readily recall.

Ruess† renders this: "Mais vous avez porté la tente de votre roi, et le reposoir de vos idoles," etc.

Schrader‡ translates: "So werdet ihr denn den Sakkûth, euren König, und den Kēwān euren Sternengott, eure Bilder, die ihr euch gemacht," etc.

Georg Hoffmann§ renders it: "Wehrend ihr gleichzeitig umhertrugt (Jer. x. 5), den SKWT euren König, und den Kēwān eur Idol, einen Stern euren selbst gemachten Gott." While the Revised Version of 1885 renders it: "Yea ye have borne Siccuth your king and Chiun your images, the star of your God which ye made to yourselves." These various renderings exhibit the difficulty of the passage. SKWT and KYWN may be rendered as common nouns as Reuss takes them, or, as the other translations quoted would have them, as proper names. In either case there remains the definite reference to a *star*, "the star of your god." Early Jewish

---

* This I have shown in my *"Semitic Ishtar Cult,"* the publication of which has been delayed, but which is now in press. It will appear in *Hebraica*.

† Cf. *La Bible* in loco.

‡ Keilinschriften und das A. T., p. 442.

§ In Z. A. W., 1883.

and Syriac expositors take KYWN as the proper name of
a star and identify it with the Arabic *keiwân*, the name
of the planet Saturn.* We now know that *kaimanu* or
kaivanu was the name for this planet in Assyrian.†
W. R. Smith's objection that this name is of non-Sem-
itic origin,‡ has really no bearing on the case if only we
can feel sure that it was in general use among the Semites at the time of Amos. I hope soon to show good
reason for making this supposition. We should then
probably read *Kaiwan* here. From the analogy of the
other languages the Massoretic pointing *Kiyyûn* would
seem to be erroneous. Notwithstanding the testimony
of the ancient versions, therefore, there is strong reason
for taking KYWN as the proper name of a planet.
Indeed I think we may claim the LXX as a witness for
this reading, as 'Ραιφάν. would naturally arise through a
palæographical error from *Kaiwân*, if in the translator's
exemplar the lower part of the K were erased or dim.
It seems therefore tolerably certain that Amos refers to
Saturn. If so, this gives us the clue to the explanation
of SKWT. Jensen has shown that in Assyrian *Ninib*
is one of the names of the planet Saturn.§ He has also
shown that *Ninib* is the same as the god *Anu*.‖ Now
in II. R., 57, 40 cd., we have "*Sakkut = Anu.*"¶ The
worship of Sakkut and Saturn were therefore, as Schrader
long ago pointed out, connected in Assyria,** and this

---

* See W. R. Smith's "*Prophets of Israel*," p. 400.

† Cf. III. R., 57, 66a, also Jensen's *Kosmologie*, p. 101.

‡ See Op. Cit., p. 401.

§ See *Kosmologie*, p. 136 sq.

‖ Ibid., pp. 136 sq. and 191 sq.

¶ Cf. III. R., 69, 5a, and Brünnow, *Cuneiform Ideographs*, No. 11097.

** *Stud und Krit.*, pp. 324–332, and *K. A. T.*, 412 sq.

was probably also the case in Israel. Thus it was no mere chance that Amos mentioned *Sakkût* (perhaps pronounced by the Israelites *Sikkût*) in connection with "Keiwan the star of your god." This *Anu* who is equal to *Sakkut* is the god who in 2 Kings xvii. 31, is called "*Anam-melech*" or "Anu is king." Hence the significance of Amos's language, "Sakkut, your king." The prophet evidently refers here to a cultus which was at least possible in Israel, and I can hardly think that it was not already present.* It is true that the account given in 2 Kings xvii., represents the introduction of this cult into Palestine as having taken place after the days of Amos. This has reference, however, not to the cult as practised by Israelites, but as practised by the colonists with whom the Assyrian kings re-peopled Samaria after having carried captive the kingdom of Israel. It does not prove that in some form the cult had not been practised by the Israelites themselves in former times. In favor of the supposition that it had, we have a bit of evidence in one of the tablets from El-Amarna. In one of the letters from Jerusalem there is mention of a city *Beth-Ninib*,† (perhaps better read *Beth-Anath*‡), the name of which is evidence that in very early times the worship of Ninib or Saturn found its way to Palestine. The references in Amos would seem to indicate that some traces of it remained until his day.

While it seems certain therefore that Sakkut and Kaiwan were known to the Israelites as deities, there seems to be little or no evidence that they were native

---

* Cf. however, Driver's, *Hebrew Tenses*, p. 167, for a different view.

† See Winckler & Abel's *Thontafelfund* No. 106, 15.

‡ Cf. Prof. Jastrow in *Hebraica*, Vol. IX. p. 37.

in Israel.   The evidence would rather indicate that the
deities were Babylonian, and that the cultus was in
Israel a borrowed one.   In the course of the centuries
they probably became quite thoroughly naturalized in
Israel, but still we can hardly regard them as native
Israelitish deities.

A LEGAL DOCUMENT OF BABYLONIA DEAL-
ING WITH THE REVOCATION OF
AN ILLEGAL SALE.

BY MORRIS JASTROW, JR.

THE interesting tablet which forms the subject of
this article was kindly placed at my disposal by its
present owner—Mr. Mayer Sulzberger, of Philadelphia,
who purchased it in London during the summer of 1890,
of Joseph Shemtob, the well-known dealer in Babylonian antiquities. The measurements of the tablet are
in centimeters 1.2 (breadth) 5.9 (length) 3.2 (thick-
ness). It is in an excellent state of preservation, the
neo-Babylonian characters being beautiful as well as
clear. The color of the firmly baked clay is dark gray.
Three nail-marks are distinguishable on the margin.
Evidently great care was bestowed upon the preparation
of the document, which is an unusually fine specimen of
the scribe's art. The tablet itself is a legal document,
and I trust that it will not seem superfluous to preface
my explanation of it with some remarks of a general
character on the legal literature of the Babylonians.

I.

The term "Contract Tablets," so commonly applied
to this branch of Babylonian literature, is not satisfactory. It is open to the objection of being too narrow.
In place of the term, I would suggest "legal and commercial documents," or more briefly, "legal documents," for such in the proper sense of the word, the

little clay objects are, that supply us with such a wonderful insight into the private life and public doings of the ancient inhabitants of Mesopotamia. It is estimated that there are at present known to exist in the museums of Europe and America, and in private hands, upwards of 50,000 such legal documents. They may for the sake of convenience be grouped into four large divisions: (1) Acknowledgments of loans and of payments. These are usually couched in brief terms. The sum involved is set down together with the time and conditions on which the money is loaned—the usual interest being 20 per cent. In the case of a payment, the customary phrase is, so and so many minas for work done, for oxen, for goods delivered, as the case may be; and occasionally some further details are added. The names of witnesses, though frequently found, are not essential, nor is the date always given; (2) Memorandums of commercial transactions, such as sales of fields, of slaves, of houses, or exchange of one commodity for another. These are more elaborate in form, and the names of witnesses, varying in number from 3 to 10, are attached, together with the date according to the year of the reigning king or dynasty; (3) Contracts in the proper sense of the word, that is, an agreement of some kind between two parties in which the terms are stated with more or less precision, and the transaction regularly attested in the presence of witnesses, the scribe as a general thing being included in the number. In this class are to be ranged, rent agreements, deeds, marriage settlements, deeds of real or personal property, deeds of adoption, agreements between parent and child as to the disposal and use of property, and—as a natural development from the latter—last testaments and wills. (4) Judicial decisions, including agreements based on them. These constitute perhaps the most interesting class. After a clear statement of the point at issue between two or more parties, involving at times an elaborate history of a disputed piece of real property or a slave, as the case may be, the decision of the court is entered or indirectly assumed, and in the presence of witnesses, the interested parties concerned bind themselves to abide by it. ·

These legal documents carry us back to a very early period of Babylonian history—the oldest dating from about 2500 B. C.—and they extend, though with many gaps,* through the days of Persian rule into the period of Greek supremacy, down to within a few decades of our era. During this long period, legal forms and terms as well as formalities continued to develop,† and one cannot but admire the extreme nicety with which increasing legal complications were regulated. Dr. Peiser has called attention to a series of some 80 tablets,‡ all dealing with the same piece of real property, and the complications arising both from changing hands and through reverses in the business affairs of the successive owners. By means of such a series we are enabled to follow the history of the property in dispute through a period of about 140 years, and it seems plausible, as Peiser sug-

---

* See Oppert Les Inscriptions Juridiques de l'Assyrie et de la Chaldee (VII. Orientalisten Congress, Semitische Section, pp. 167-9.)

Some of these gaps are now filled by the collections of the University of Pennsylvania, which are especially rich in tablets found at Niffer that date from the Cossæan period of Babylonian history.

† Meissner and Tallqvist in the Wiener Zeitschrift fuer die Kunde des Morgenlandes (IV., pp. 111-130), furnish some interesting illustrations of the changes in the use and meaning of legal terms during the various periods of Babylonian history.

‡ Monatsberichte d. Berliner Akademie d. Wiss., 1889, pp. 813-828.

gests, that the entire series was brought together on one occasion to serve as the basis for the judges in rendering their decision.

The indirect bearings of this legal literature in furnishing illustrations of the social conditions prevailing in Babylonia, are scarcely less important than the direct ones. The documents being the outcome of actual occurrences, offer authentic information regarding the position occupied by the various classes of inhabitants,—the officials, the slaves, the parent, the child, woman—the methods in vogue for transacting business, the fluctuating value of property, and the like. It may safely be said that when once the large material now at our disposal shall have been thoroughly studied, there will be but few phases of public and private life in ancient Babylonia, that will not find illustration from the little clay tablets. The task involves the most careful attention to details, and it is only by noting all the points in each case as presented, that on the basis of a clear view of the situation thus obtained, the proper conclusions may be drawn. Incidental references will prove to be of especial significance in following this method. Thus, to take as an example a group of tablets, which involve the legal and social status of woman in Babylonia, we find by an application of the method referred to, that she could hold property in her own name, and that she could dispose of this property. Furthermore, she could enter a claim for payment of a debt, could bring suit against a member of the male sex, and could receive the slave of her debtor as a pledge. We have an interesting case on record of a woman who acts as a witness in an agreement in which her daughter is involved, and another of a mother-in-law becoming surety for her son-in-law in a business transaction. Woman did not lose her independent legal status upon marriage. She could be associated with her husband in contracting a debt. It appears indeed that the wife could hold property in her name, for we find her deeding slaves both to her husband and her son. In the case of adopting a child, her consent had to be obtained. True, a daughter could not marry without her father's consent, but neither could the son. On the other hand, it does not appear that the mother's consent was necessary to the marriage of her child if the father was alive, though in the event of the husband's death, the rights of the latter were transferred to his widow. In accordance with this principle, the widow retains control of her children, whom indeed she is required to take care of till they reach man's estate; and even after that time she retains a certain control over her husband's estate, the presence of the mother being required in order to enable the son to dispose of any portion of the paternal inheritance. In the event, however, of the widow's remarrying, the property of her first husband falls to the sons without any conditions. Infidelity on the part of the wife was severely punished. Death by the sword was her fate. Some measure of protection was accorded to the divorced woman. The husband pays an indemnity on dismissing his wife, the sum stipulated in one case being six minas. Again, if the husband takes unto himself a second wife not agreeable to the first, the latter may resume her former state,* and also receives an indemnity—one mina being put down in a certain

---

* This, I take it, is the sense of the phrase, *aſar maḥri tallaka* (e. g., Nbk., 101, 12).

case of this character. Finally, as a rather remarkable illustration of the independent position occupied by woman before the law, the case may be instanced of a mother and daughter associated in the purchase of a slave and entering upon an agreement that the slave should belong to the daughter upon her mother's death, and should not become part of the paternal estate.

In the same way, by collecting the references in the documents to slaves, to loans, to houses, and the like, we are able to amass facts interesting in themselves and of the greatest import in a study of the social conditions prevailing in Babylonia.

II.

The specimen before us belongs to the fourth class, according to the above enumeration, viz., that of judicial decisions or agreements based thereon. The features connected with the settlement of the dispute in question are unusually interesting, and in some respects unique.

The tablet reads in transliteration as follows:

(Obverse.)

11 ŠA ḫipu kane bitu ip-šu
ša Nur-e-a apil amelu bâ'iru ina kâtâ
Aplâ apilšu ša Bel-aḫe-ir-ba
apil Ili-ia ki-i bar ma-na 7 šiklu
ribitu (tu) kaspi im-ḫu-ru Bel-ikiša (ša)
aḫu-šu ša Bel-aḫe-ir-ba apil Ili-ia
bitu ki-i bit abu-u-tu
u-pak-kir ma kakkad
kaspi-šu Nur-e-a i-tir
ú kanaku ša bit Nur-e-a
u-tir-ma a-na Bel-ikiša (ša)
id-din ta-a-ru ú da-ba-ba
ša Nur-e-a a-na
eli biti il-ti

(Reverse.)

Bel-ikiša (ša) ia-a-nu
ina ka-nak duppi šu-a-tim
mahar Nergal-uballit (it) amelu Pa-še (ki)
mahar Nabu-ib-ni apil Bel-napšâte
Babil-â apil amelu šangu Adar
Arad-Marduk apil Al-pin-nu
Šamas-iddinna (na) apil amelu bel abulli
Nabu-bel-šu-nu apil Bel-napšâte
E-rib (?)-šu apil amelu bâ'iru
Nabu-ikiša (ša) apil amelu re'u alpi
ú amelu dup-šar ša-tir duppi
Marduk-ah-a-ni apil šangu Rammanu
Babili (ki) arah Nisan ûmu 18 (kan)
šattu 6 (kan) Kan-dal-a-ni šar Babili (ki)
su-pur Nur-e-a mar bâ'iru
kima kunukišu. *

I translate as follows:

Eleven *ŠA* and no "reeds," a productive property which *Nurea* son of the fisherman purchased from the *Aplâ* the son of *Bel-ahe-irba*, son of *Ili-ia* at the rate of ½ mina 7¼ shekels of silver.

Bel-ikiša the brother of *Bel-ahe-irba* son of *Ili-ia* claimed the property as a paternal property, and *Nurea* having been paid back his capital, and having surrendered the deed of the house and given it to *Bel-ikiša*, there shall not be any further claim on the part of *Nurea* against *Bel-ikiša* for that house.

By this document sealed in the presence of
    Nergal-uballit of *Paše*
    Nabu-ibni the son of *Bel-napšâte*
    Babilâ the son of the priest of Adar

* Written IM DUP as in Peiser Babylonische Vertraege, No. 116.

Arad-Marduk the son of *Alpinuu*
Šamaš-iddinna the son of the gate-keeper
Nabu-bel-šunu the son of *Bel-napšâte*
Eribšu the son of the fisherman
Nabu-ikiša, the son of the ox-herd
and the scribe, the writer of the tablet
Marduk-aḥa-ni the son of the priest of Ramman
Babylon, month of Nisan, 18th day
6th year of Kandalanu, King of Babylon.

Nail mark of *Nurea* son of the fisherman, in place of his seal.

Before taking up the interpretation of the document, it will be necessary to discuss a number of terms occurring in it.

The first line presents a real difficulty, owing to a term that appears here for the first time in a legal document, so far as I have been able to ascertain. I refer to the sign preceding the ideogram GI. The latter which is the equivalent of the land measure *ķanu* * "reed" is of frequent occurrence in connection with a *bîtu ipšu* as here (e. g. Peiser Babyl. Vertr. No. XCIV. and CXVII. Nab., 85, 1, 356, 6 sc) and in all cases the notation, whatever it be, is joined directly to the measure. The number 11 therefore, cannot belong to GI. In view of this, it will be admitted that *ŠA* in this line cannot be anything else but the measure, which as Oppert first showed, is equivalent to 2 GI.† Its use, especially at the beginning of a tablet, is exceptional, the GI being ordinarily the highest measure employed.‡

* GI as ideogram is evidently to be deduced from *ķanu*, in accordance with Halevy's "acrologistic" theory.

† cf. Peiser Keils. Actenst, p. 91. Baby. Vert., p. 236.

‡ e. g. Peiser B. V. CXVII., Nab. No. 85 etc. May ŠA perhaps be connected with Hebrew *Sea ?*

For examples of $\check{S}A$ see Peiser Keils. Act.. No. III. and B. V., No. XCIV, and CXVIII. Moreover, the standard according to which property was sold, was invariably the GI, and even when as. in B. V. No. XCIV, the $\check{S}A$ is introduced, the rate of sale (l. 13) is given according to ½ SA, i. e. one GI. The use of $\check{S}A$ as a double GI reminds one of *kasbu* as the "double hour," but whatever its origin may be, it is quite natural that as a standard it should have fallen into disuse. We may, therefore, assume that in our document likewise the rate of 37¾ shekels is according to the GI and not the $\check{S}A$. So much being clear, the reason for the introduction of GI, depends of course on the meaning of the sign preceding. In the Syllabary II. R., 27, No. 2, there is a passage which bears directly on the point involved.

Lines 55–58, left-hand column, the word *ḫipu* is found, the general sense of which is to "destroy." In the left-hand column three ideographic equivalents are given, together with specifications, as follows:

ll 55.   TIR=ḫipu

56.   GAZ=ḫipu ša ekli=ḫipu of the field

57.   AK AK*=ḫuppu ša GI=ḫipu of the "reed"

The second of these signs is the same as in our tablet, and the specification in this case means that the stem *ḫipu* has a meaning which may be applied to a "field;" and correspondingly, the double AK means *ḫipu*, said of a reed. There can be no reasonable doubt that the latter is the sense in which *ḫipu* (or the piel of it, *ḫuppu*) is used in our document. As for the rather curious interchange, GAZ being used in our document with GI,

---

* A gloss informs us that the double sign is to be read *ša ša*.

whereas in the syllabary the sign is brought in connection with "field," there are two explanations possible, either that GAZ and AK AK are used interchangeably for either sense of *ḫipu*, or the scribe has confused "ekli" with GI and their position should be reversed. I am strongly inclined to the latter alternative, for to judge from other instances, when three equivalents for a stem are given in a syllabary, three different meanings of the stem are intended. The *ḫipu* when used of "field" must be distinct from *ḫipu* when used of a "reed;" and since, in our document, GAZ is connected with GI, it is the *ḫipu* of l. 57 and not that of l. 56 for which GAZ is the ideographic equivalent. In further support of this supposition, the Talmudic usage of the Piel form of *ḫapâ* may be instanced, namely, the "harrowing" of a field (lit: "covering up;" see Jastrow's Talmudic Dictionary, p. 491). This is so common a use of the Piel in Talmudic parlance that one is strongly inclined to suspect an Assyrian *ḫuppu ša ekli* to be the equivalent to it. But it is likewise evident that this meaning of the verbal stem does not in any case apply to GI as "reed."

Thrown back as we are to the Assyrian, for determining the specific meaning of *ḫipu ša GI*, an examination of its occurrence in cuneiform literature shows that in the historical and poetical texts, it has the general meaning of "destroy" (*Ašurn* I, 51; 4th creation Tablet Rev. 22 sc.). Secondly, in both historical texts and in syllabaries the word *ḫipi* is a frequent gloss to indicate that a word or a passage has been "obliterated" in the copy which the scribe uses as his model. Thirdly, the stem is frequently met with in legal documents in the phrase that the *nantim*, i. e., indebtedness of such and such a person against another is *ḫipatu* or *ḫuppâ'* (Nab.

311, 8; 605, 10; NbK 42, 25; 60, 7, sc.). Delitzsch (Assyr. Woert., pp. 423 and 441) renders the term correctly as "wiped out," or, as we might put it, "settled."

It is from these meanings that we must endeavor to advance to an interpretation of our term, for Haupt's suggestion (Sumer. Famil., p. 34) for the passage of the syllabary in question, viz.: "cutting off" taking GI literally as a "reed," and not as a measure, does not at all suit the conditions of our document, and the latter, moreover, conclusively points to the use of GI in the syllabary also as a measure and nothing else. My proposition is to take the term as an indication that the notation 11 ŠA represents the exact and full measurements of the property in question. In other words its measurements are 11 $\breve{S}A$ without any fraction of a GI. *Hipu* I take it, is equivalent to our "blank" or "nought." It will be seen that this use of the stem comes nearest to the gloss *hipi* above instanced, which might with equal propriety be rendered as "blank" or "*deest.*" It would appear indeed that this term *hipi* forms a connecting link leading to the use of *hipu* in the sense proposed. *Hipu* originally applied to an "obliterated" passage because it was "wiped out," would naturally lead to the notion of "blank" or "nought," when once the cause for the "wiping out" would be dissociated from the result. Upon examining the legal literature of the Babylonians so far as published, it appears that the case must have been a rare one indeed when the measurements of a property were exactly so and so many GI or $\breve{S}A$. Peiser Babyl. Vertr. No. XCIV. is such a case, and there may be one or two more; but in the great majority of instances, the measurements include, beside the full GI

fractional amounts given in *ammatu* or "ells" and
uban "finger-breadths."* In view of this extreme
nicety with which measurements were made, it would
be quite natural in the case of an official document,
where precision was of course a pre-requisite, to note the
unusual circumstance that a property covered a round
number of "double GI s," without any fraction whatsoever. The use of $\bar{S}A$ or "double GI" instead of the
ordinary single GI as the unit would of course furnish
an additional motive for specifying that the property
contains exactly so and so many $\bar{S}A$ and "o GI." A
modern parallel to this use of *hipu*, would be our notation ".oo" in the case of an even sum of dollars and
"no cents" or the English custom of writing 5£. o. o.
to emphasize the even sum, without any shillings or
pence.

Passing on, the proposed rendering for *bitu ipšu* requires a few words in justification. *Bitu*, as has already
been recognized by others, is employed in the legal
documents of the Babylonians in a double sense; (1)
for a house proper, and (2) for a piece of property without reference to the fact whether there be a house on the
ground or not. This double usage is co-ordinate with
agricultural life. In the nomadic state of Semitic culture, the *bitu* is simply the place wherein one spends the
night. A permanent structure, no matter how primitive,
used as a dwelling, carries with it the condition of being
surrounded by some ground which naturally becomes
the means of furnishing sustenance to the household.
This advance accordingly leads from the restricted to
the wider sense of the term. The *bitu* becomes synon-

---

* e. g. Peiser B. V. CXVII. 5 G I. 10 uban, Nab., 85 ; 7 G I 5 Ammatu 18 uban, etc., etc.

ymous with "land." The ambiguity which, it might
be supposed, arises from this double application, is removed through the internal evidence furnished by the
documents themselves. It is possible, moreover, to set
up certain criteria for distinguishing between the use
of *bitu* as house and as land. We find in connection with legal documents relating to real estate that
either the measurements are given in the ordinary notation or the boundaries on the various sides are given;
and in some cases both metes and bounds are given.
In the case of the boundaries, moreover, the description is either complete by an indication of the properties
situated on the four sides, or it is incomplete, the general situation alone being noted. Thirdly, there are
cases in which neither metes nor bounds are given. An
analysis shows that when land measures are employed,
a piece of land, with or without a house, is invariably
meant; and likewise when a complete description of
boundaries is furnished. If, however, the boundaries
are only partially given or these are merely general
indications of the situation, the transaction refers
strictly to a house. Thus to confine the illustrations to Peiser's Babylonische Vertraege, No. CXVII,
where both metes and bounds occur, internal evidence proves that a piece of land is involved and not
a house. The document is interesting also as furnishing a definite confirmation of the extended use of
bitu of land. A comparison of l. 14 with No. XCIV,
10—treating of the same property—shows that *bitu* is
synonymous with "measurement." * Again, No.
CXXVI, with complete boundaries, and No. LXXXIX,
with measurements, refer to land, whereas Nos.

---

* *Bitu ïualim=miïihtum ïualim.*

LVIII, LXVIII, LXXII, XLI, XLVII, where neither measurements nor boundaries occur, deal with house-rent; and likewise XLIV, where the boundary line on only one side is noted, CXXXIV, where the situation is indicated by naming the street, CXXXV, where two streets constitute the description, houses are involved. Of course in such cases where produce is spoken of, as in No. CXXVIII, "bitu" can only mean "land." The addition of "*ipšu*" to "bitu" is also of quite frequent occurrence in these legal documents, but an examination of the passages shows that its use is restricted to cases where "bitu" means "land."* It is clear, therefore, that any translations which connect the term with "house," are erroneous. Tallqvist's rendering of "angebaut," and Peiser's "bebautes," while correct in so far as they make the term applicable to a piece of land, yet are not altogether satisfactory. It seems to me that *ipšu*, in accord with the usage of the stem in Assyrian, indicates simply that the property is in some way productive, whether by being cultivated, or used as pasture ground, or yielding a profit in any other way, if such there be. The term is vague, intentionally so, and therefore a rendering such as "productive," which was kindly suggested to me by a legal friend, is to be preferred, just because it mirrors this vagueness. As a matter of fact, *bitu* without the addition of *ipšu*, is also used for land yielding a profit, and the specification *bitu ipšu* is only introduced when special emphasis is to be laid upon the "productiveness" of the property, and when this productiveness forms an essential item in the transaction. Thus in the

* See the passages in Tallqvist Sprache d. Contr. aud Peiser's Keils Aktenst and Babyl. Ver. (index).

case of our document, the property is described as
"*iṭṣu*," to account for the fact that in the return of
it which is arranged (ll. 8–9) the purchaser receives the
purchase money back, but no interest, because he has
enjoyed the profit from the "productive" property.
Fully in keeping with this interpretation is the use of
the phrase, "*epiši ša biti*,"* that is occasionally met
with.   It may be rendered as "use" or "usufruct" of
the property, and as Babyl. Vertr., No. III, 5, shows, is
considered equivalent to and offered in lieu of "interest."   Correspondingly the expression *bitu šuatu ša
nakaru u epišu* in the Berlin Sargon Stone (Peiser
Keils-Akt., p. 14), must be understood as implying that
the property in question which is transferred by the
owners in lieu of a debt is handed over unconditionally,
to lie idle or to be made productive.†

Another point calling for notice is is the manner in
which the value of the property is indicated.   It is clear
that 37¼ shekels would be entirely too small a sum for
the entire estate.   According to Oppert's calculation
(Zeits. für Assyriologie, IV, p. 98), one GI may be worth
as much as 75 shekels, and, on the other hand, in No.
III. of Peiser's Keils. Aktens (p. 91), the price per G I is
(about) 35 shekels and again 13½ shekels (Beitraege zur
Assyriol., I, p. 133).   Assuming even that the latter is
above the average, it is certainly out of the question
that the price of a large piece of land containing 22
G I should be as low as 37¼ shekels.   The word *ki*,
therefore, must be taken in the sense of "at the rate

---

* Nab. 232, 3.   Baby. Vertr. III, 5, &c.

† Note however that the Šafel of *epišu* in the phrase *mnš piši sa
biti* (Peiser, B. V., LXXIX., 7) appears from the context to mean
simply "the building of the house."

of," and for which elsewhere (e. g. Peiser *ib.*) *ša* occurs. This would bring the full value of the property up to 819 shekels. Attention might also be directed to the phrase *bit abûtu.* The existence of the latter word is vouched for by the syllabary II. R., 33, No. 2, 9. Oppert, in his Documents Juridiques (p. 63), has already suspected the term to be a legal one, and it is interesting to find it now occurring in a document. No justification is required for the rendering that is proposed. The fact that the property in question is a *bit abûtu* furnishes, as will be seen, the key to the situation.

Lastly, a few words as to the notation. Two measures are found in the contract tablets for estimating the size of a piece of land—one a long measure by reeds,* cubits and finger-breadths, the other a notation of capacity according to the average yield of sown land. Of the two, the measure of capacity is the more primitive and, presumably, the older. It dates from the period when the chief value of land lay in the produce that it was expected to yield, whereas the measurement by actual size would apply to the house erected on a piece of land, together with the surrounding ground. That the two systems should have continued to exist side by side at a time when the long measure might have sufficed for both is somewhat of a surprise, though, no doubt, the apparently unstable character of the notation of capacity was as accurately regulated as the *homer* or *imeru*, i. e., the "ass-load" was, or as in our days horse-power is.

---

* One GI=7 ammatu (ells)—168 uban (finger-breadths)=⅓ ŠA.

III.

Coming now to the interpretation of the document, the circumstances are as follows : A certain Nurea has bought a piece of land from Aplâ and has paid for it in full, at the rate of 37¼ shekels for the GI or *kanu*. It appears, however, that Aplâ had no right to dispose of the property, for the reason that it formed part of the paternal estate. *Belikiša*, the uncle of Aplâ, steps forward as a claimant. A decision it appears has been rendered in favor of *Belikiša*, and Nurea is obliged to give up the property and to surrender the deed to *Belikiša*. Nurea receives back the sum paid by him for the property, but, be it noted, without interest. This can only be accounted for satisfactorily on the assumption that Nurea actually enjoyed the use of it from the time of the original sale, the productiveness of the property being silently assumed or perhaps expressly adjudged to be the full equivalent for the interest. Nurea accordingly does not lose anything, which is only proper, on the theory that he is in no way responsible for the illegality of the sale. The deed consists of the document by which Aplâ made over the property to Nurea, and the latter, after receiving his money, solemnly agrees upon surrendering the deed to forever renounce all claims upon the property. This is the force of the phrase so frequently added at the close of transactions, *târu u dababu* * * * *ianu*, "there shall not be any further claim." Very much like our legal term, quitclaim. This is done in our tablet, in the presence of nine witnesses, the ninth being, as is customary, the scribe himself; and Nurea imprints his nail-mark (which is distinctly to be seen) on the tablet in lieu of his seal.

The case involved is a new one. It is the first time, as

stated, that the term *bit abûtu* occurs, and the tablet thus
constitutes a real addition to our knowledge of the Babylonian law of inheritance. According to the document,
the son, it would appear, had no right to dispose of the *bit
abûtu*. Evidently then it was not a possession that his
father could have bequeathed to him for complete control. Now it is to be noted that both when Aplâ and
when *Belikiša* are mentioned, the name of Ilîa is added.
Aplâ is the grandson of Ilîa and *Belikiša*, being the
brother of Aplâ's father, *Belaheirba*, Ilîa is the father of
Belikiša; and it must, therefore, be Ilîa who is the "father" implied in the *bit abûtu*. The property we may,
therefore, conclude is one that *Belaheirba* and *Belikiša*
have inherited in common from their father Ilîa, and, as
a consequence, Aplâ could at most have had his father's
share in it and not full control. His action in disposing of
it is either an infringement upon the rights of the co-
heir, his uncle, or it is possible that his uncle, Bel-ikisa
was the sole heir of Ilia, as his eldest son or as the sur-
vivor of his brother Bel-ahe-irba. Fortunately we have
another document which illustrates the point involved
—the absolute necessity of securing the consent of co-
owners for the sale of land. I refer to the Berlin
"Sargon-Stone" already mentioned, where three sons
in payment of a debt contracted by their father, and
which they as heirs are obliged to pay, agree to give up
their father's land (*bit abini*), receiving 50 shekels in
return for the excess of the value of the land over
the debt. The offer which is accepted by the creditor
is made by *all three* of the sons, and special stress appears to be laid on this circumstance. It is not necessary to assume that Aplâ wilfully sought to defraud
his uncle of his rights, for it may be that he only sold to

Nurea his share in the estate,* or if he sold it in its entirety, was willing to give the uncle a share due to him; but his action in either case would be illegal without the express concurrence of the uncle, or rather any disposition of the property could only be made conjointly. This not having been done, the sale is annulled by order of the court. Instances of such annulment were not rare in Babylonian courts, and, no doubt, in such a case as ours, neither the express stipulation that there shall be no revocation nor the solemn invocation of the gods against him who should put in a claim—so often added to give greater solemnity to a transaction—was of any real utility. The only way of ensuring one's self against all possible trouble was to have all persons present who might rise up as claimants, and by their presence concur in the transaction. So we find a son summoned to bear witness as the future heir to an agreement entered into by his father with a third party; and again quite an array of relations appear in another case and agree not to put in any claim whatsoever against the legality of a sale. It is the seller who takes the risk, and the Babylonian law appears to have been that, in the case of an enforced annulment, he is obliged to refund the purchase money, together with the usual interest of 20 per cent. calculated from the time of the sale. In accordance with this, the purchaser frequently stipulates that, if a claim by the brother, sons, or any relation, male or female, of the seller be established, he, the purchaser, is also to receive the interest on his money. We have already seen why, in the present instance, Nurea receives only the princi- without interest.

---

* According to Talmudic law this could be done if the property was large enough for two parties.

Strictly speaking, therefore, the document before us is the statement of the agreement reached between Nurea and *Belikiša*, on the basis of a judicial decision that had been rendered.* The main purpose of the document is to assure *Belikiša* against being disturbed in his possession through the illegal act of Aplâ. The latter, therefore, receives only a bare mention. The property has been given up, and Nurea being the person to be bound, is called upon to give his assent to the settlement. Whether there was an additional document stipulating the terms of agreement between Aplâ and Nurea, it is of course impossible to say, though it may be put down as more than probable.

IV.

In conclusion, a word of explanation in regard to the date and royal name attached. In the canon of Ptolemy, Kineladan appears as a King of Babylonia as the successor of Saosdouchin. Until the discovery of legal documents bearing the name like ours of Kan-dal-a-ni (written also Kan-da-la-nu, and Kan-da-la-ni, and Kandala †), the passage in Ptolemy was a puzzle that tried the patience of scholars. The solution of the mystery is due to Prof. Schrader,‡ who starting from the statement of Berossus (preserved through Alexander Polyhistor) that Sammuges—identical with Saosduchin—

---

* Cf. Meissner's Beitr. z. Altbabyl. Privatrecht, No. 79, where we have an instance of an agreement in which the decision upon which it is based is specified.

† Pinches Proc. Soc. Bib. Ar., 1882, p. 6.

‡ Eb. Schrader, Kineladan and Asurbanipal Zeits. fuer Keilschr., II. pp. 222-232. Schrader's view has been accepted by all scholars except Oppert. See Lehman Samassumukin, p. 6.

was followed by his brother Sardanapalus, showed conclusively the identity of Kineladan and the famous
Sardanapalus, or to give the more correct forms, Kandalani and *Ašurbanabal*. The latter tried the experiment of giving the Babylonians a semblance of in-
dependence, by placing the government of the country
in the hands of his brother, whose name appears in
cuneiform documents as *Samaš-šum-ûkin*. It is rather
strange to find the King entering upon such a policy, for
several of his predecessors—Sargon and Sennacherib—
who had tried the same experiment, had to pay dearly
for it. *Samaš-šum-ukin* organized a rebellion in Babylonia, which was only put down after a severe conflict.
Ašurbanabal thereupon took the government of Babylonia into his own hands, just as Sargon and Esar-haddon
were obliged to do before him. Continuing an ancient
tradition, he assumed a different name as King of Babylonia from the one he bore as ruler of Assyria. This
appears to have been a concession to a theoretical in-
dependence of Babylonia and Assyria, which was never
entirely lost sight of. For the Babylonians, *Ašurbanabal*, the King of Assyria, did not exist, but only
Kineladan. Official documents were dated according
to the reign of the latter, precisely as Tiglethpileser
III. was known as Pulu in Babylonia, and Shalmaneser
IV. as Ululu. *Ašurbanibal's* reign over Assyria begins
in 668 B. C. It was not until 647 that he also assumes
the title of King of Babylonia. Our document was accordingly drawn up in the year 642 B. C.*

---

* Other documents dated in the reign of Kandalani, range from the
10th to the 22d year—the year of the King's death (626 B. C.). See
Strassmaier's recent publication of additional tablets of the reign of
Kandalanu in the Proceed. of the 8th Orient. Congress, Vol. I.

REVERSE.

OBVERSE.

A LEGAL DOCUMENT OF BABYLONIA, DEALING WITH THE
REVOCATION OF AN ILLEGAL SALE.

A NEW NUMERICAL FRAGMENT FROM NIPPUR.

BY H. V. HILPRECHT.

In his "Assyriologische Miscellen" (*Erste Reihe :*
I.–III.)* p. 193 ff., Delitzsch discusses the numerical
fragment K. 2014,† known through Schrader's *A. B. K.*,
p. 237, and places it in its proper light. Simultane-
ously with the printing of that essay, in the course of
my work on the Nippur tablets, I came across a small
brown clay fragment, measuring 6.65 cm. in its longest,
and 3.5 cm. in its widest part. On both sides, the tablet—to which I gave the number, Ni. 1893—shows
remains of lines of cuneiform writing in Neo-Babylonian
characters. Although apparently only the portion of a
so-called "contract tablet," it derives especial importance from the fact that it contains several Assyrian.
numerals in phonetic writing which up to the present
had not been found elsewhere.

As an exact reproduction of the fragment will appear in
one of the forthcoming volumes of my series of *Cuneiform
Texts*, giving the results of the Babylonian Expedition
of the University of Pennsylvania, I shall confine myself
here to a short description of what is essentially new in
the fragment. The obverse alone needs to be considered

---

* Reprint from the *Berichte d. Philolog.-Histor. Classe d. K. S.
Gesell. d. Wiss.*, 8 Juli., 1893.

† Bezold, *Catalogue of the Cuneiform Tablets in the Kouyunjik Collection of the British Museum*, I., p. 385.

for our purposes. In its fragmentary condition it consists of two columns. Of the left-hand column only a
few signs at the end of the first seven lines are preserved,
namely: l.1: ME; l.2: A–AN; l.3: I*kan*; l.4: II*kan*; l.5:
III*kan*; l.6 and 7, merely *kan* or remains of that sign.
It is impossible to determine at present what may have
stood at the beginning of these single lines. At all
events the right-hand column makes it probable that the
numerical signs followed by *kan* continued in uninterrupted succession, at least till IX, and perhaps still
further.

It is to be regretted that the right-hand column,
which, among other things, contains the masculine or
feminine forms of the Babylono-Assyrian cardinal numbers, is only preserved up to the numeral VIII or IX.
Of course there is still a possibility that the remaining
portions of the tablet may be found among the fragments not yet cleaned, or may be furnished by the ex-
cavations continued with such success at Nippur.

I need not stop to consider the numerals I to V, since
such forms as *šelóšu, irbit, ḥamilti,* have been known
for some time. For number II, we find instead of
the usual *šiná, ši-nu-u = šinû.** The numerals VI–IX,
appear as follows:

   l. 8: *siš šit-ti*
   l. 9: *sib-ti*
   l. 10: *sa-man-ti*
   l. 11: [*ti*]*t†-ti*

* Scarcely to be regarded as the ordinal number=*šanû*. The feminine of the numeral II, which Delitzsch omits in his enumeration,
Assyr. Gram., § 75, is found in Strassmaier, *Nabonidus,* 258, 12 : II-*it,*
i. e., *šinit.*

† Cf. Bruennow, *A Classified List,* No. 1486.

The last line may doubtless be completed to *til-ti*, the traces pointing to this character, and there being only space for one character between the ruling at the edge and the break. *Tilti* or *têlti* = *tišti* = *tišati* = *tiš-šati* = *tiš'ati*, is therefore the form *fi'latu*. The well-known form *ti-šil* on the other hand is a formation *fi'iltu*.* In the case of the numeral VII there are also two complementary formations of the feminine occurring side by side, as will be shown below. The masculine form for IX is, as Delitzsch has already correctly put it, *ti-šu*, i. e., *tišu* (=*tiššu*=*tiš'u*).

The number *samânti*=VIII appears here for the first time. It coincides fully (especially when ending in *a* = *samânta*) with the Ethiopic accusative form *samânta*.† From the feminine form the masculine *samânu* may be readily deduced. Cf. also Bezold, *Oriental Diplomacy*, § 32.

It is interesting to note the feminine form *sibti* or *sêbti* by the side of the one hitherto known *sebilti*.‡ Just as in the case of the numeral IX, so we have for VII two distinct formations, *fa'latu* and *fa'altu*, i. e., on the one hand *sêbti*=*sêbi(a)ti*=*sâbatu*=*sabbatu*=*sab'atu*, on the other *sibilti* or *sebilti*=*sebatti*=*saba'ti*.‖ The corresponding masculine *si-ba*, i. e., *sêba*‖ was previously known.

* Cf. Delitzsch, *Assyr. Gram.*, *ibid.*

† Occurring at a late period, though in reality a more primitive form, from which the customary *samânta* was deduced according to the Ethiopic Phonetic Laws. By the side of the latter we also find the older samânita (acc.), cf. Praetorius, *Aethiopische Grammatik*, §§ 135, 136 and 15.

‡ Cf. Delitzsch *Assyr. Gram.*, *ibid.*

‖ Delitzsch, *ibid.*, §65, 6, Anmerkung.

The feminine form of the numeral VI *sîššitti* is abnormal. The shortened form *sîš-šit* is found, 82, 7–14, 864, col. III, 14 ab. (Meissner, *Z. A.*, VII, pp. 28 and 20, and the same author's *De servitute Babylonico-Assyriaca*, p. 6). The passage reads: VI, *gin guškin ni-lal·e=sîš·šit sik-lu kaspu i-šak-kal*, "six shekels of silver shall he pay." Inasmuch as the Assyrian stem for the word is *s·d·š*,[*] we should have expected a form *sidšati=sîšša(i)ti*, which, indeed, Bertin, in his Assyro-Babylonian grammar, p. 34, adopts. The form *sîššitti* can only be accounted for as a secondary formation due to analogy and arising under the influence of the form *fi'iltu*, which, as it appears, was predominantly employed in numerals such as *sebitti, tîšitti* (cf. also *šinitti*, probably pronounced thus) and *irbitti*. In other words, just as the stem *š-d-š* becoming through dissimilation *s-d-š* (but cf. the ordinal *ši-iš-ši* and the cardinal *ši-ib-i* or *ši-bi* in Bezold, *Oriental Diplomacy*, § 32), led to pronouncing "seven" and "eight" as a rule with initial *s*, so conversely the feminine forms like *sebitti* and *tîšitti* (by the side of *sêbti* and *tîšti* or *têlti*) superinduced *sîššitti* as the feminine formation for "six." The masculine form must have been *sîššu* in Assyrian, conformably to the Semitic ground-form *šidth*;[†] and *sîššu* again would, in appearance and pronunciation, be identical with the cardinal of six, inasmuch as the latter appears as *sadušu*[‡]*=sadšu=sedšu=seššu* (written *sîššu*).

---

[*] Delitzsch, *ibid.*, § 75, and *Assyriologische Miscellen*, p. 196.

[†] Noeldeke *Die Semitischen Sprachen*, p. 7, Anmerk 1.

[‡] *Fa'ul* in Assyrian in accordance with Delitzsch, *Assyr. Gram.*, § 76, close.

THE HOLY NUMBERS OF THE RIG-VEDA.

BY EDWARD WASHBURN HOPKINS.

[For further details than are given in this paper, and for the questions of the Indo-Semitic Duodecimal system, see the author's account of all the Vedic numbers, given in full in Journ. Am. Or. Soc. For the holiness of one in "one god," etc., see a paper by the same, published in the Drisler Memorial Volume (1894), on Henotheism in the Rig-Veda.]

THE most revered cardinals of the Rig-Veda are three and seven. The origin and application of these numerical groups form the study of this paper. The chief questions involved, are the antiquity of their sacred character, and the effect produced upon theosophic speculation by their employment as holy numbers. To give some examples of the employment of each in turn: there are three heavens and three earths; heaven is threefold with apportioned realms. There are seven seers, rivers, rays. But more complex, including the atmosphere, is the later division of the fifth book: Three heavens, three light-spaces, three rain-spaces, are the places of the highest gods. The simplest and earliest form, as I conceive, of a threefold division is that of earth, air and heaven—of which we have an example in I, 95, 3: "Three are the birth-places of the fire-god, in air, in heaven, in water," where "water" stands for cloud, since Agni's third form is the lightning. Important is one result of this division, viz.: that according to several passages the gods collect in threes, *i. e.* there are gods in earth, air, and heaven; although this is sometimes varied so that "in the realm of light the gods stand in threes," *i. e.*, in each of the three heavens. Yet no passage that seems to belong to the earliest period would indicate a formal three-fold division into groups of all the gods. Sub-divisions of earth itself are left to the imagination, though a curse in one passage suggests that the third earth is super-imposed on a sort of hell, for the enemy is cursed "to lie under all the three earths."

Particularly in the constant application to the gods, and to many liturgical reckonings, is three the holiest of holy numbers. Three are the strides of Vishnu across heaven; thrice a day, morning, noon and night, the gods descend to the sacrifice (oblation). In one passage this is extended to three nightly benefits of Agni (VII, 11, 3). Even where the dual character of the gods is characteristic, as in the case of the two Açvins (Horsemen), the Dioskouroi of India, three is applied, as it were mechanically, in their praise: "Thrice come to us to-day, three tires are on your chariot, three supports; thrice by day ye come, thrice by night; when dawn ascends the chariot that has three seats then give us thrice your heavenly refreshment . . . Thrice ye compass earth and through three distances ye come; in threefold way is the oblation poured out; thrice are the three vessels filled; three are the wheels of your three-fold chariot, three are the seats; upon this three-fold chariot come, O Açvins, together with the thrice-eleven gods" (I, 34). Though this is rather an extreme instance of harping upon three, it shows compactly what may be illustrated at length from many passages, that three is a number peculiarly holy and of especially di-

vine application. Compare especially Om = a, u, m
(See Av. XIII, 3, 6). Omitting here a vast number of
details (which will be found elsewhere) I call especial
attention to the use of three in the formation, first of
divine triads and then of an early trinity. Agni, the
fire-god, makes a triad with Soma and Gandharva; he
makes with Wind and Sun another and very important
triad. Of other groups of three may be mentioned the
gods Aryaman, Mitra, Varuna; the goddesses Ilā,
Sarasvatī, Mahī (these are given in various orders and
with the substitution at times of Bharatī for Mahī); also
the three Ribhus; the three mother-goddesses of Agni;
the three Fates or Destructions (but this is quite unique);
"the three that cause increase;" "the three fires that
follow dawn," etc. (human are "the three Aryan races,"
"the three ages past," etc.). There is but one clearly
defined trinity, interesting as a prototype of the later
trinity (Brahma, Vishnu, Siva), and that is from Fire—
Sun—Lightning. For there is a certain homoousian
tendency, which leads to the union of different gods,
notably of Agni with Indra and Savitar by means of the
identification of their respective attributes, flame, sun-
light, lightning. Eventually the middle factor, Indra
(lightning and its spiritual *causa movens*), is formally
stated to be the same with the sun, and with Agni, the
sacrificial fire.

Almost all the cases of threes are of divine or ritual-
istic application. Apart from this and certain rare instances of earth (above), three is used in a superlative
sense, but generally as the limit of an unbroken series,
as "for one, for two, for three, or for many;" where it
is important to note that three is not used for many, but
only as leading up to it; and as an adverb, in the sense

of "much" or "very," though probably with no more evanescence of the original meaning than is to be seen in Τριφίληπτος, ter felix, etc. In proper names it is interesting to note parallels to Τριπτόλεμος, etc., such as Trivrishan, Trimántu, etc.

In later literature three is much employed in witchcraft, as in Greece and Rome. In the Rig-Veda itself, examples of this may be seen in X, 87, 10–11; VIII, 91 (80), 5–7.

SEVEN.

The use of seven is not the same with that of three. The difference should be carefully noticed. In the first place three is too small a number to be used as an equivalent for "many," except in such adverbial phrases as "thrice red," etc., parallel to ter felix, whereas seven is constantly used in the sense of "many." In the second place three is a holier number than seven.

In regard to the first point we have such expressions as that used by Indra: "I am a seven-slayer," i. e., a slayer of many; and also "the seven fortresses" of the sky as equivalent to an indefinite plurality, something like our generalized use of "dozen;" though even in English the use of seven as an indefinite number is not unknown. Compare Shakespeare's "a vile thief this seven year." Such also is the significance of saptápada in the phrase "food for seven places" (i. e., many), which leads to the expression "a friend for seven places" (Atharva Veda) i. e., in many or in all circumstances, while this in turn gives place to the later legal term saptapadī, the bride or new wife, who, from forgetfulness of the original meaning and in consequence of a literal translation of the ancient formula, was by Hindu law, in order to be true to her title, obliged to take seven

steps around the altar at the time of the wedding cere-
mony.   The same indefinite meaning is to be seen in
sapta-budhna, the "seven-bottomed" sea, a companion
piece to the Nile *ἱππάρροος*.   So again "better than
seven" means better than many.

The prototype of three as a holy or at any rate mystic
number is given in nature.   There are obvious threes
all around us—earth, air, and sky; land, water, and air;
sun, moon, and stars; morning, noon, and night, etc.,
to which came also the thought of completeness in three,
a Pythagorean notion exemplified in the Rig-Veda by
the "three bonds" of Varuna, and in general by the
beginning, middle, and end of anything.

Now if we look for a counterpart to this in seven, we
shall find only two groups that could have caused seven
to be used as it is; one, the group of seven stars called
the seven seers (compare Latin septentriones); the other
the seven streams (distinct from the five, the Pun-jab),
which in the Rig-Veda, as well as in the Persian Avesta,
give the name to the country.   In many cases it is impossible to say whether the application of seven is derived
from its indefinite sense or from analogy with these
often-alluded-to seven stars and seven streams.   The
former view is the usual one, yet it seems to me natural
that in the second case, that of the seven streams of
heavenly *soma* and their earthly counterparts, we have
only analogy with the seven rivers of earth.

Indra subdues seven fortresses (evidently like *saptahá*
(X, 49, 8), a designation of many; so too the *vrájam
saptásyam*, "seven mouthed enclosure," just like
ἑπτάστομος=ἑπτάπυλος.   There are seven priests of Agni, but
the number is not constant (five and four are elsewhere
spoken of), and these seem to be earthly equivalents of

the seven seers in the sky. Out of this conception,
however, is developed an important result. Each of
the seven seers has his own path, and Agni follows each
path. For this reason, I think, Agni is credited with
"seven flames," and from the theosophic identification
of Agni with the Sun and with Indra we find that the
beams of the one and the accompanying spirits of the
other are also originally reckoned as seven (Compare in
Greek ἑπτάπορος of the stars). As support for this interpretation I may adduce IV, 1, 12, where the seven friends
of Agni are his beams. Apart from these instances the
sevenfold song and seven kinds of music deserve notice,
as perhaps indicative of an original division into seven
notes, but this is in a very late hymn. Theologically
important is the evident derivation of the seven Ādityās
(later twelve) from the idea of the sun's seven rays, for
we find them given as five, six or seven (this is the usual
number) in exact parallelism to the raising of Agni's
priests to seven. And so later the priests become twelve,
as do the Ādityās. As to Indra, we find his rays are also
seven, and contemporaneously seven are his friends.
The expression *saptá-tantu*, used of the sacrifice, "with
seven strands," is apparently from the same source.
Although these conceptions are couched under various
metaphors (seven steeds, reins, sisters, etc.), they are
all at bottom applicable to light-rays alone when applied
to light-divinities.

Other uses of seven are rare: most conspicuous are
the "seven places" of various gods, and the therewith
connected "seven mights" (or "seven places," *dhámani*
certainly means the same with *padáni* in X, 122, 3).

The cardinal points are four or five as a general thing,
but once (only IX, 114, 3), they are reckoned as seven

(possibly on account of being grouped with the seven priests and seven Ādityas) a view that prevailed, however, in later literature (A. V.), In two passages seven plays a mystic role, but in the first only in conjunction with other cardinals likewise employed in a sort of hocus-pocus (IV, 58, 3; X, 99, 2). In the second passage it may perhaps refer to the seventh Āditya.

Proper names made of "seven" are Saptágu, Saptávadhri. Compare Snooks (= sen = seven oaks); Simrock (= sieben röcke), etc.

THREE AND SEVEN UNITED.

Before comparing the holiness of three and seven it is necessary to remark on the association of these numbers. Some of the sevens are the same in application with the threes. Three, again, is simply grouped with seven, at other times it is multiplied into seven—the latter case is of especial interest. I begin with the simpler case. Three beside seven, juxtaposition, seems to be the starting point of the later union of three and seven multiplied into each other. The Açvins come thrice and find three vessels thrice filled with *soma*-streams which have seven mothers (I, 34, 8). Varuna rules seven streams and looks on three heavens, three earths (VIII, 41, 9). There are a few other similar instances.

THE THRICE–SEVEN.

Far more important is the raising of an original seven to thrice its original value. Thus the seven rivers are made twenty-one (X, 75, 1); thus too the *soma*-streams are trebled, from seven to thrice-seven, and so also are the heavenly streams. An instance later than the Rig-Veda may be seen in the Atharva, where Varuna's three fetters become twenty-one ("seven thrice," AV, IV, 16, 6–7).

I have said that this is an important alteration of the original conception. The theosophic bearing of the change will occupy us presently. But first I would call attention to the aid furnished by these statements to literary criticism, in particular to the question of the relative age of certain books of the Rig-Veda. For it is to be taken for granted if the rivers of earth or of heaven are usually alluded to as seven and occasionally as thrice seven, and if the latter number is chiefly found in later parts of the Rig-Veda, that, conversely, the rare occurrence of thrice seven in passages of which the age is doubtful should help us in estimating the period to which we are to refer the books where are found these thrice-sevens. Now with two exceptions, all the cases of thrice-seven are in books I, VIII, IX, X, which from this point of view almost form a group by themselves; since the two exceptions are of such a mystical sort that they bear on their face evidence of belonging rather to the Brahmanic than to the early Vedic period. Both, moreover, refer to the same point, and both are confessedly of esoteric darkness: "Varuna declared unto me the wise one (that) the not-to-be-slain one (viz., the cow) bears thrice seven names," and it is added that this piece of esoteric wisdom should not (?) be revealed (VII, 87, 4). Compare IV, 1, 16: "They observed the first name of the cow, they found the thrice-seven highest name of the mother." In I, 164, 3, there are "seven names of the cow," and in each of these cases we have to do with the raising of the number of the Maruts from seven to thrice-seven; who are thus described in an old verse apparently added (out of place) in VIII, 28, 5:

"The spears of the seven are seven; seven are their
lights; seven, the glories they don." That this is the
older idea stands recorded in the Revelation (*çruti*)
quoted by Ludwig: "According to Revelation the
Maruts are hosts of seven." It is evident that the
"lightning-handed" Maruts were once identical in
number with the seven beams of Indra's car.

The first instance, in order, of the raising of seven to
3x7 is that of I, 20, 7. Here "thrice seven" gifts are
begged for, instead of the "seven gifts" elsewhere (V.
1, 5; VI. 74, 1) requested.

In the same way the "seven secret places" of Agni
(see above) are in I, 72, 6, raised to "thrice seven."
Again in a late and mystic hymn of the same book we
read: "The three times seven *vishpulingakâs* swallow
poison and die not; the thrice seven peacocks (Maruts?)
and the seven sister streams have removed the poison"
(I, 191, 12–14).

Our next instance is from the ninth book: "Thrice
seven cows milk for him," (IX, 70, 1) probably the
thrice seven streams of VIII, 46, 26. Again we find as
above the "thrice seven cows" opposed to "seven
cows" (IX, 86, 21, 25).

In the tenth book "we call the thrice seven streams"
(X, 64, 8) and "seven fences, thrice seven woodpiles"
(mystic application of liturgical rites), X, 90, 15.

In VIII, 46, 26, (this book is the chief point of interest) we find first that "Vāyu (?) has *tris saptá sapta-
linâm, i. e.*, 3x7x70, where there is an effort to render
more holy a phrase perhaps already too trite to produce
the requisite effect. Compare in St. Matthew, 18, 21 :
Οὐ λέγω σοι ἕως ἑπτάκις ἀλλ' ἕως ἑβδομηκοντάκις ἑπτα; and in one of the
later gift-lauds of X, 93, 15; "seventy and seven,"
with the "three seventies" of VIII, 19, 37.

In VIII, 69 (58), 7 another allusion to the Maruts as "thrice seven;" and in Ib., 96 (85), 2: "the thrice seven mountain tops" are destroyed by Indra, who is elsewhere wont to destroy "seven." Bergaigne takes both VIII, 96, 2 and I, 72, 6, as referring to worlds. As is well known, the "thrice sevens" as one word, are common later (e. g. in the Athava). Of this use we have in the Rig-Veda only I, 133, 6, and Vāl., 11, 5: "the thrice seven beings" and "help us by the thrice seven."

In another passage of this eighth book, which from many numerical coincidences I consider to be in age on a par with the later part of the rest of the Rig-Veda, we find the Maruts raised again to thrice sixty, VIII, 96 (85), 8.

THE THRICE—ELEVEN.

The gods are currently cited as being thrice-eleven. In Vāl., 9, 2, and in IX, 92, 4, all the gods are included in this sum (so in the late passage I, 34, 11). In one other passage where the gods "with their wives," are mentioned (III, 6, 9) we find the last mention of the thirty-three gods outside of the group books I, IX, and VIII (28, 1; 30, 2; 35, 3; 39, 9). One of the passages in the first book seems to be peculiarly late, I, 139, 11, and here the three elevens are distributed as "eleven in heaven, eleven on earth, eleven in the waters" (compare X, 65, 9). Without division they are mentioned in I, 34, 11; 45, 2 ("three and thirty"). In III, 9, 9, the gods are 3339, a late passage, really belonging to X, 52, 6.

I shall now attempt to show that this number of thirty-three gods, which obtains in the Rig-Veda, being a parallel case to that which we have noticed in the case of the Maruts, is a development from an original pantheon of ten gods.

Thirty-three gods is an odd number to select. What caused it? In the first place, we see in several instances that groups are raised by multiplying with three, and as this has been demonstrated for other groups it seems not forced to see the same process here. Of later growth is perhaps the distribution of the gods in general into groups of three (in earth, air, heaven). The same distribution is found in the case of twenty-one worlds, and of the Maruts, who like the thrice-eleven were originally seven and then thrice-seven.

If then we conceive of the host indicated by thrice-eleven as having passed through the same development with that of the parallel thrice-seven Maruts, thrice-seven rivers, etc., which is a natural and justified assumption, we arrive at an a priori group of eleven as the origin of the thrice-eleven.

Now comes in play a curious tendency. The Hindus, like other peoples, were very apt to close or fasten a number by the addition of one as a sort of head. This is the δυοῖν τρίτος idea (O. T., 581), which is found with us in the "baker's dozen" of thirteen. In the North compare the Gudhrūnakvidha fyrsta: "seven sons, and my husband the eighth." In Greece, compare Alcman (Frg. 49):

> ὥρας δ᾽ ἔθηκε τρεῖς, θέρος
> καὶ χεῖμα κ᾽ ὠπώραν τρίτην,
> καὶ τέτρατον τὸ ἦρ

In other circumstances compare in the Rig-Veda VIII, 3, 24: "Drink is life; clothing, body; ornaments, power; as the fourth (good thing) I name the donor of this horse," where we have a triad increased (as shown by the phraseology) by the "fourth," a later thought. So again we find "the seven rays, and Agni as the eighth" (II, 5, 2); and "seven sons of Aditi with the sun as the eighth" (X, 72, 8). Exactly like the example from the Edda cited above is the prayer of the marriage ritual: "May she have ten sons, her husband the eleventh." So also we find instead of one hundred that "one hundred and one" are enumerated (X, 130, 1). Compare 1001 Arabian Nights Tales and our popular collection of 101 songs. Now just as *ékaçatam* really means *çatám* (this is quite frequently the case in AV.), so *ékādaça* means, as it seems to me, originally *dáça*, or *dáça* with a leader added. An humble parallel of *ékādaça* (ten gods with a leader) would be οἱ ἕνδεκα of Athens, *i. e.*, ten men with a captain. For another case of thrice eleven evolved from eleven, compare TS., 1, 4, 11, 1: "There are thirty-three Rudras; of which eleven (the older number) are in the waters." Either solely from the tendency to reduplicate with three, or from the later division of gods (as those of three places) being united with this tendency, we have an original group of eleven raised to thrice-eleven. And it is to be noticed that the mention of thrice-eleven coincides in time pretty closely with the other groups raised by the same multiplication.

A very good example of this additional one is given by a passage in which, in accordance with a much later method of identifying the gods with the heavenly bodies, we find them counted in the same breath as thirty-four and thirty-five, their leader being omitted in

. the first count and being really not represented in the system.*

If this theory of an original group of ten gods be accepted, it will at least explain some very obscure passages in the Atharva-Veda. Here, namely, although the gods are often reckoned as countless (all groups of gods tend to become greater, *e. g.*, in TS, 5, 5, 2, 5, the eight Vasus become 333), we yet find a formal utterance to the effect that there were originally ten gods. Or how else shall we interpret the statements AV. XI, 8, 3: "Before the gods there were born ten gods together," and Ib. 10: "The gods that were born before the (present) gods gave over the world to their sons?" The poet of the Veda explains it philosophically, mystically. But to me it seems to be a bit of theosophic tradition. Moreover, another point, although the thrice-eleven gods are often met with in the Epic, yet in the popular phraseology they are consistently called, not the thrice-eleven but the thrice-ten, *tridaça*, a word the difficulty in the interpretation of which has led the Petersburg Lexicon to render *tridaca* as "a simplified expression for thirty-three." But here *Brahmâ tridacais saha*, etc., can mean only "Brahma with the thrice-ten," where the head of the group is again reckoned extra. Compare *dvidaça* "twenty."

There are enough obsolescent gods in the Rig-Veda to support this view—gods of older dignity than the popular—Dyaus, Earth, Varuna, Mitra, Trita, Bhaga, Yama,

---

* Cf. ÇBr., IV, 5, 7, 2: "There are thirty-three gods, and Prajâpati is the thirty-fourth." In the other case twenty-seven lunar stations (as stars) are combined with the five planets, the sun and the moon = 34, the real number. Compare RV. I, 162, 18, where, as Ludwig thinks, and X, 27. 15-16, where, as I think, the thirty-four gods are again alluded to (all late).

Sūrya the Sun, the Wind, and Pūshan are less modern than are Agni, Indra, the Moon, Dawn, Rudra, the Maruts, the Vasus, the Ribhus, the Ādityās, Soma-plant, the Fashioner, the All-maker, the Creator, Vishnu, Savitar, Brihaspati, the All-gods, the Waters, and the host of lesser mights.

The later interpretation of the "thrice-eleven," including in its reckoning twelve Ādityās (instead of eight or seven) is palpably worthless.

I would suggest in closing that as the Návagvās, the Tuneful Nine of the Rig-Veda, may be associated with the *Novensiles* and perhaps with the Nine Muses, so the Dáçagvās, decemviri, are not at first "ten months" as will Weber, but possibly a survival of this older pantheon of ten, named in bulk, and kept as a group. They are to the Vedic age what were to the Epic the *devās* of the Rig-Veda, the shadows of departed divinities, the ghosts of gods.*

NINE AND NINETY.

It is odd that the holiness of 3x3 is implicitly or explicitly stated as a matter of course, while nine in and for itself seems to remain in an abeyance of sanctity. In later times this is not the case. Kaegi, Die Neunzahl, has given liturgical and legal illustrations of nine as a holy number after the Vedic Age, but in the Rig-

---

* As the seven Ādityās were afterwards fitted to the new arrangement of a twelve-month year and became a dozen, so the twelve gods (at least two of which may be Semitic) of the Greek pantheon may originally have coincided with the ten-month year of which we hear in Rome. In Northern mythology Simrock says that of the twelve gods two are certainly late. For another passage in AV. where "ten creators" are spoken of, compare XI, 7, 4; and with this possibly the ten in RV. VII, 104, 15=AV, VIII, 4, 15.

Veda with the exception of the Návagvās it is only 3×3 or 99 that are peculiarly holy. Nine alone is little regarded. The word scarcely occurs except as a factor in ninety-nine. Even the resultant nine of thrice three is rare, and it is evident that the sum was not so sacred as the factor. Thus in I, 163, 4: "They say there are three bindings in heaven, three in waters (air), three in the sea," which make nine, but only by inference. With the exception of a casual allusion or two to nine as a metrical element in a series, and of the nine of the thirty-four (gods) in X, 27, 15 (see above) the only independent nine in the Rig-Veda, is, if I do not err, the "nine days and ten nights" when Rebha, a protegé of the Açvins, lay in the water; but this appears to have no special significance (I, 116, 24). Nine-and-ninety has the plain function of producing an indefinitely magnified effect, and the illustrations go hand in hand with the cases just mentioned of three times seven. Thus the streams of heaven become ninety-nine in X, 104, 8 (in I, 80, 8; 121, 13, they are ninety); and the citadels destroyed by Indra are either ninety or nine and ninety; once nine and ninety and then "the hundredth" (VII, 19, 5). As simpler equivalent of many "ninety-nine strengths" may serve (X, 49, 8; 39, 10). Most of the examples (but there is little variety) are those of the thrice-seven group. A Briarean monster with ninety-nine arms is once (II, 14, 4) mentioned; and Indra's steeds in ever-varying numbers are also so counted; so we find one thousand and ninety-nine loads. The Návagvās and Návavāstva alone remain. In V, 27, 3 "ninth" is doubtful.

COMPARISON OF THREE AND NINE WITH SEVEN.

I propose now to take a somewhat wider point of view, and by comparing the use of three, nine, and seven in other Aryan languages, seek to discover whether there was from the beginning a difference in the holiness attaching to these numbers. But I may say at once that, while it may not be denied that seven in the primitive Aryan period was a number looked upon with peculiar respect, it will yet be found that there is a striking contrast between the sacredness of seven and that of three and nine.

In Greece exact references neither for three nor for nine will be necessary to establish their respective holiness. The τρίζυγοι θεαί are but a type of the one; the ἐννεαπήχεες ἐννεόργυιοι, and ἐννέωρος, (Od. XI, 311), of the other. Compare Zeus' three-forked lightning; Poseidon's three-forked spear (trident); the three (or five) rivers of hell; and around hell the Styx thrice three times; the three Fates, three Furies, three Graces; the three judges of hell; the three-headed dog of Pluto; and certain triads of Hesiod (Theog., 149, 890, 902, sq.) Eunomia, Dike, Eirene; Notos, Boreas, Zephyros; Kottos, Briareus, Gyas; while in regard to nine, compare the Ark of Deucalion floating nine days; nine muses; the nine days' plague; the nine days' visit of the Iliad; Pindar's nine years of purgatory, etc. As in India, to treble is to produce greater holiness, τρὶς ἐννέα κλῶνας τιθείς, in O. C., 483. In the Iliad nine oxen are sacrificed for the nine days' feast, etc. Three is divinely holy.

Now on examining the use of seven the contrast in Hellas is marked: Almost all the triads and enneads are applied in Homer to gods or divine things and events. But notice to what seven is applied: a shield of seven

hides; a town of seven gates; a year of seven seasons; a
lyre of seven strings; life divided into seven stages
(Solon); the seven wise men of earth; a rower's bench,
θρῆνς, seven feet long; seven wonders; seven sleepers;
seven senses (due to planets), sons, ships, etc.   In almost
every instance in sharp contrast to three (nine), seven is
of earth earthly, until we come to Orphic, and perhaps
foreign influence.   There is in the early literature
scarcely a link connecting seven with the gods (an exception somewhat vague may be seen in ἑπταχα πάντα διεμοιράτο
Od., XIV, 434).   It is not too much to say that until we
come to Æschylus seven is by far not so holy as three—
and this is putting it mildly.   The seven seers of
heaven are here the Wain—earthly.   The seven planets
(ἑπτάπορος) are known in the Homeric hymns, but no
sacred application is made of them.   There is no group
of seven in the pantheon, and ἑπτάκτις, ἑπταφαίς, ἑπτάζωνος, etc.,
are all late.   The holiness of seven is not aboriginal with
the Greek.   Nor is it in Rome.   For here, except for
the Seven Oxen (Septemtriones), the Septemviri, the
Septempagium (all earthly and worldly in their conception, even including the oxen), there are no native
sevens of any moment.   Now let us turn to Northern
mythology.   All the holiness which may be claimed for
seven belongs, so far as I can judge, not to the older Edda,
but to the younger, and even this is vague.   "Seven
sons of sobriety," "seven mysterious knives" are noticed; but in the older Edda there are only seven eagles,
kings, halls, sisters, sons, and seasons of years (misseri).
We find here in combination with three a parallel to the
use of the Rig-Veda: "for seven days we trotted through
cold land; seven more over the sea, and the third seven
we went over dry steppes" (Gudhrûnakvidha önnur).
Evidently here we have only a round number, as in the

younger Edda "sevenfold council." There is no more
mystery in regard to seven than there is in other numbers of a character not at all sacred, as for instance eight
(brothers, sisters, knights, nobles, seasons, etc.). But
as soon as we reach three, we come up to the same level
of divine application as that on which stands this number in classic lands. The Nornen are three, the Walkuren are three, or nine; there are nine worlds and nine
heavens, nine magic formulas. Odin's ring drops eight
others every nine days. In Thrym's song Thor's ham-
mer is in the eighth depth below (*i. e.*, there are nine
strata). See especially Völuspâ, passim (in 24 the Nornen and Walkuren are identified).

The general character of nine and three contrasts
strongly with that of seven. One is essentially divine;
the other is humanly perfect, and so shades into completeness, thence into mystery and holiness.

I cannot but think that in India the same state of
affairs obtained. Seven is here also an indefinitely complete number, and as there are no heavenly prototypes
for seven save in the seven stars, we are driven to look
upon these as the origin for all the sevenhood of seven
as a heavenly number, for the streams seven are palpably
earthly, and, perhaps, pre-Indian. It seems, therefore,
much more reasonable to take the divine application of
seven in India as originally arising from the indefinite
and so complete sense conveyed by it. And even the
seven stars may have originally been conceived of as the
many departed seers (this is the opinion of Roth), *i. e.*,
the Manes, until they became limited by a strict interpretation to seven, and the seven stars were then taken
as their representative—exactly such a procedure as we
can trace historically in the case of the word *septápada*
(above). Even in India the application of seven in

divine circumstances is till late (seven islands, etc.)
much more contracted than that of three.

Our religious sense has been affected by the ecclesias-
tical use of seven, so that with the exception of the tri-
une, seven is to-day rather more a sacred number than
is three, although the popularity of nine lingers in vulgar sayings and proverbs.   Examples of each will show
how modern, comparatively, is the sacredness of seven,
and how thorough-going (popular) the use of nine.   Thus
"possession is nine-tenths of the law;" "cat o'nine
tails;" the "ninth wave;" a "nine days' wonder;" "a
cat has nine lives" (compare the dog, ἐννεάψυχος); "it
takes nine tailors to make a man;" "rigged to the
nines;" "a stitch in time saves nine," etc.   Leases
run for 99 or 999 years.   On the other hand, as the
effect of ecclesiasticism (that of astrology in seven
zones, planets, senses), may be cited: The seven
spirits before God's throne; seven graces of God; seven
divisions of the Lord's prayer; seven Levitical purifica-
tions; Churches in Asia; candlesticks; trumpets; horns;
eyes of the Lamb; exile of Israel; Pharaoh's kine;
ears of corn, etc.   One question arises here which
is outside the limits of this paper, and can only be
broached.   The seven above are Semitic, not Aryan.
But the Sabbatical year and the seven days of creation
seem to be made by analogy with seven days of the
week.   Now later than the Rig-Veda, a week of seven
days is in India (Atharva Veda) obtained by dividing
into quarters the lunar month of twenty-eight days.   Is
not this the origin of the Semitic sacredness of seven?

In Scandinavia the week was, I believe, one of nine
days.*

* For previous literature see the author's article referred to above.

THE CHANGE FROM SURD TO SONANT IN JAPANESE COMPOUNDS.

BY BENJAMIN SMITH LYMAN.

THE main object of this paper is to place on record in detail the more important facts at the base of certain euphonic rules briefly given in the short published abstract of a paper of mine on "The Japanese Nigori of Composition," read before the American Oriental Society in 1883.

At the beginning of the second part of very many Japanese compound words the surds *ch, f, h, k, s, sh* and *t* are changed to sonants. The Japanese call a sonant the *nigori*, that is, the turbid, or impure form, of its corresponding surd. They have at times even insisted that all the sonant consonants of the purely Japanese part of the language are only derived from surds; and, although that has seemed impossible to some foreigners, on account of the occurrence of sonants at the beginning of many apparently simple words, we shall see, in the light of some cases at least, the Japanese view is not so wholly inconceivable.

It has sometimes seemed to European students of Japanese that the nigori of composition was as inexplicable as it appears to be in our words hurdy-gurdy, hurly-burly and the like, or that it was a mere matter of the ear, and might be used or not at will. But it will be found that its use depends on the meaning instead of wholly on the ear, and that the Japanese do not, like

(160)

foreigners, use it indifferently or drop it.   In some cases,
however, both forms may be allowable, according to difference of meaning or derivation.

The rule in general for purely Japanese words is that
the second part of a compound word takes the nigori ;
that is, if beginning with *ch*, *f*, *h*, *k*, *s*, *sh* or *t*, those
consonants are changed to the corresponding sonant
ones ; yet with only a slight preponderance, about 2361
cases against about 2316; and the general rule does not
apply : (1) when *b*, *d*, *g*, *j*, *p*, or *z* already occurs anywhere
in the second part of the compound ; nor (2) when the
second part is a Chinese word; nor (3) where the word,
though given by Hepburn as a compound, is really made
up of words in regular grammatical connection (without
ellipsis), such as juxtaposed verbal forms, or Chinese
words followed by verbal forms denoting doing or action
(*shi*, *suru*, and the like), or words connected by *no* or
followed by *to*, *te*, or any of the syllables used for the
terminations of verbal forms ; and (4) there are 1000
other cases where the nigori is not taken against 2220
where it is, or one case out of three.

It is not probably worth while to record here the very
numerous words that conform to these general and special rules, but only the much less bulky lists of exceptions to them.   The rules are based on a review, made
sixteen years ago, of all the words in Hepburn's dictionary, second edition, and some two or three hundred
more, in all about 23,000 words; and though an over-
sight here and there may have taken place, and though
his third edition may have added further material, it is
hoped that the present results may be exact enough for
practical purposes.

In reading the lists it is to be borne in mind that

under the general rule *h*, as representing an ancient surd labial, is changed to *b*, or sometimes to *p*, "half nigori."—*Hu*, instead of *fu*, would correctly give the pronunciation of Tokio; but at Kiyoto the sound is really *fu*, with the *f* exactly like the English *f*; and Kiyoto, from its central situation and other circumstances, rightly gives the standard for the language in general.— In transliterating (not anglicising), *oo* (like the other vowels) is not used with the same force as most often in English, but to represent .two successive, yet not audibly separated, long o's, as each would commonly be called, much like *oo* in *oolite, oolitic, oological, zoological, zoophyte.* Such a mode of writing the sound, so far from being an innovation, as some have considered it, is as old as any systematic rule of Japanese transliteration, and was explicitly adopted about two hundred years ago by Kaempfer, and has been in use ever since. —In the lists of exceptions a dash is used to save repetition of the corresponding part of the preceding word.

1.—*B*, *d*, *g*, *j*, *p*, or *z* in the next syllable (363 cases), or any following one (35, in all 398 cases), prevents the nigori. The only exception is amagappa.

A sonant in the syllable before has no effect on the nigori (about 150 words with, and about 150 without).

2.—Compounds with the final part Chinese do not take the nigori in about 2090 cases (besides 81 cases where a following nigori would have prevented at any rate) ; but in 287 (about one case in seven) it is taken, namely:

(*a*)—Where immediately preceded by the letter n, in the following 186 cases:

(*aa*)—All those (131, and excepting one?—zenhai, which also has zempai,) in which *n* in the first part of the compound comes before *h* or *f* in the second, of which 120 change *nh* or *nf* to *mp* (half nigori), against the 11 following, which change *nh* or *nf* to *mb:* Jim BEN, mam—, nin—, sam— (4); SAM-biyaku, —bon (2); hambitsu, hombuku, imban, kembeki, membaku (5).

(*ab*)—And the following 55, in which a surd consonant following *n* takes the nigori (against 515 in which it does not): Jin-DZUU, yuu— (2); han-GOKU, hon—, kin—, on—, ran—, rin—, san—, sen— (8); en-JA, han—, in—, kan—, sen—, shin— (6); ban-JAKU, en—, on—, ren—, san—, tan— (6); ren-JI, zen— (2); baken-JO, kan—, kin—, nan—, shin— (5); nan-ZAN, rin—, san— (3); EN-doo, —gi (2); HAN-dan, —doo, —zatsu (3); SAN-dzui, —gai, —jiki, —zai, —zashi, —ze, —zen (7); SEN-zankoo, —zen (2); bushinjin, injn, konjiki, manzai, nenjin, shinzoo, tenden, unjinkitsu, yunzei (9).

(*b*)—And the following 106 cases: Do-BEI, ishi—, ita—, neri— (4); ashi-BIYOOSHI, ita—, ma—, shira—, te— (5); ue-BOOSOO, uma—, ushi— (3); go-BUKU, imi—, ki— (3); cha-DANSU, choo— (2); ishi-DOOROO, mawari—, taka—, tsuri— (4); boo-DZU, joo— (2); kakure-GA, me—, utsuri—, waki— (4); otoko-GI, utsuri—na, yowa— (3); Ei-GOKU, Futsu—, riyoo—(3); kuchi-GIREI, te—(2); cha-GUWASHI, hi—, midzu— (3); annai-JA, choo—, moo—, ninsoo—, shugiyoo—, uranai— (6); doo-JI, e—, hana—, hashiri—, hei—, too—(6); e-JIKI, kotsu—, moku—, ni—, niku—, so— (6); bareki-JIN, sadai—, sui—, ubai—, yoo— (5); kawai-JO, niroku— (2); gin-ZAIKU, mugiwara—, te— (3); kake-ZAN, kuwa—, menoko—, muna—yoo, nagare—, sa—, tatami—, wari— (8); hei-ZEI, fu—, oo—, sei— (4); atsugan, chiwagenka, doozen, gobatsu, funagassen, fuuzetsu, giyodzni, hatsugoori, hayabikiyaku, koogaku, kajichi, katsudatsu, midzujaku, nezoo, otamajakushi,

3

saguwan, shigedoo, soodegooro, tooguwa, usugeshoo, yakiban, yasejotai, yudoofu (23).

3.—About 670 cases given by Hepburn as compound verbs do not take the nigori (besides 148 similar cases where it would be prevented at any rate by a following nigori consonant), but in the following 35 cases it is taken, namely: Aomi-DACHI, hooke—, tsure— (3); mamori-DOOSHI, yomi— (2); ike-DORI, tsukami— (2); name-DZURI, sae—(2); karon-JI, sakin—, uton—, yasun— (4); SHI-bari, —bori, —buri, —bomi, —dare, —goki, —gumi, —gure (8); FUM-bari, —batakari (2); degire, iregomi, kikigane, kuribiki, nezame, nibami, oibore, sashigumi, saegiri, tsuibami, ukegai, yasegare (12).

The following 99 words, given by Hepburn as nouns, of which both parts are verbal, take the nigori (against 96 that do not): Otoshi-BANASHI, tatoe—, yari— (3); ai-BORE, ne— (2); sukashi-BORI, uki— (2); (aomi-DACHI) are—, suki— (2); ki-DOOSHI, kiri— (2); kiri-DORI, kogiri—ni, oshi—, tsukuri—, uri— (5); sashi-DZUME, tachi—(2); baitori-GACHI, kane—, itsuwari—, okitari—, wasure— (5); kake-GAE, nori— (2); ate-GAI, oshi— (2); kaeri-GAKE, kai—, ki—, nuke—, omoi—ni, tasshi—, tomari—, toori—, yuki— (9); furi-GAKI, hashiri—, hikae—, kiki—, misebi—, nijiri—, nuki—, soe—, tsumori—, wari— (10); (ire-GOMI), ki—, ue— (2); hanare-JINI, kubire—, obore—, tachi—, ue—, yake— (6); mi-ZAME, ne— (2); maki-ZOE, sashi— (2); de-ZOME, kaki—, nori— (3); hanarebanare, harebare, karegare, kiregire, shimijimito, taedaeni (6); akegure, aibiki, hanarezakari, kakeberi, kakedzukuri, kaigakari, kaigui, kashidzuki, kiribari, machibuse, makigari, midate, mi-kakedaoshi, namege, nebie, neboke, nedzumai, negaeri, nurigome, okurebuse, okizari, soibushi, tachigare, tachigiki, tachigie, tachigurami, tachigiri, tatakibarai, uttegawashini, waidame, yoigurui, yukidomari (32).

The following 31 cases of Chinese words followed by *shi* or *suru* take the nigori: Benji (dzuru), danji (dzuru), enji (dzuru), gaenji (dzuru), genji (dzuru), hanji (ru, dzuru), henji, junji (ru, dzuru), kenji (dzuru), kunji (ru, dzuru), menji (ru, dzuru), nenji (dzuru), ninji (dzuru), ronji (dzuru), sanji (ru, dzuru), senji (dzuru), shinji (dzuru), sonji (dzuru), soranji (dzuru), tanji (dzuru), tenji (dzuru), zonji (dzuru), (22 ending in *n*); chooji (dzuru), dooji (dzuru), hooji (dzuru), jooji (dzuru), kooji (dzuru), ooji (dzuru), shooji (ru, dzuru), tooji (dzuru), (8 ending in *oo*): ei-ji (dzuru), (1).

The following 11 words compounded with Chinese ones ending in tsu and the verbal ending shi (suru) do not take the nigori: Besshite, esshi, kesshi (shite), kusshi, resshi, sesshi, sosshi, tasshi, tesshi, usshi, zesshi. Also gese and geshi do not take the nigori. Other Chinese words followed by shi (suru) are not given as compounds, and are not followed by the nigori.

In about 151 other cases which, though given by Hepburn as compounds, are really words in grammatical connection without ellipsis or contraction, there is no nigori of composition. The six apparent exceptions are: Amanogawa (of which, however, *no* = prairie ?), michinobe, nanigana, osoiba, sainogawara, unabara (for "umi no hara").

Of so-called verbal terminations, the change from a surd to the nigori occurs in: *Ba*, in the so-called conjunctive and conditional forms; *do* and *domo*, in concessive ones; *de*, *dzu*, *ji*, *zaru*, in negative ones; *de*, in affirmative ones where the root ends in *gi*, and the *g* is dropped in contraction, or where *mi* at the end of the root is changed to *n*.

· 4.—The following 1000 compounds do not take the nigori (against 2220 that do):

(*a*)—353 with verbal endings (against 681 that do take the nigori): Charumera-FUKI, furo—, hai—, hora—, kane—, midzu—, sorauso—, (7); ame-FURI, hire—, (2); ei-FUSHI, hire—, (2); chiri-HARAI, kushi—, tsuchi—, yaku—, (4); kasa-HARI, joo—nokami, taiko—, (3); ami-HIKI, edzu—, fune—michi, ha—, midzu—, momo—, mosa—, yado—, (8); ido-HORI, kane—, (2); midzu-KAI, tsuchi—, ushi—, yak—, (4); fude-KAKE, hara—, hashi—, katana—, koshi—, mae—, me—, midzu—, ron—, te—, sudzu—, yari—, yodare—, (13); e-KAKI, hanshita—, hi—, kago—, kai—, kasa—, koshi—, mae—, masu—, meso—, mimi—, mono—, sumi—, te—, to—, beso-kaku, (16); kugi-KAKUSHI, me—, (2); hana-KAMI, oo—, yak—, (3); me-KARI, midzu—, (2); cha-KASHI, gura—, kane—, me—, (4); hi-KESHI, sumi—, (2); kuchi-KIKI, me—, te—, (3); choo-KIRI, en—, ishi—, kama—, kichak—, kubi—, soba—, shin—, yajiri—, (9); cha-KOSHI, midzu—, toshi—, (3); miru-KUI, mono—, mushi—, ki—mushi, (4); ara-KURE, chobo—, kai—, nani—, o—, saka—, shiraba—, ta—, (8); ito-KURI, kara—, ta—, wata—, (4); ei-SAME, haru—, me—, mura—, (4); abura-SASHI, bin—, e—, fuda—, hata—, midzu—, mono—, sumi—, tatami—, tori—, zeni—, (11); tadzu-SAWARI, yu—, (2); abumi-SHI, e—, fude—, gura—, hata—, ikada—, ikake—, imono—, ireba—, kagami—, ka-wara—, kazari—, koshaku—, koto—, kusu—, kuji—, makie—, megane—, nage—, nani—ni, nani—ka, nani—oo, nurimono—, sashimono—, sato—(se), shiru—, sora—, sugo—, yatsu—, makoto—yakani, tai—ta, nami-suru, (32); ato-SHIKI, kana—, kata—, kore—, kura—, naga—, utto—, ya—, za—, (9); abura-SHIME,

haji—, karo—, midzu—, obi—, soo—, yama—, (7);
mono-SHIRI, us—, soo-shiranukao, (3); dara-SUKE,
darani—, fuku—, kumo—, san—, (5); goma-SURI,
han—, ko—, mimi—, te—, (5); kara-TACHI, kit—,
kunitoko—, mono—, (4); shiro-TAE, uro—, ut—,
yoko—, (4); hi-TAKI, meshi—, (2); hana-TARE, shio—,
shita—, (3); hachi-TATAKI, ishi—, ma—, niwa—,
shiba—, (5); fude-TATE, me—, ya—, (3); shito-TOME,
sode—, (2); akari-TORI, aka—, amma—, ase—, ato—,
chiri—, hiyoo—, kaji—, koi—, kuchi—, me—, nomi—,
o—, ondo—, sai—, sao—, seki—, shaku—(mushi), shi—,
sumi—, sumoo—, tema—, yu—, zoo—, midzutorn-
tama, toshi-totta, (26); boo-TSUKAI, hebi—, idzuna—,
sora—, (4); bin-TSUKE, hada—, hi—, kado—, kako—,
kane—, ishi—, jin—, ki—, me—, muku—, ne—,
shimo—, te—, (14); aka-TSUKI, basa—, beta—, biku—,
bira—, biri—, bura—, chira—, fu—ai, fuda—, fura—,
giro—, gota—, gura—, gudo—, gudzu—, guta—,
hiyoro—, iki—, ira—, jara—, ji—, kabi—, kidzu—,
kira—, kitsu—, kiyoro—, kome—, kose—, maga—,
me—, na—, nawa—, nicha—, nura—, otoko—, seka—,
sen—, set—, soko—, sowa—, ta—, teratsu—, uka—,
uro—, uwa—, kentsuku, shaa-tsuku,(48); hana-TSUKURI,
niwa—, yumi—, (3); cha-TSUMI, na—, (2); eishire,
eitaore, etoki, fusoroi, futemawari, futsuriai, asakaranu,
hanahiri, hoofukurashi, hookamuri, iwotsuri, karisome,
kikori, komekami, kotokire, kotokawari, kotosaranu,
kototari, kubikukuri, kuchisui, mekuramashi, midzu-
sumashi, midzutamari, midzutame, miotsukushi, mu-
kabaratatsu, nedzumikoroshi, netsusamashi, omohoe,
saikaeri, sayofuke, shiohi, shirake, shirokae, shitashimi,
shitatame, tadzusae, takumi, takuromi, takuwae, tasuke,
tasukari, tekihaki, tesuki, tokoroseki, yatsure, yoko-
tawari, yoosuki, yuusuki, yuusari, (50).

(*b*)—83 reduplicated words (against 67 with the nigori): chikuchiku, chirachira, chirichiri, chirochiro, chokochoko, furafura, fuwafuwa, hakihaki, haraharato, hatahata, hekoheko, hetahetato, hihi, hirahirato, hiri-hiri, hitahita, hiyokohiyoko, hiyorohiyoroto, hokohoko, horohoro, hotehote, hotohototo, kachikachi, kakukaku, karakara(to), katakata, kechikechi, kirakirato, kirikiri-(to), kiyakiya, kiyorokiyoroto, kokekoke, korokoroto, kosekose, kosokoso, kotekote, kunkunto, kurakura, ku-rukuruto, kushakusha, kusukusuto, kutsukutsuwarau, kuyokuyo, sakusakuto, sarasara(to), sashitsumesashi-tsume, satemosatemo, satesate, sawasawato, saetsuo-saetsu, sekaseka, sekiseki, sewasewashii, shaashaa, sharisharito, shikashika, shikushiku, shioshioto, shito-shito, sokosokoni, sokusoku, somosomo, soresore, sorosoroto, soosoo, sowasowa(shite), soyosoyoto, sura-surato, surusuruto, suyasuyatoneru, takatakayubi, taka-takatsuki, tamatama (tamadama), taratarato, teratera, teriteriboodzu, torotoroto, tonton, tootoo, tsukatsuka, tsuratsura, tsurutsuru, tsuyatsuya.

(*c*)—34 compounds with adjective endings (against 106 that do take the nigori): akarui, anakashiki, aoshiroi, arakuroshii, aramahoshii, furukusai, futokutakama-shiki, hashikashii, hinatakusai, ikikusai, ikuhisashii, jimankusai, kashikamashii, katakurushii, kirakirashii, kogarekusai, mimahoshii, mimishii, mudzukashii, musakurushii, semahoshii, shibutoi, shiohayui, shio-karai, sharakusai, shisomonai, shitsukoi, tattoi, tootoi, tsumetai, utsukushii, wakawakashii, yofukai, yuyushii, besides others compounded with mahoshii, shii, tai, and toi, which do not appear as separate words.

(*d*)—29 juxtaposed words of allied or contrasted mean-ing: achikochi, anakashiko, atosaki, hirarikururito, iroka, itotake, kagehinata, kakasoso, kakute, karekore, muchakucha, musakusa, norarikurari, norakurato, oyako, sakoso, sosokusato, tokaku, tokoo, tomokakumo, tomokoomo, tonikakuni, toosamakoosama, tosenka-kusen, toyakakuto, toyakooto, unekune, ushitora, uwoosawoo.

(c)—Also the following 501 words (against 1366 with the nigori): a-CHI, ko—, nama—, shira—, so—, idzu—, (6); haya-FUNE, hiki—, kawa—, yo—, (4); de-HA, ori—, saka—, shira—, yudzuru—, (5); naga-HAMA, shio—, yoko—, yoshi, (4); aka-HARA, ato—, hi—, kata—, name—, suki—, ura—, (7); kata-HASHI, me—, (2); kiza-HASHI, mi—, sori—, (3); iri-HI, tobi—, (2); kumi-HIMO, uchi—, (2); ma-HO, midzu—, tsugi—, (3); hanashi-KA, hoshi—, (2); kawa-KAMI, kaza—, kome—, (3); kiri-KAMI, ori—, shibu—, (3); furu-KANE, shiro—, midzu—, (3); ai-KASA, matsu—, midzu—, oribetsu—, toshi—, (5); ashi-KASE, kubi—, maro—, te—, (4); abura-KASU, cha—, soba—, tabe—, tare—, (5); ai-KATA, ara—, ato—, de—, fuchi—, funa—, haha—, hake—, hiyooro—, hisa—, idzu—, kari—, kashi—, koshi—, kure—, kawase—, mae—, me—, mi—, moto—, ni—, mochii—, ori—, oya—, sabake—, saki—, sato—, sen—, shiire—, shi—, shitate—, shite—, tana—, tsukai—, uchi—, uma—, ura—, ya—, yu—, yuu— (40); nari-KATACHI, shina— (2); abura-KAWA, atsu—dzura, kata—, ni—, oo—, shibu—, togi—, totsu—, tsukuri—, usu—, uwa— (11); abura-KE, ara—nai, chiri—, hata—, iro—, kawara—, koshi—, midzu—, mukai—, mushi—, nebari—, nigo—, nodo—, oomi—, saku—, shiru—, sori—, tawa—, tsuyu—ki, ubu—, yata— (21); chi-KEMURI, midzu—, uma—(3); kabu-KI, karasu—, kare—, koshi—, kuchi—, kusu—, ma—, maru—, masa— nadzu—, nama—, nami—, saka—, shira—, taru—

tori—, tsugi—, ubu—, ue—, waka—, yak— (21); arai-KO,
arashi—, asu—, dada—, funa—, hari—, haru—, iri—,
ishi—, ko—, kumi—, kushi—, mai—, mama—, midzu—,
mi—, migaki—, moro—, nama—, ne—, nicha—, nuna—,
obo—, shiro—, shiru—, so—, tana—, te—, tera—ya,
tori—, tsure—, udon—, uji—, uro—, yak— (35); hiki-
KOTO, kata—, mi—, tawa—, uwa—, wabi— (6); ai-KUCHI,
de—, ho—, iri—, karu—, kata—, mitsu—, mochi—,
muki—, oo—, ore—, sabake—, sode—, tobo—, ure—,
uri—, waru—, yatsu—, yoi—, yomi— (20); ashitaka-
KUMO, mura—, shira—, yami— (4); kami-KURA, kari—,
nama— (3); haya-KUSA, kara—, midzu—, mi—, omo—,
saki—, shichi—, some—, to—, ume—, yake— (11);
kuchi-KUSE, shi—, te— (3); hana-KUSO, kani—, kana—,
me—, mimi—, mune—, mushi— (7); abumi-KUWA,
kuro— (2); aka-SAKA, ko— (and kozaka), kudari—,
nobori—, tama—, to— (6); akari-SAKI, he—, hoko—,
kuchi—, mi—, muna—, te—, toto—, uri—, ya—, yoo—
(11); ari-SAMA, akara—ni, ashi—ni, ika—, midai—,
mina—, nani—, ne—, ni—, noke—ni, oku—, saka—,
saki—, tono—, too—koo—, toto—, yoko—, nesan, nisan,
obaasan, okamisan, ototsan (22); hi-SAO, kara— (2); ima-
SARA, nao— (2); furu-SATO, tori— (2); asa-SE, fuka—,
hada—, kugu— (4); saka-SHIMA, te—ishi, yoko—, (3);
chi-SHIO, ha—, hi—, hiki—, michi—, sashi— (6); kawa-
SHIRI, mayu— (2); kawa-SHIMO, kaza— (2); kata-SHIRO,
nawa—, toji—, uri— (4); chi-SHIRU, hana— (2); kaze-
SHITA, me—, obi— (3); ami-SO, nanori— (2); ao-TA,
ara—, are—, fuke—, kawa—, midzu— (6); ko-TACHI,
kodomo—, kunitoko—, nan—, omae—, yakunin— (6);
ara-TAKA, kuma—, ashi—kumo (3); ari-TAKE (and ari-
dake), hana—, hatsu— (and hatsudake), iwa—, kawa—,
kure—, matsu— (and matsudake), mimi—, shii— (9);

ara-TAMA, kin—, kuro—, kubi—, midzu— (5); kakobi-
TE, hama—, hiki—, hineri—, hon—, ho—, i—, kai—,
kara-me—, kara—, kata—, kawariban—, kiri—, kit—,
ko—, me—, naka—, nawa—, oi—, oku—, oo—, saka—,
saki—, sawa—, sen—, shimo—, shita—, shi—, sho—,
tori—, tsukai—, tsuri—, uri—, uwa—, yaki—, yari—,
yose— (37); ao-TO, e—, mune— (3); kana-TOKO, niwa—
(2); ko-TORI, niwa—, oo— (3); ma-TSUCHI, masa—,
neba—, yase— (4); mu-TSUKI, shimo—, sa— (3); kiba-
TSUTSU, ko—, moto-gome—, o—, oo—, tan— (6); hanshita, —toki (2); KARA-kami, —kane, —kasa (—sao),
—sumi (4); KATA-ho, —kana, —sumi, —toki (4); KO-
sawa, (—saka and —zaka) (1); MAMA-chichi, —haha
(—ko), —samurai (3); MI-hakase (—hashi), (—kata),
(oo—ke), —koshi (—koto), —sora, —takara, —tama
(iki—tama), —tarashi, —toohoo, takamikura (8); o-
fukuro, —hayoo, —hari, —hiya, —hiyarakashi, —hie,
—kan, —ketsu, —tamaya, —tori (—totsan), (—tsutsu),
—tsuyu (11); (oo-kawa), —kimi (—kuchi), —kurashoo,
—sawa (3); aburahi, aohiki, aosora, aoto, asahaka, edaha,
fusasakura, hakoromo, hanafuyu, inukoro, irotsuya,
i(h)e, kamashika, kamisakayaki, katatsumuri, kirikishi,
marutoshi, mekao, morotomoni, muneto, narisoo, nori-
kumi, okusokonai, orifushi, orihima, ototoi, ototsui, rai-
haru, sahachi, sahari, satsuhito, shookachi, wakatono,
dzukuni, jisaka, midzukame, midzusaki, midzuseki, sabi-
tsue, shattsura, shinobitsuma, shiosu, shiratsuya, tobihi,
tookarasu, uminechima, ubusuna, yabuka, yobikoe,
yohoro, yubukarashi, yumahiko, yurumekusuri (53).

If the complete lists of compounds with the nigori
and without be carefully examined, it is found that:
When the first part indicates the origin, source, cause
or the like, possession or ownership, superiority, preva-

lence, pervasion, inclusion (either physical or ideal or a classifying feature) of the second part, in short domination over it as a subordinate thing, there is no nigori of composition.   These are the very qualities possessed in English by a substantive following the word *of*, as compared with the one that precedes.

But when those qualities are rather possessed by the following part of the compound, of which the first part indicates a subordinate or a more or less imperfectly, partially, superficially, temporarily, occasionally applying characteristic or feature, there is nigori.   When, for example, the nigori compound has an adjective ending, the first part shows in what respect the quality is meant; and when both parts are verbal forms, the first likewise shows with reference to what the action of the second takes place, instead of there being something else to which both actions concomitantly refer.

It is clear that the nigori invariably arises from the disappearance of a sonant consonant, almost always an *n*, and generally the word *no* (of), but sometimes *ni* (in, to, especially in re-duplicated words), sometimes the negative *n*, and sometimes other sonants or syllables, as perhaps occasionally *de* (at or with), which appears to be on the same principle a contraction either of *nite* (with, by, in) or of *motte* (having).   It can now be understood why the sound *n* is so often heard in colloquial and rustic Japanese before a dental nigori and *m* before a labial one, and still oftener the sound *ng* instead of simple *g*.   The significance of such sounds is a very strong argument for specially marking them in any system of transliteration in Roman letters; and for writing, say, *Nangasaki* in the time-honored European way, instead of the recent *Nagasaki*.   The very existence of the argument, too, is proof that investigations like the present one, though seeming perhaps remote and trivial, may nevertheless have useful bearings upon a question ,of such pressing importance as the best method of adapting our alphabet to the use of the Japanese.

It is probable that some of the Japanese themselves are not altogether conscious of any difference in meaning, owing to the presence or absence of the nigori of composition, or disregard it on account of inability to explain it or formulate it.   At any rate the famous spot for the manufacture of porcelain called generally by the Japanese *Kutani* (that is, not nine valleys, as some one has mistakenly imagined, but *Ku-no-tani*, or ninth valley, corresponding to the uncontracted *ichi-no-tani*, first valley, and several other numbered small valleys that with it branch out of a single large one) is in the neighborhood itself called *Kutani*, without the nigori. It seems to be an illustration of the fact that the attempts of the partially informed to carry out what they conceive to be grammatical rules, are often less correct than the unquestioning instinct of the wholly ignorant.

The real significance and character of the word *no*, of such extremely frequent occurrence, is of some interest and consequence.   It appears to be the last syllable of the word *mono* (thing) ; for in Japanese not merely is the last part of a word dropped in derivation, as in many western languages, but it is very common that the first part is dropped ; as Mr. E. M. Satow has also remarked (Trans. As. Soc. Jap., VI, 472).   The form *no* is very often used after adjective and verbal forms (frequently contracted to simple *n*), with obviously the same meaning as *mono* (thing).   It is plain that in the form of the postposition *no* (of) it has in reality the same meaning (thing), and helps to carry out the universal Japanese rule of letting general words precede the particular. If a subordinate feature has to precede, it is brought about through the interposition of the word *no* (that is, *mono*, itself a particularizing word in reference to the foregoing one), in order to make the expression so general that the otherwise principal word may follow as a subordinate, or a possession, or a limiting or defining word. This corresponds well with common idioms in so distant a language as Chinese, and supports the view that even in western languages the possessive and genitive terminations originally had likewise essentially the same meaning (thing).

The rule of the nigori in composition helps very much towards tracing the derivation and primitive meaning of many Japanese words. For example, *Terashima* would be an island belonging to a temple; whereas *Terajima* would be an island with a temple on it. *Akindo* (trader) is *akinai no hito* (man of trade); *shirooto* (one not skilled in a profession) is *shiro-hito* (man of whiteness); while *kurooto* (one skilled in a profession) is *kuro-hito* (man of blackness). But *kuromboo* (negro) is perhaps *kuro na hito* (a man that has become black or tanned); and likewise *akamboo* (baby) is *aka na hito* (red man, but not permanently or fully so); and *shiwamboo* (miser) is *shiwa na hito*. It should be remembered that the Japanese *h* in these cases is to be reckoned as a labial. The last syllable of *kaeriji* (return journey), *kawaji* (river road), *mikkaji* (three days' journey), and *kooji* (small streets) is clearly *michi* (road). The first part of *kadzu* or *koodzu* (the paper mulberry) is apparently derived from *kami* (paper). *Koodzuke*, the name of a province, is evidently *Kami-tsuke* (this *kami* meaning upper), cor-

responding to *Shimo-tsuke* (*shimo* meaning lower), without the nigori. *Koobe*, the name of a town, would be
Kami-he (upper place or dwelling). *Oozaka*, the name
of the great city, is *Ooki na saka* (the great steep-road) ;
whereas *Oosaka*, as it is often called, would be *Ooki saka*,
nearly the same in meaning, but perhaps differing in the
degree of emphasis. The monosyllable *ga*, pronounced
nga, may be derived from *no ka*, with the *ka* meaning
emanation. *Ga*, like *ji* from *michi*, also given as a
separate word, and like *de*, already mentioned, is an instance where the nigori begins a word ; and it seems
not wholly impossible that all the comparatively few
cases where purely Japanese words so begin might have
some similar explanation, and that the other cases of
nigori, in the middle of a word, may have arisen from
compounding.

The word *hidari* (left hand), often *hindari* in the
country, appears to be the direction of the sunrise; *hi
no detari ;* while *migi* (right hand), often in the country
migiri, is possibly *miru no o kiri*, or *miru n' kiri*, the
direction of the cutting (*kiri*) off of seeing (*miru no*), or
sunset ; or from *mi kagiri* (limiting of sight) ; or again
from *mi kagiri*, that is, *kami kagiri* (the august setting,
or the god's setting). The derivation that has been
proposed (As. Soc. Jap., VI, 473) from *nigiri*, to grasp,
is rather impossible ; for, besides the difficulty of changing *n* to *m* in such a case, the word *nigiri* as a concrete
substantive applies to the part of the bow that is
grasped, and that with the left hand. The words for
left and right in Japan appear, then, to be derived from
the position of the sunrise and sunset, with reference to
the favorite and ordinary outlook of dwellings there.
This would seem to suggest a reasonable and natural

explanation why in India the South is reckoned to be on the right hand ; not by any worship of the rising sun, such as exists even in Japan, but by the fact, discovered with little camping experience in those tropics, that tents or other dwellings, whenever possible, are made to look towards the east, so as to have the rising sun take off the morning chill, and to be in the shade the rest of the day. It seems to be one of those cases where points in one langage are made clear by the investigation of another very distant one.

It is certain that a thorough collation of what may seem very dry Japanese grammatical facts, aside from mere euphonic changes, would lead to the elucidation, not only of the derivation and true meaning of words, but to a better understanding of the structure of the language ; so that the acquisition of the tongue could be made easier for future students. It can hardly be doubted, too, that useful light would be thrown in many ways upon the derivations and grammar of our western languages, and on grammar in general. It is highly probable, moreover, that research of that kind would uncover several more or less hidden grammatical features that would guide towards a more satisfactory method than any yet common for the rational and completely practical phonetic adaptation of Roman letters to Japanese, a matter of the greatest moment. But perhaps that might require first the still more needed improvement of the transliteration of Chinese, considering the very large number of words that have been taken from Chinese into Japanese, especially among scholars.

THE ARYAN NAME OF THE TONGUE.

BY H. COLLITZ.

My main object in this paper is to show that the
Greek name of the tongue, γλῶσσα, is identical with Sanskrit *jihvā'*, Latin *lingua*, and the rest of the words
which are generally held to be the lineal descendants of
the Old Aryan name of the tongue. This etymology
occurred to me several years ago, but for various reasons
I refrained from publishing it. I am fully aware that
at first it may seem venturesome, since, e. g., Skt. *jihvā'*
and Greek γλῶσσα do not apparently agree in a single
sound except the final *a*, and that this very agreement is
rendered somewhat problematic by the fact that the *a*
in Sanskrit is long while in Greek it is short. Moreover
I found some difficulty in explaining the υ of the Greek
word and I hesitated in regard to some other points. So
it seemed more advisable to wait, in the hope that renewed consideration or perhaps new material might
yield additional proof. In the meantime new material
has been derived from a source from which it could be
least expected. Among the papyri recently brought
from Egypt to the British Museum are the fragments of
Herondas' (or Herodas') mimiambs. Among the interesting additions to Greek vocabulary and Greek
grammar to be gathered from this newly-discovered
monument of ancient literature is the word γλάσσα
"tongue." If I am not mistaken we are furnished by

this form with the missing link between Greek γλῶσσα
and the words for "tongue" in the cognate languages.

.The comparison of Skt. *jihvā'*, "tongue," with Latin
lingua and Gothic *tuggo* finds a place among the earliest
etymologies in comparative philology. See e. g., Bopp,
Vergl. Grammatik I', p. 165 ; Pott, Etymol. Forsch. I',
p. 88, 119 ; Benfey, Allgem. Lit. Ztg., 1837, p. 909
(=Kleinere Schriften I, 2, p. 8), and Griech. Wurzel-
lexikon II, p. 201, 217 ; Graff, Ahd. Sprachschatz V, p.
681 ; Diefenbach, Vergl. Wörterb. d. Got. Spr. II, p.
673.   But almost as old as this etymology is the doubt
whether Skt. *jihvā'* ought to be identified with the Latin
and the Gothic word.   So Jacob Grimm, although holding that *lingua* (for *dingua*) and *tuggo* are identical (e.
g., Deutsche Gramm. I', p. 586, 590), and combining
with these Lit. *lëžùwis* and O. Slav. *językŭ* = Russ.
jazýkŭ (D. Gramm. III, p. 400 ; Gesch. d. D. Spr., p.
320, 354), nevertheless omits any reference to Skt. *jihvā'*.
Furthermore, Pott, who was among the first to suggest
the identity of Skt. *jihvā'* and Lat. *lingua*, is later on
(Et. Forsch. I', p. 230), inclined to abandon this etymology for the derivation of *jihvā'* from root *hvā* "to call."
Pott's uncertainty and Grimm's silent disapproval were
followed by Lottner's positive statement (Kuhn's
Zeitschr. 7, p. 185), that Skt. *jihvā'* could not be identified with *lingua* and *tuggo*.   Similar opinions were also
expressed by Delbrück in Zacher's Zeitschr. I, p. 70,
and by Pott in the second edition of his Etymologische
Forsch. II, 2 (=Wz.-Wtb. I), p. 570, and III, p. 1013.
More recently Lottner's standpoint was endorsed by
Schade, Altdeutsches Wtb.' s. v. *zungâ*, by Bartholomae in Kuhn's Zeitschr. 27, p. 207 sqq, and by Merin-

ger, Beiträge z. Gesch. d. indog. Declination (in the Sitzungsber. d. K. Akad. d. W. in Wien, Ph.-H. Cl., Bd. CXXV), Wien, 1891, p. 38 sq. The chief objections raised by these scholars will have to be considered later on in this article. Suffice it for the present to refer to K. F. Johansson's discussion of the points in question in Indog. Forsch. II, p. 1 sqq. I entirely agree with Johansson in claiming that the identical meaning and the striking similarity in form—especially in regard to the derivation and inflection—are in favor of identifying with Lat. *lingua*, the Indian and Iranian words for "tongue."

Let us now try to reconstruct the original form of the name of the tongue in the Aryan languages. The material on which the reconstruction is mainly to be based, is the following:

Sanskrit. In addition to *jihvā'* f. in the Rigveda the word *juhū'* f. (Instr. sg. *juhv'ā*, i. e. *juhúā* or *juhúvā*, Instr. pl. *juhū'bhis*) is found, the latter coinciding in form with *juhū'* f. "sacrificial ladle." The sacrificial ladle may have originally been tongue-shaped (see Böhtlingk-Roth s. v. 2 *juhū'*).[1]

[1] I hold with Roth, Grassmann and von Bradke, in "Festgruss an R. v. Roth," 1893, p. 125, that *juhū'* has in the Rigveda both the meanings "tongue" and "sacrificial ladle," while Bergaigne, Rel. Ved. I, p. 40, and Pischel, Ved. Studien II, p. 110 sqq., claim that it is confined to the latter meaning. If we were to adopt Bergaigne's and Pischel's opinion, it would mean that in Indian the one theme of the Aryan word for "tongue" (that one which is identical with Avest. *hizū*, O. Slav. *jezy-kŭ*, O. High Germ. *zungŭ-n*, etc.,) adopted throughout the secondary meaning, "sacrificial ladle," while its other theme (the one agreeing with Avest. *hizva*, Lat. *lingua*, Goth. *luggò-n-*, etc.,) preserved the original meaning "tongue." In my opinion Pischel is probably right in his interpretation of certain passages, but I do not

Iranian.   The Avesta has two forms exactly parallel to those found in the RV., viz. *hizvā-* f. and *hizu-* (Gen. *hizvō*, Instr. pl. *hizubīš*) f. and m. Comp. Justi, Handb. d. Zendspr. s. v. *hizu* and *hizva*, Bartholomae in Bezzenb. Beitr. 8, p. 210 and 13, p. 89 sq.   In Old Persian the Acc. sg. [*hiz*]*āvam* (or [*iz*]*uvam*?) is found Beh. II, 74, cp. Bartholomae in K. Z. 27, p. 208, N. 3 and Fr. Müller in Wien. Ztschr. f. d. K. d. Orients I, p. 223. It is of some interest to compare with these forms those of the Middle Iranian and the Modern Iranian dialects, viz., Pahlavi *huzvān*, Parsi *hizvan*, Mod. Pers. *zabān*, (*zubān*, *zuwān*), Gabri *izvūn* (Justi in ZDMG. 35, p. 414), Kurd. *ezmān*, Osset. *äwzág* (Hübschmann, Etymologie u. Lautl. d. Osset. Spr., p. 18), Pāmir dial. of Wachan *zik*, dial. of Sirikul *ziv*, dial. of Shugnan *zev*, (see Tomaschek, Centralasiat. Studien II, Wien, 1880), Yigdhāh (or Mungī) *zevir* (from *zevin*? see Tomaschek in Bezz. Beitr. 7, p. 200), Afghan *jiba*.   Balūcī *zavān*, *zuvān* is according to Geiger, Lautlehre des Balūcī, p. 68, a loan-word from Mod. Persian.

Armenian.   Lezu (Gen. *lezui*, an *i*-stem).   See Benfey, Kl. Schr. I, 2, p. 8, and Hübschmann, Armen. Studien I, p. 32.

Latin.   In addition to *lingua*, there existed in Early Latin the form *dingua*, quoted twice by Marius Victor-

---

see sufficient evidence for entirely denying to *juhū'* the meaning "tongue."   The relation of the meaning "ladle" and "tongue" is seen in Lat. *lingula* or *ligula*, "spoon, ladle, skimmer," dimin. of *lingua* "tongue" and Ir. *liagh*, "ladle" — Welsh *llwy*, "spoon," Bret. *loa*, alongside of Ir. *ligur* "tongue", Welsh *llyaw* "to lick," Bret. *leat* (cp. Stokes in K. Beitr. 8, p.323).   In view of such examples it is hard to believe with Bechtel, Sinnl. Wahrnehmungen, (Weimar, 1879), p. 41 sq., that *juhū'* is derived from root *hu*, "to pour," and is not originally connected with *jihvā'*, "tongue."

inus (4th cent., A. D.) in Keil's Grammatici Latini,
Vol. VI, p. 9, 17, and p. 26, 2.

Celtic. There are two words in Old Irish that may
belong here, viz., *tenge*, Gen. *tengad* (a *t*-stem, see
Zeuss-Ebel, p. 255 sqq.; Stokes in Bezz. Beitr. 11, p.
88, reckons it among the stems in -*ial*) and *ligur* (in
Cormac's Glossary, p. 26, cp. Stokes, On the Bodleian
fragm. of Cormac's Glossary, p. 8).[1] It has been
doubted, however, whether either of the two may be
claimed as a relative of Skt. *jihvā'* and Lat. *lingua. ligur*
is generally held to be connected with Skt. *lih-*, Gr.
λείχω, Ir. *ligim* (see Stokes in K. Beitr. 8, p. 323; Win-
disch in Curtius' Greek Etym.[5], p. 194; Brugmann,
Grundriss I, p. 296, 383) and identified with Armen.
lezu and Lit. *lëżùwis* by Hübschmann, Armen. Studien
I, p. 32. The combination of *tenge* with Lat. *lingua*
(which has the support, e. g., of Fick, Vergl. Wörterb.
[3]II, p. 123, and [4]I, p. 71) is rendered doubtful by the
initial *t* of the Irish word, for which we should rather
expect to find a *d.* Johansson, in Indog. Forsch. II,
p. 4, tries to meet the difficulty by presupposing a Prim.
Aryan form *zdṇghvā*=Proto-Celtic *tṇg(v)a*. Stokes,
on the other hand, in Fick's Vergl. Wtb. [3]II, p. 121,
is in favor of abandoning the comparison with *lingua*
by connecting *tenge* with Old Irish *tongu*, "I swear,"
and Lat. *tangere*, "to touch." In my opinion the view
held by Fick and Johansson is more probable, although
I doubt whether Johansson's explanation of the initial *t*,
ingenious as it is, finds support in any Aryan language

[1] Cp. *ligair ·i· tenga* in Duil Laithne. From *ligur* is derived *ligrad*
in Forus Focal, Nr. 57=*lioghra*, O'Reilly. See Stokes, On the metrical glossaries of the Mediæval Irish (in Transactions of the Philolog-
ical Society for 1891), p. 81 (Bezz. Beitr. 19, p. 91).

other than Celtic. We shall be again concerned with this latter question later on.

Teutonic. Gothic *tuggō* (Gen. *tuggōn-s*), O. Norse *tunga* (Gen. *tungu*), Ag. S. *tunge* (Gen. *tungan*), Engl. *tongue*, O. Sax. *tunga* (Dat. *tungun*), O. High Germ. *zunga* (Gen. *zungûn*), Mod. Germ. *zunge*. All of these words are "weak" feminines, i. e., feminine *n*-stems. It is of importance to notice the genitives (and datives) in *-*ûn* in O. Norse, O. Sax. and O. H. G., whose origin from an Aryan form ending in -*û*- has been recognized by H. Möller in Paul & Braune's Beitr. 8, p. 543 sq. The original inflection in Teutonic seems to have been: Nom. **tung(w)ō*, [1] Gen. *tungûn-s*, Dat. & Acc. *tungûn*. In other words, the inflection of the word for "tongue" in the Teutonic languages is built upon the two stems **tungwō-n-* and *tungû-n-*, which are parallel to the pair *jihvā' : juhû'*-in Sanskrit or *hizvā-: hizu-* in the Avesta.

Slavonic. O. Slav. *język̄ŭ* (Masc.). The words for "tongue" in the modern Slavonic languages are regular descendants of the Old Slavonic form. Especially noteworthy among these are the Russian and the Serbian words, since by their aid the Old Slavonic accent may be reconstructed. Russ. *jazýkŭ* shows that the accent originally rested on the second syllable. This is confirmed by Serb. *jèzik*, since the accent ` in Serbian is always a secondary accent, found on the syllable which precedes the one that originally bore the accent. The

---

[1] The *w* may have been lost in Primitive Teutonic, as *w*, where it was kept after consonants in the Prim. Teut. period, is generally preserved in Gothic. There are, however, a few cases in which *w* must be ascribed to Prim. Teut., although it is not found in Gothic, e. g., Teut. *priskwan "to thrash" = O. Norse *pryskva*, Goth. *priskan* (cp. Gr. τρίβω for *trizgvō, Fick in Bezz. Beitr. 7, p. 95).

initial group *jęz* has been explained from orig. **dņz-* by Bezzenberger in his Beitr. 3, p. 135.[1]

Baltic. Old Pruss. *insuwis* (Vocab. 94) has lost the original initial dental for the same reason as Old Slav. *językŭ* (see Bezzenberger, l. c.). Apart from this difference in the treatment of the initial consonant, the word agrees with Lituanian *lëżùwis*, and is to be regarded, like the latter, as a mascul. *ja*-stem.[2] Notice the following special points of coincidence between Slavonic and Baltic (in addition to those phonetic peculiarities in which the two branches otherwise agree): 1. Both point to an original theme in *-ņ-*, not in *-va-* (or in neither of the two is the original theme in *-va-* preserved). 2. The gender in both has been changed from feminine to masculine. 3. The original initial consonant has been dropped in all of the Slavonic and in part of the Baltic dialects. To the Primitive Slavo-Baltic period may be ascribed the two forms, *inżņ-* (for *dęnżņ-*) and *lįnżņ-* (= Lit. *lëżuw-*).

---

[1] O. Slav. *językŭ* and Pruss. *insuwis* are reckoned by Bezzenberger among the chief evidences for a Prim. Aryan syllabic nasal (in distinction from reduced vowel + nasal). This opinion, which for some time was generally adopted, has recently been combatted by Bechtel, Die Hauptprobleme der indog. Lautlehre, p. 134 sq. This scholar denies that syllabic nasals or syllabic liquids were known either to the Prim. Aryan or to the Baltoslavic period, and proposes to substitute in both cases for the alleged "sonant" nasal or "sonant" liquid a combination of weak vowel + nasal or weak vowel + liquid. Bechtel's conception seems to me on the whole preferable, at least in regard to the nasals. The decision of this question, however, is not of material consequence for my present purpose, and I have for this reason retained the current sign *ņ* alongside of the perhaps more correct form *ęn*.

[2] In Lettic the original name of the tongue has given way to the word *mēle* (a fem. *ja*-stem, see Bielenstein, Lett. Spr. 2, p. 46), for which an etymology, to my knowledge, has not yet been found.

How are we to discover in such manifold variation
the quality of the ground form in Primitive Aryan?
So overwhelming is the variety of forms, and so perplexing are often their changes, that we cannot wonder
that several scholars have so despaired of the task of
establishing their union as to prefer to ascribe to Prim.
Aryan various words for the tongue.[1] But even if we
were willing to admit that Primitive Aryan, in distinction from most of the existing languages, may have
designated the tongue by more than one name: the various forms that we should have to ascribe to Prim.
Aryan, would be so much alike in their sounds, their
accent and their inflection, that it would seem impossible to deny their origin from one and the same word.

The chief stumbling-block in the way of those who

---

[1] e. g. Meringer in his Beiträge z. Gesch. d. indog. Decl., p. 38
sq., arrives at three Prim. Aryan names, viz.: I. * *nghū.* II.
* *d-nghvā.* III. * *s-ighvā* or *s-nghvā.* But he has not taken into
account the *ū* forms OHG. *zungū-n-* and Skt. *juhū'-* (Av. *hizu-*). In
order to include these, Nr. II. ought to be given (from Meringer's
standpoint) as * *d-nghū* and * *d-nghvā,* and Nr. III. as * *s-ighū* and
* *s-ighvā* or * *s-nghū* and * *s-nghvā.* Moreover the *l*-forms (Arm.
lezu, Lat. *lingua,* Ir. *ligur,* Lit. *lēžùwis*), which Meringer regards as
younger developments, are probably not younger than the forms
upon which he bases his Nr. I.; so that we may add a Nr. IV:
* *l-nghū* and *l-nghvā.* There is a further chance for increasing the
primitive forms of this kind by ascribing to Prim. Aryan, on account
of Irish *tenge,* a form with initial *t.* If we were to carry on the same
method in regard to other differences, (e. g., in regard to the syllabic
element of the first syllable), there would be no end of Aryan names
of the tongue. Still all of these would agree in the form *-nghū* or
-nghvā (or at least *-ghū* and *-ghvā*), that is to say, in everything except
the first or the two first sounds. And even in these the words would
be very much alike, as the first sound in all would be some kind of a
dental (sometimes assimilated to the following nasal), and the second
generally a syllabic nasal.

denied the identity of Skt. *jihvā'* with Lat. *lingua*, has been the initial *j* in the Indian word. Skt. *j*, it is argued, cannot be regarded as the regular descendant of the Prim. Aryan *d*, which is presupposed by Lat. *dingua* and Goth. *tuggo*. No doubt Prim. Aryan *d* is in Sanskrit generally represented not by *j* but by *d*. Yet we ought not to overlook the fact that the second syllable of *jihvā'* and *juhū'*- begins with a *palatal* spirant, through whose influence the initial dental media of the first syllable may have been replaced by the palatal media *j*. In favor of this view we may cite the well-known words in which in Sanskrit initial dental and palatal sibilants of neighboring syllables have attracted each other, e. g., *çvāçuras* for **svá-çuras* = Lat. *socer*, Germ. *Schwäher;* *çvaçrū's* for **sva-çrū's* = Lat. *socrus*, Germ. *Schwieger;* *çaçás* m. "hare" for *ça-sás* = Germ. *Hase*, etc. (see e. g., Bartholomae, Ar. Forsch. I, p. 79, note 1, and p. 105, note 14; Osthoff, Z. Gesch. d. Perf., p. 494 sqq.) Moreover the change of **dihvā'* in *jihvā'* has an exact parallel in that of **dihmá* = Gr. δοχμός "slanting" into *jihmá* (see Pott, Etym. Forsch.² II, 3, p. 224 — who, however, wrongly explains Gr. δοχμός by dissimilation from **γοχμός* — and Bugge in KZ. 19, p. 422).[1]

I cannot bring myself to the conclusion that this explanation is less satisfactory or less probable than the one proposed by Bartholomae in KZ. 27, p. 207 sqq. (cp. also his Ar. Forsch. 3, p. 37, note), and adopted by

---

[1] Notice in regard to the palatal in *jihva'*, *jihmá, jyok* "a long time" from **dyok*, and *jyut* "to shine" = *dyut*, Bloomfield's remark, Amer. Journ. of Phil. 7, p. 482: "In all the cases the change occurs before *i*, and is to be regarded as an exhibition of palatalization, in principle the same with corresponding changes in the Pāli-Prākrit dialects." Comp. also Johansson in IF. II, p. 3, note.

Meringer, Beitr. z. Gesch. d. idg. Decl., p. 38, and — with
some modifications — by Johansson in IF. II, p. 2. In
claiming that Skt. *jihvā'* and Avest. *hizva* ought to be
derived from a common Indo-Iranian basis **sizhvā'*
(=Prim. Ar. **sighvā'*), Bartholomae assumed an assimilation of the alleged Prim. Indo-Iranian form (for
which we should expect in Sanskrit **sihvā'*) to Primitive
Indian **zizhvā'*, whence we finally arrive at Skt. *jihvā'*.
Osthoff, Z. Gesch. d. Perf., p. 503, rightly objected that
if there was in Sanskrit a tendency toward such an assimilation, we ought to find, e. g., a form **jah* instead
of Skt. *sah* or **jahásram* instead of Skt. *sahásram*.
Meringer, indeed (l. c.), tries to meet this objection by
ascribing the *s* of *sah* to the analogical influence of forms
like *ásākṣi* and, perhaps, *sā'dhṛ*, and that of *sahásram* to
the influence of *sakṛ́t*.   But is it probable that the numeral for 1000 should hesitate to undergo a phonetic
change for the reason that this change would deprive it
of its similarity with an adverb[1] which means "once"
or "at once?"   And is it probable that the few aorist-
forms of *sah-* and the isolated participle *sā'dhṛ-*[2] should
have influenced the whole verbal system of the root *sah*
and the long series of nouns connected with this verb?
Instances like the nominative *sā'ṭ* (RV. I, 63, 3) or the
compounds in *sā'ṭ* (*janā-sā'ṭ, purā-sā'ṭ, turā-sā'ṭ*, etc.)[3]
do not seem to imply that the Indians were very anxious
to keep the *s* in *sah* unchanged.   Meringer, in fact, has

---

[1] This adverb, by the way, is found in the Rigveda nine times, while
sahásra, with its compounds, occurs several hundred times.

[2] This participle is found in a single passage of the RV. (V, 56, 23),
where its nominative is spelled *sā'ḷhá*.

[3] Cp. Benfey, Die Quantitäts-versch. in den Saṃhitā- u. Pada-Texten,
V, 1 Abt. (Gött., 1880), p. 14.

in my opinion failed in his attempt to explain the *s* in
cases like *sah* and *sahásram* by analogy.   The assimilation supposed by Bartholomae to exist in *jihvā'*, so far
from being based upon any strict phonetic law, can only
be regarded as a sporadic phonetical change.   I, for my
part, do not entertain any theoretical objection to phonetic changes of this kind.   Yet would anything be
gained in our case by granting the exceptional assimilation assumed by Bartholomae?   It seems to me that, instead of explaining the similarity between the words for
"tongue" in Indo-Iranian and in the European languages, it would make this similarity the more mysterious; and instead of obviating the difficulty found in
the initial consonant of the Indian and the Iranian
forms, it would carry this difficulty over into the Primitive Aryan period.

I could more readily agree with Johansson's explanation (l. c.), in that it at least avoids separating the Indo-
Iranian from the European name of the tongue.
Johansson starts from a Prim. Aryan form * *zdnghū-*,
or * *zdnghvā* (based especially upon O. Ir. *tenge*),
from which he proceeds through an intermediate form   •
**zng͡hū-*, * *zng͡hvā* to Indo-Iranian **ziźhū-*, **ziźhvā*.
From the latter form he proposes to derive, on the one
hand, Skt. *jihvā* (by an intermediate form * *źiźhvā*, in
which the two sibilants were assimilated), on the other
hand, Iranian *hizvā* ("perhaps" by an intermediate
form * *siźhvā*).[1]

My objections to this theory are as follows: 1. A Prim.
Aryan form **zdnghū-* with initial *z* seems to me not
sufficiently warranted by the Irish word *tenge*.   Even

---

[1] Comp. the similar explanation of *hizvā* proposed by Bechtel,
Sinnl. Wahrnehm., p. 42.

in Irish there is no other example for initial *t* from $z+d$, and with the rest of the European languages initial *z* seems to agree so little that Johansson himself is obliged to admit in the case of these a parallel form without *z*. In presupposing an earlier form * *denge*, I prefer to hold that Irish *t* is an irregular phonetic change. I know that the scientific code of most of the philologists of the present time does not allow of any individual exceptions from so-called phonetic laws. Still exceptions of this kind are frequently met with in every language. E. g., all of the changes generally comprehended under the name of "popular etymology," are, looked at from a purely phonetical standpoint, exceptions from the regular phonetic laws. Another group of words in which exceptional phonetic changes occur very frequently consists of abbreviated proper names, e. g., in English:[1]

Bill = William.	Maud = Magdalen, Matilda.
Bob = Robert.	Moll, Molly = Maria.
Dick = Richard.	Nan, Nanny, Nancy = Anna.
Dolly = Dorothea.	
Fanny = Frances.	Ned = Edward.
Harry, Hal = Henry.	Nell = Helena.
Harriet = Henrietta.	Noll = Oliver.
Jack = John.	Pad, Paddy = Patrick.
Jim = James (Jacob).	Pat, Patty, Patsy = Martha.
Kate, Kitty = Katherine.	Peg, Peggy = Margaret.
Kit = Christopher, Christian.	Poll, Polly = Maria.
	Sal, Sally = Sarah.
Maggy, Meg = Margaret.	Ted = Edward.
Matty = Martha.	Wat = Walter.

[1] My collegue, Dr. H. W. Smyth, who has been kind enough to look over the manuscript of this paper, has called my attention to a paper by Mr. C. P. G. Scott, in the forthcoming number of the Trans-

It would be erroneous, however, to confine irregularities in sound-shifting to these two classes. Their field is perhaps as unlimited as that of regular phonetic changes, although we may naturally expect that the instances in which the common rules are observed will. always outnumber those of the exceptions. Suffice it for my present purpose to quote a few examples which are etymologically clear, and in which the irregularity cannot apparently be gainsaid. In Old High German, alongside of the regular forms, *thûsunt* and *dûsent*, "thousand" (= Goth. *pûsundi*, Ag. S. *pûsend*, etc.), is found the irregular *tûsent*, on which Mod. Germ. *tausend* is based. The verb "to thaw" (Ag. S. *pâwan*, O. Norse *peyja*), is in O. H. G. regularly *douwen*, but in M. H. G.—by an irregular change of *d* into *t*—becomes *touwen*,[1] and is accordingly Mod. Germ. *tauen*. A more recent change of *d* into *t* is observed in Mod. Ger. *Trümmer* = M. H. G. and O. H. G. *drum*, Mod. Germ. *losen* = M. H. G. *dôsen*, O. H. G. *dôsôn*, and a few other words (see Wilmanns' Deutsche Gramm. I, p. 70). In •the Mod. Low German dialect of Waldeck the words for "father" and mother," whose common Low German form is *fader* and *môder*, (or *môder*), have, by a change otherwise unheard-of in this dialect, passed into *fater* and *môter*. In Mod. Germ. *Hirsch* and *Hirse* an irregular shifting of the sibilants is noticed. The regular forms would be **Hirz* (= M. H. G. *hirz*) and **Hirsche* (= M. H. G. *hirse*), as is clear from a comparison of e. g. *Herz* = M. H. G. *herze* and *herrschen* = M. H. G.

actions of the Amer. Philol. Society, which deals with these abbreviated names.

[1] The regular form *douwen*, however, is kept in M. H. G. in the meaning "to digest," Mod. Germ. *ver-dauen*.

hersen. The initial group *spr* is in Anglo-Saxon and English generally kept (*to spring* = Germ. *springen, to spread* = Germ. *spreiten*, etc.), but has lost its *r* in Ag. S. *specan* = Engl. *to speak* (found in Ag. S. alongside of *sprecan* = Germ. *sprechen*).[1]

As in examples like these irregular phonetic changes are taking place, as it were, before our eyes, I cannot see any sufficient reason for excluding irregularities from the development of sounds in pre-historic times.   And I would prefer the explanation of O. Ir. *tenge* from **dengc*, by an irregular change, to that from **zdenge* by an alleged regular change, so long as no definite traces of an initial *zd* have been found in other Aryan languages.

2. Johansson indeed claims (l. c., p. 2), that a prim. form with initial *zd* is—at least to some extent—supported also by Indo-Iranian.   Yet I doubt whether by presupposing, as he does, an Indo-Iranian prim. form ** zizhū* or ** zizhvā*, the forms are sufficiently explained which we actually find in Indian and more especially in Iranian. The change in Iranian of *voiced z* into *h*, the regular descendant of *unvoiced s*, would be without a parallel.[*] Moreover the sound *z* is found to a large extent as the representative in Iranian of Prim. Aryan palatals and sibilants.   Certainly we should expect Johansson's primitive Indo-Iranian form to have become in Iranian nothing else but **zizū-, *zizvā.*

3. Johansson's theory would lead to presupposing not one, but two primitive words for the tongue, viz., the

---

[1] Kluge, Etym. Wörterb d. nhd. Sprache, s. v. *sprechen*, tries to account for the loss of *r* in Ag. S. *specan* by presupposing a Germanic root "*spek.*"   But M. H. G. *spehten*, to which he refers, belongs to M. H. G. *spahen* and is not originally connected with *sprechen*.   Nor can I agree with Kluge's derivation of Mod. Germ. *Spuk* from *sprechen*.

one with an initial sibilant and another one without this
sibilant. In my opinion, it is doubtful whether dupli-
cates of this kind were known to the Prim. Aryan
tongue, although their existence in that language is
generally agreed upon. It is true that in several instances an initial *s* is found in one or more than one of
the Aryan languages, for whose origin we are unable to
account. Yet is anything gained by ascribing to Primitive Aryan in such cases both the existence of the *s* and
its non-existence, thus making that period the scape-
goat for the lack of our knowledge? Such an explanation would be possible if any conditions were recogniz-
able in Primitive Aryan leading to an interchange of
forms with and without *s*, or if a tendency were apparent
in some of the Aryan languages to preserve, and in others
to lose, the *s*. But as the matter stands, the treatment
of initial *s* would not be in harmony with the rules of
Prim. Aryan Sandhi ; and its preservation or its loss in
the single Aryan languages would seem not less arbitrary should we start from a double Aryan form than if
we presupposed in each case a single primitive form (be
it a form with or without initial *s*). The theory of Prim.
Aryan double forms, differing in an initial sibilant, is,
in brief, ground too unsafe to build upon.

If we reject the theories by which the Aryan name of
the tongue is considered as beginning with a sibilant,
and equate Skt. *jihvā'* with **dihvā'*, are we obliged to re-
tain the prim. form **dughvā'*, a form usually accepted
by scholars at the present time (cp., e. g., Fick, Vgl.
Wtb. 'I, p. 71)? I think not. There is no other word
in which an initial Prim. Aryan *d* has assumed, in the
single Aryan languages, so many various forms as are

found in the initial sounds of the words for "tongue."
Although this variety may to some extent be attributed
to the peculiar sequence of sounds (*d-n-gh*) found in the
first syllable of our word, yet it is perhaps more probable that the Proteus-like initial sound was other than
d. There is in particular one group of words that
seems to call for a different explanation, viz., those with
initial *l*: Armen. *lezu*, Lat. *lingua*, Old Irish *ligur*, Lit.
lëžùwis. It is generally held that in these instances the
word for "tongue" was influenced by the Old Aryan
verb **leigh(e)-: ligh(e)-*, "to lick," found in Armen.
lizum, *lezum*, Lat. *lingere*, Old Irish *ligim*, Lit. *lëžiù*.
Of course, there is a distinct parallelism between the
two groups, and there is no doubt that the noun meaning
"tongue" has in these instances been influenced by the
verb meaning "to lick." Yet analogical changes in
form cannot, as is well known, be explained, as a rule,
by mere resemblance in meaning. In addition to the
similar meaning (the general likeness, as it were, in the
inner form) some special agreement in outside form is
required, and it is by the united action of the two that a
further approach in form is achieved. Now if we were
to assume the Aryan word for "tongue" to have been
*dṇghū', the only point of agreement with the verb
*ligh(e)-, *leigh(e)-*, would have been the aspirated media
gh. I doubt whether this minute likeness would have
been powerful enough to produce independently, in four
different languages, by means of analogy, one and the
same radical change. It seems preferable and almost
necessary to presuppose that, from the outset, a closer
similarity was found between the noun and the verb.
If this is granted it will easily be seen that there is only
one way of solving the problem, viz., by admitting the

l in Lat. *lingua*, etc. to be of an early date and the name of the tongue to have been Prim. Aryan **dlŭghvā'* (resp. *dlŭghū'-*) or perhaps more exactly (cp. above p. 183, note) **dlᵉnghvā'* (resp. *dlᵉnghū'-*). In the single Aryan languages accordingly either the *d* or the following *l* was lost, the result being in the former instance **lᵉnghvā'* (=Lat. *lingua*, Old Ir. *ligur*, etc.), in the latter instance *dᵉnghvā'* (=Lat. *dingua*, Old Ir. *tenge*, etc.). This double set of forms reminds us of the Aryan name for another part of the body, viz., the liver, where part of the Aryan languages point to a prim. form **yᵉqr̥* (=Skt. *yakṛt*, Old Iran. *yakarc*, Gr. ἧπαρ, Lat. *jecur*, Lit. *jeknos*, pl.), the other part to a prim. form **lᵉqr̥* (=Arm. *leard*, OHG. *lebara*, Ag.S. *lifer*), while the original form was probably **lyᵉqr̥* with both *l* and *y*.

In the case of the word for "tongue" we are fortunate in finding one or two words in which both of the initial consonants are kept, the dental, however, having been transformed into a guttural. These words are Greek γλῶσσα (or γλῶσσα) and perhaps Albanian (Toscan) *ǵuhᵉ* (= Gegan *ǵuhᵉ*, Calabr. *gl'ujᵉ*, Sicil. *gl'unzᵉ*, comp. G. Meyer, Albanes. Wörterb., p. 142, s. v. *ǵuan*).

There are in Albanian several words in which initial *g'* is found alongside of *gl'*, the two forms varying with different dialects. I follow Gustav Meyer (Albanes. Studien III,[1] Vienna, 1892, p. 9), in assuming that in these instances *gl'* is the more original sound. This seems certain, e. g., in the case of the words for "knee," Toscan *ǵuri*, Gegan *ǵuni*, Greek and Sicil. *gl'uri*, where

---

[1] Sitzungsberichte d. K. Akademie d. Wiss. in Wien, Bd. CXXV, Abh. 11.

the *l* is endorsed by Old Ir. *glún* "knee" (see G. Meyer,
Alb. Wtb., p. 142).[1]

The variety of the intermediate consonants in *g̓uhε*,
gl'uγε and *gl'unzε* finds a parallel in the words for
"roof": Tosc. *strehε*, Ital. Alb. *štrejε* and *štrezε* (G.
Meyer, Alb. Wtb., 394). As *štrezε* is explained by G.
Meyer from **strejεzε*, we may conclude from this parallel that the difference in both cases is probably not phonetic merely. *gl'unzε* may likewise be traced back to
*gl'unγε-zε and regarded as a diminutive, formed by the
ending *-zε*, which in Albanian is frequently met with ;
comp. *pu̓χizε* (Cal. Sic.)=*pu̓χī* f. "air, draught," *šokεzε*
= *šokε* f. "woman's girdle," *šolεzε* = *šolε* f. "sole, san-
dal," *tsabjεzε* = *tsabjε*, *tsabεjε* "sword," *vašεzε* (*vaizε*,
varzε) = *vašε* "maid, girl," *bezεzε* ("mit doppelter
Dem.-Endung," G. Meyer, Alb. Wtb., 23) = *bê*, *bahε*
"sling" and many others. The γ of Calabr. *gl'uγε*
seems in that dialect to be the regular representative of
an earlier intermediate *h*, comp. e. g., *tsoγε* "woolen
cloth, shawl" = Tosc. *tsohε*, Geg. *tsoho*, Mod. Gr. τσόχα,
Turk. *tšoha* (G. Meyer, Wtb., 442) and *l'eγonï* "child-
bed" = Tosc. *l'ehonï*, Mod. Gr. λεχωνιά (ibid., 240.)

The forms of the different Albanian dialects may then
be traced back to a common basis *gl'unhe*. If we admit
in the case of this form a substitution of *gl'* for *dl'*, similar to the one found in Sicil. *glεgóni* (Cal. *g̓eg'εñ*, Geg.

---

[1] These words may be connected with the Old Aryan name of
"knee" (Skt. *já'nu*, *jñu-*, Gr. γόνυ-, γνυ-, Lat. *genu*, etc.), if we assume
that in both Old Irish and Albanian *glun-* arose by dissimilation from
gnun-. Comp. Lit. *lĕndrë* f. and *lendrinë* f. = *nĕndrë* and *nendrinč*
"reed, cane;" Lit. *glinda* from **gninda* and Lat. *lens*, G. *lendis* from
*(c)nens, **(c)nendis* = κονίς, G. κονίδος "nit;" Lat. *luscinia* for **nus-
cinia*, i. e. **noctis-cinia* "nightingale" (Pott in Bezz. B. 8, p. 56) ;
sterquilinium for **sterquininium*, etc.

pt. *g'eg'un*, pass. *g'eg'em*) = *ndl'egóñ*, *ndil'góñ*, *dilgóñ*,
"to hear" from Lat. *intelligere* (G. Meyer, l. c., 67),
we arrive at **dl'unhe* or earlier **dlunhū* (since initial
cons. + *l'* regularly replaces Prim. Aryan cons. + *l*,[1]
and *e* is the regular form of the Prim. Ar. ending -*ā*).
This form bears such a close similarity to the Prim.
Aryan groundform **dlenghva* that it seems scarcely possible to deny their inter-connection.

There are, however, two phonetic changes assumed
in this etymology for which an explanation is required,
viz.: that of orig. *len* into Albanian *lun* and that of
orig. *ghv* into Alb. *h*.

The spirant *h* is found as a representative of Prim.
Aryan *gh* in Alb. *l'ch* "easy" = Skt. *raghú-*, Gr.
ἐλαχύς, etc.; see G. Meyer, Alb. Stud. 3, p. 10 sq. The
orig. *gh* here belongs to the Prim. Aryan "velar"
series, while in the word for "tongue," it belongs to
the Prim. Aryan palatal series. This distinction, however, is counterbalanced by the fact that in the word for
"tongue" *gh* is followed by *v*. It seems possible to
assume that the group palatal + *v* in our word passed
into the velar series in the same way as in Greek Prim.
Aryan **ecvo-s*, "horse," was changed into ** éqo-s* =
ἵππος, and Prim. Aryan **cvant-* "every, all" into
* qant- = πάντ-.[2]

The *u* in *g'lun-* for Prim. Aryan *dlen-* I regard as the
representative of a Prim. Aryan weak vowel. This

---

[1] See G. Meyer, Alb. Stud. 3, p. 77.

[2] The irregular *k* in Old Slav. *svekrū* "socer," = Lituan. *szeszúras*,
may be similarly explained from the group palatal + *u*. Old Slav.
svekry "socrus" apparently adopted the guttural of *svekrū*, while in
Gothic *swaihra* "socer" received its *h* (instead of *hu* = orig. *cu*) from
swaihrô "socrus."

assumption may at first sight seem to be at variance
with the fact that Prim. Aryan weak vowels (or vowels
developed from Prim. Aryan syllabic liquids) are in
Albanian generally represented by i; comp. the examples (given by G. Meyer, Alb. Stud. 3, p. 78 sq.) of
Alb. ri = Prim. Ar. $\underset{\circ}{r}$. The apparent contradiction,
however, may be removed by assuming that $gl'un$- replaces an earlier form *$gl'in$- and that u instead of i is
due to the influence of the preceding l', as in Alb. $l'ut$-
= Gr. λίτομαι or in $l'ul'e$ f. = Lat. $lilium$[1] (see G. Meyer,
Alb. Wtb., p. 250 s. v. $l'ul'e$ and Alb. Stud. 3, p. 28).

We may now consider Greek γλῶσσα and γλάσσα. Every
etymology of these words must start from the fact that
in Greek itself there are several nouns which in both
form and meaning are closely related to γλῶσσα. These
nouns are the plural γλῶχες "beard of corn" (Hesiod
Scut. 398), and the feminine γλωχίν- "point of an arrow,
end of a yoke-strap"[2] with its compounds τανυγλώχιν,
"with long point," τριγλώχιν, "three-barbed, three-
forked," χαλκογλώχιν, "with point or barbs of brass."
The similarity between these words is generally explained by presupposing an early root γλωχ- "to be
pointed." In my opinion, they are derived from a
basis γλωχ- "tongue," which, by a change in suffix or
in inflection, originated from the Prim. Aryan name of
the tongue. I adopt this view for the reason that
no certain trace of the alleged root γλωχ- has been met

---

[1] The latter example would have to be dropped, if G. Meyer's
identification (Alb. Stud. 3, p. 92) of $l'ul'e$ with Lat. $flórem$ is preferable to his former etymology.

[2] According to Hesychios s. v. γλωχίνα (γλωχῖνα· τὴν γωνίαν τοῦ βέλους.
—καὶ γλῶσσαν. καὶ ἄκρον) it may also mean "tongue."

with outside of Greek,[1] and that in Greek itself we find
vocables that are undoubtedly derived from the word
for "tongue" with a similar meaning to those mentioned above. E. g. γλωσσίς (as sometimes γλῶσσα itself)
may mean "the end of a (shoe-) strap (see Lobeck ad
Phryn., 229) and γλώσσημα is quoted from Aischylos (frg.
141 = schol. Pind. N. 6, 85) in the phrase γλώσσημα κάμακος
"the pointed end of a pole."[2] But whether the one or
the other conception is adhered to : in either case this
comparison entitles us to explain the σσ in γλῶσσα from
$x + j.$[3]

Let us now turn to γλάσσα.[4] Until very recently this
form was known only by one or two quotations of ancient lexicographers. In the Etymol. Magn., p. 558, 50,

---

[1] Brugmann in Curt. Stud. 7, p. 291, derived Greek γλωχ- from root
kark, which he explained by "broken reduplication" from root *kar*;
while Bechtel, Sinnl. Wahrnehm., p. 23, equated γλωχ- with the root
ghalgh (amplified from *ghal*). I doubt, however, whether these
scholars adhere to their earlier etymologies, as neither Brugmann in
his "Grundriss," nor Bechtel in his "Hauptprobleme" refers to his
former opinion. Suffice it to say, whether we followed the one or the
other, we should expect to find in Greek initial κλ- instead of γλ-.

[2] It is noteworthy that Lat. *li(n)gula* shares the meanings "end of
a shoe-strap," and "pointed end of a pole."

[3] The origin of γλῶσσα from γλῶχja is, to my knowledge, generally
approved of except by Wiedemann, who in Kuhn's Ztschr. 33, p.
164, proposes to derive γλῶσσα from *glŏdhiä*. This he compares with
O. Irish *ad-glädur* "to speak." But the origin in Irish of *glad-* is
so doubtful (it may be explained from *glad*, or *ghlad*, or *gladh*,
or *ghlādh*, or *glŏd*, or *ghlŏd*, or *glŏdh* or *ghlŏdh*) that it is scarcely
advisable to base an etymology of a Greek word on the Irish verb
alone. Moreover, Wiedemann's etymology is improbable for the
reason that in the Aryan languages nouns meaning "tongue" are
not as a rule derived from verbs meaning "to speak."

[4] Comp. for the sources in which γλάσσα is found and for its accent
especially R. Meister, Die Mimiamben des Herodas, p. 698 sq.

γλῶσσα· γλάσσα is mentioned s. v. λαῖφος. · The gloss γλάσσων. μωρός· ἀνοίστατος (which, of course, presupposes the existence of γλάσσα) is handed down by Zonaras, p. 439. These statements have been confirmed by the papyrus in which the poems of Herondas, or Herodas (who lived in the 3d cent. B. C.), were discovered.[1] In these the word γλάσσα is found no less than seven times (III. 84, 93, V. 8, 37, VI. 16, VII. 77, 110), so that there cannot be any doubt as to its authenticity.[2] Since Herondas uses the Ionic dialect (see Meister, p. 771), the form γλάσσα is to be regarded as Ionic. In this dialect, however, the form γλάσσα was not exclusively used, as γλῶσσα occurs, e. g., in Homer, in Herodotos, in Hippokrates and in an inscription from Miletos (Bechtel, Die Inschriften des ionischen Dialekts, Göttingen, 1887, Nr. 100; comp. Meister, p. 699).

If γλῶσσα originated from *γλῶχ-ja, γλάσσα will have to be explained from *γλάχ-γα. The latter form may be traced further back to *δλάχ-ja, because in the case of disyllabic words, whose first syllable begins with the group media + l and whose second syllable begins with a guttural,

---

[1] The papyrus was first read by Kenyon in "Classical Texts from Papyri, in the British Museum, including the newly discovered poems of Herodas" (London, 1891). This publication was followed by the editions of Rutherford (Lond., 1891), van Herwerden (in Mnemosyne, 1892, p. 41 sqq.), Bücheler (2d ed., Bonn, 1892), Crusius (Leipzig, 1892), R. Meister (Leipz., 1893, = Abhandlungen der phil.-hist. Cl. d. K. Sächs. Gesellsch. d. Wiss., Vol. XIII, Nr. VII, p. 611 sqq.). Meister's edition is especially useful on account of its commentary and its thorough investigation of Herondas' dialect. It also contains (on p. 877 sq.) a complete list of the considerable literature (up to June, 1893) which has soon gathered around these poems.

[2] The common form γλῶσσα, which occurs only once (VI. 41), is probably due to a scribal error (see Meister, p. 699).

there is in Greek a strong tendency to assimilate the
initial labial or dental media into the guttural media γ.
Examples of this tendency are : γλάγος ntr. "milk" from
*βλάγος and this from *μλάγος, cp. ἀμέλγω and Goth. *miluk-s;*
γλακτ- in Hom. γλακτ-ο-φάγος and with anaptyctic vowel
γάλακτ- ntr. from *βλακτ- and this from *mlact- = Lat. *lact-*
"milk ;" γλήχων (hymn Cer. 209) "pennyroyal" (mentha
pulegium) = βλήχων ; γλυκίς from *δλυκίς = Lat. *dulcis.* In
*δλάχ-ja the stem syllable of our Prim. Aryan form
dlĕngh-vā' or *dlĕnghū'-* is easily recognized, since Greek
α is the regular representative of Prim. Aryan *en*, as in
ἑ-κατόν = Skt. *çatám,* Lat. *centum,* Germanic *hund,* and
in many other well known examples.

As regards the suffixes of Gr. γλάσσα = *dlĕ'ngh-ja* and
Skt. *jihvā'* or Lat. *lingua* = *dlĕngh-vā',* it may seem that
the original *v-* suffix had been replaced in Greek by a
j- suffix. A similar exchange of endings may indeed
be observed, e. g. in Gr. υἱύς [1] (later on υἱός) as compared with Skt. *sū-nú-s,* Goth. *su-nu-s,* or in Gr. ἀκτ-ίν- f.
"ray, splendor," as compared with Ved. *aktú-* m. "day-
light, splendor," and Goth. *ūhtwō* f. "morning, day-
light." Yet there is another way of explaining the
difference, which to my mind is preferable. Since in
Greek the group palatal + F often moves on the same
line with velars (cp. above p. 195), we may assume that
χ in γλωχίν- represents earlier χ + F, and that σσ in γλάσσα,
γλῶσσα, represents the combination of χF + *j* in the same
way as e. g., the χ of ἐλαχύς, ἐλάχιστος represents an earlier
velar, and σσ in ἐλάσσων represents the combination of
velar + *j.* If the latter explanation is correct, the difference between the ending in Greek γλάσσα, γλῶσσα, and

[1] See G. Meyer's Greek grammar [2] § 320, or Blass-Kühner I, p.
506 sqq.

Skt. *jihvā'* would simply amount to a change of the two feminine suffixes *ā* and *i*.[1] The difference is so slight as to be indistinguishable in the case of several derivative formations such as Ved. *dīrgha-jihvyà-* (RV. IX, 101, 1) and Greek τανύ-γλωσσο-ς (Hom. ε 66) "long-tongued."

There remains to be considered the difference in the vowel between the two Greek forms γλάσσα and γλῶσσα. The most probable explanation is perhaps that λω in γλῶσσα represents an earlier long syllabic *l*,[2] which arose in **dlᵉnghvā'* by an assimilation of *n* to *l* similar to that of *l* to *n*, which is observed in O. Slav. *jezy-kŭ* and O. Pruss. *insuwis*.

Another way of accounting for the varying vowel would be to explain ω with R. Meister (l. c., 699) as "Ablaut" of *a*. Yet if I am right in regarding the *a* of γλάσσα as the representative of a syllabic nasal, the instances quoted by Meister (ῥάξ "grape," and ἐρράγην) are no longer quite parallel. γλῶσσα, indeed, might be explained from **γλῶγχja (as ἀσσον stands for ἀγχjον) and the interchange between ων and *a* (= *n̥* or *en*) compared with that seen in πρόφρων : πρόφρασσα, ἀπείρων : πείρατα, μνήμων : μνῆμα, etc. But since no trace of a long vowel appears in any other Aryan language, it would be rather venturesome

[1] Comp. for similar fluctuations in the declension of feminines K. F. Johansson in Gött. Gel. Anz., 1890, p. 752 sqq.

[2] See on the origin of Gr. ρω, λω, from long syllabic *r l* de Saussure, Système prim. des voyelles indo-eur., p. 263, and Brugmann, Grundriss I, p. 243 sqq. A different opinion on this subject has recently been expressed by Bechtel, Hauptprobleme, p. 203 sqq. It would be too long to discuss in this paper the whole complicated question of long syllabic liquids. I will only say that the existence in Greek of the group ρω in the function of a Prim. Aryan ‾ρ (or, as Bechtel prefers, in the function of a Prim. Ar. weak vowel + long *r*) cannot well be denied in the case of the adverb πρώϊον = Ved. *pūrvyàm*.

to ascribe to Primitive Aryan an interchange in our word between different grades of "Ablaut." The *ω*-form is more probably due to an innovation which in Greek took place at a comparatively recent period.

Note 1.—The learned author of the Dictionary of the Talmud, the Rev. Dr. Marcus Jastrow, who was present when I read the above paper before the Oriental Club, called my attention to the interesting fact that in Talmudic and Midrashic transliteration, Latin words beginning with *l*, are often spelled with a guttural preceding the *l* sound. E. g. *lectica* is found as *glegdica* (*glugd'ka*), *chlechtica*, *klectica*, and also as *lektica* (see Jastrow, Dict. of the Talmud, etc., p. 246); *Lesbii* (Lesbian figs, also olives), is found as *glufsin, chlufsin, klufsin*, and also as *libsim*, and *libsin* (see *ibid.*, p. 640); *Lesbiaca* (a white and delicate bread, and also a superior sort of olives), appears as *gluska, kluska, gluskin* (see *ibid.*, p. 246). It seems scarcely possible to deny that in these and similar cases *l* passes into *gl*. Since, however, the above are loan-words, and in loan-words phonetics are generally treated more freely than in words that are indigenous, I should not like to draw from these examples the conclusion that the initial *gl* of the Greek or 'Albanese words for "tongue" originated from forms with simple initial *l*.

Note 2.—Since sending an abstract of this paper to the Secretary of the Oriental Club, I heard from Professor Bloomfield that the same etymology of γλῶσσα had been communicated to him by one of his former pupils, Dr. Edwin W. Fay. I hope that the latter will publish the reasons that have led him to identify γλῶσσα with the rest of the words for "tongue" in the Aryan languages. The fact that Dr. Fay and I have arrived at the same result independently of each other is, I trust, a guarantee of its correctness.

THE FEATHER AND THE WING IN EARLY
MYTHOLOGY.

BY SARA YORKE STEVENSON.

OWING to the abuse which, in the early days of Philology, was made of myths and symbols for the purpose of tracing contact and even ethnic affinity between different races of men, the attention of students has, of late years, to a great extent been drawn away from their study, and there seems to exist among the best scholars a decided disinclination to allow them any special importance.

Yet, if in themselves they are of little use in the discussion of questions of origin, they afford invaluable assistance for a fuller understanding of man's intellectual evolution.

Fanciful and disconnected as the myths of primitive races appear to be, their creation is nevertheless subject to a law which connects them with the ideas and notions proper to a given stage of culture. They are born of man's effort to find an explanation, however crude it may be, of certain phenomena, which, owing to the external conditions of his life, are brought more directly under his observation, and as such they bear a definite relation to his intellectual and material condition.

One of the most brilliant minds of our time, the late Ernest Renan, has said : * " Mythology is life lent to

* " La mythologie, c'est la vie prêtée aux mots."—Le peuple d'Israel, I, p. 46.

words." Is it not on the contrary names given to life? At all events, primitive myths generally represent metaphysical theories, which in their origin necessarily depend upon the extent of the experience and upon the intellectual horizon of the metaphysician.

Certain myths frequently survive in a modified form the stage of civilization which produced them, and the symbolism to which they gave rise often outlives the thought to which it originally owed its existence. We have a striking instance of this in the ancient forms of pagan symbolism that have survived in the modern Christian Church.

But, nevertheless, if they can be traced back to their origin, they may be classified by the student of primitive thought according to the intellectual stratum to which they owed their origin ; and a fair test is obtained if we come across similar ideas among races who, at different periods of the world's history, have passed through the same stage of culture ; or who at the present day, from some cause or other, have remained unprogressive.

In order to give expression to his religious aspirations, man early found three principal vehicles : The Myth, from which was later evolved the dogma ; the Rite, which gave rise to Liturgy ; and the Fetish, image or embodiment, which eventually became the Symbol.*

---

* The Count Goblet d'Alviella (Hibbert Lectures, 1891), makes of the Rite a subdivision of Symbolism. The word "Symbol," however, implies an abstraction unknown to the primitive mind. Such a classification must tend to obscure the practical difference existing between the concrete significance of the fetish or of the imitative Rite for the naive worshiper, and the later religious feeling which may find expression in the Symbol or in the symbolical representation.

The Symbol is the visible form in which is coined the idea.

The myth is the work of the poet; the rite is the work of the priest; the symbol, that of the artist.

In the stage that precedes the birth of art, the primitive thinker uses natural objects to serve as vehicles to the ideas which he has made unto himself of the forces of nature. For him a hidden power resides in the tree and causes it to bud forth each year; in the stone, and bursts out of it in a spark; in short, wherever he finds motion and life. Animals, especially those whose ways seem mysterious, such as birds who fly high into the heavens, and serpents who burrow deep into the earth, seem to him especially to be the incarnate spirits of these elements. This is what modern science calls animism.

Later, the artist steps upon the scene and fashions more or less fanciful simulacra—fetishes wherein he establishes the supernatural power which he dreads or reveres, thus obtaining over him, through personal ownership, a certain occult influence. Then the shapeless stone becomes an axe, a cone or a column; the tree becomes an asherah—and after the imagination has once entered upon this path, religious art adapts itself to the higher level of a more idealistic mythology, and anthropomorphism appears. At first we find mixed forms: upon the tree-trunk appear the features or characteristics of a female form; the pillar assumes a head, arms, or a phallus: in Greece and in the Mediterranean xoana define themselves; in Egypt, the animal assumes a human form—in Mesopotamia it takes a human head or a bird's wings; and as the human intellect develops itself and becomes capable of conceiving an abstraction,

the fetish more and more detaches itself from the idea of
the power of which it once was the embodiment—it ceases
to be its earthly form and becomes its symbol.   When, at
last, artistic genius having attained its highest expression, the chisel of a Phidias shows us the Heavenly
Power which in primeval times may have been worshiped as an eagle * or a stone transformed into the
Olympian Zeus ; the Hermes of Praxiteles replaces the
archaic cippa and the asherah of deified nature becomes
the Aphrodite of Milo.†

A careful study of the subject brings out the fact that
the myths of the Historical period must generally be regarded as developments of elementary myths which
originated in an inferior intellectual stratum.‡   These
are so similar in various parts of the world that they
may broadly be said to be common to mankind ; the differences observable in various localities being mainly
due to special environment, when they are not simply
due to the particular stage of a myth's evolution at
which we may happen to consider it.

The symbol is as it were a mile-post on the way.   It
points out the road to follow in order to reach the idea
of which it may once have been the embodiment.   As
Mr. Clermont-Ganneau truly says :‖   "There must be a
mythology of images as there is a mythology of words,"
and as the image changes less than the original, the

---

* C. P. Tiele, "Manual de l' Histoire des Religions," p. 291.   1885.

† M. Collignon, "Mythologie figurée de la Grèce," pp. 9–13.   1884.

‡ Tiele, Rer. de l' Hre des Relig., II, 153: " Elements exotiques de la
Religion Grecque," has demonstrated that certain ideas at the basis of
ancient myths, belong to the human stratum that precedes the division
of races.

‖ "Coupe de Palestrina," Introd., p. VI.   Paris, 1890.

student who has the good fortune to find one to guide him in his researches, may use it with success to retrace the characteristic features of ideas which have become transformed in the course of centuries.

It is a fact that a religious thought once embodied in an artistic form has a tendency to lose itself into the material object which represents it, in the eyes of the masses. The idea, free and living, develops in the minds of thinkers in each generation; the old nature-myth may become purer and more idealistic in the hands of poets; but it remains crystallized in the artistic symbol, which remains more or less unchanged. Once created by art and admitted into the religious life of a people, the artists of subsequent generations, as pointed out by Lessing in his celebrated treatise upon "death,"* hesitate to depart from it for fear of not being understood. It becomes a part of its traditional stock; of its customs, of its commerce, and often, under this concrete form, the symbolism of one race passes into foreign countries, where, without understanding its real meaning, men adapt it to conceptions absolutely different in their character and origin from those of which elsewhere and at another epoch it was the legitimate expression.†

It would therefore seem that, in endeavoring to grasp the ideas embodied in any given myth and in its sym-

---

* "Wie die Alten den Todgebildet," pub. in 1769.

† For instance, the human-headed bird, symbol of the soul in Egypt, of which the Greeks borrowed the form to give it to their Harpyies, or the grotesque lion-killing hero of Babylonian art, which, in Egypt, became the deformed god Bes, and under Phœnician influence became Melqart; or to come down to our own civilization, St. George and the Dragon, the Mother and Child, the Eye, the Solar Rays, the Dove, and many other symbols of early times adopted into the modern Church, and before which to-day the priest still bows his head.

bols, and detect their origin, one may legitimately make use of the traces that similar ideas, result of like circumstances, have left among other races who, at different epochs of the world's history, have passed through the same moral and intellectual vicissitudes.

If we find among races of low culture, pure and unaltered, the idea which is at the basis of myths, the symbols of which are discovered upon the earliest monuments of the historical period, we may without impropriety use the information thus obtained to cast light upon the conditions under which that idea was evolved at a time preceding the development of art.* If, after this, we find among historical races whose civilization presents intermediate degrees, the same idea embodied in myths the character of which corresponds to the industrial and social development of the people, it is probable that we are on the right trail, and that, whilst making allowance for the different milieu in which the primitive thought was developed, we hold the thread that must guide us through our labyrinth. To resume: we may here apply the Platonic method as formulated by J. Stuart Mill,† and seek the sense of the abstract in the concrete.

By following the line indicated above, and carrying the inquiry to the confines of the prehistoric, I shall endeavor to trace the pedigree of the feather symbol, which among the ancient Egyptians was not only the emblem, but also the hieroglyph of light and of truth, and at the same time offer a suggestion as to the origin of the winged sun-disk and of other winged emblems.

* Comp. Ottfried Müller, "Prolegomena," p. 282, and M. de Littré, "Revue des deux Mondes," Mars, 1858, "Étude d'Hist. primitive."

† "Essay on Nature," p. 4.

Although the embodiment of an abstraction, the feather was already used in this sense at the opening of monumental history. It is obvious that the origin of an association of ideas apparently so incongruous must be sought in the prehistoric intellectual and religious development of the people ; for unless we admit for it some powerful reason now lost in the mist of an unknown past, it were difficult to understand why a feather should have been used in this connection by men as exact as the Egyptians generally were in their selection of the objects used as signs in their graphic system.

We shall see that the whole order of ideas concealed in the winged and feather symbols is connected with the beliefs and knowledge proper to men in the stone-age ; that they represent in their original form the myths fitted into their intellectual horizon, and were but the mode of expression by which they gave utterance to their naive explanation of celestial phenomena, which were closely associated in their minds with phenomena of an igneous nature.

Those who have studied the beliefs of non-civilized races know that, with few exceptions,* they look up

* The Hottentots, the Bosjemen, the inhabitants of Tierra-del-Fuego, who seem more especially to worship the moon, the Australians and a few inferior American tribes—as, for example, the send d'Oreilles of Oregon—whose notions are vague, and who even have no funeral rites, and perhaps a few other tribes in a very low stage of culture. In looking over the works of Messrs. Tyler, "Researches into the Primitive History of Mankind," and "Primitive Culture," Albert Réville, "Religions des Non-Civilisés," D'Alviella, "Prolégoménes," and "Histoire du Feu," Brinton's "Myths of the New World," Lubbock's "Origin of Civilization," Spencer's "Principles of Sociology," etc., and many narratives of ancient and modern travelers, with a view to tabulating the principal objects of worship of various non-developed races, it was found that with the few excep-

with reverence to a Power above. They conceive it as
residing in the upper space; his voice is heard in the
thunder; his anger strikes in the lightning; and the
manifestation of his good-will is practically displayed
in the light and life-dispensing rays of the sun. In a
word, and if we may adapt the happy expression applied
by Burnouf to the Vedic god Indra, they worship "the
atmospheric energies of the heavenly" light.*

tions above-mentioned, and a few races who—having advanced to the
agricultural stage—honor more particularly the sun—and in this case
it is often easy to perceive that we have a secondary development of
the primitive idea by which the sun is made the principal manifestation of the Spirit or Power governing the heavenly vault—the worship of the latter may be regarded as quasi-universal. In Polynesia,
and among peoples in whose existence the sea plays a conspicuous
rôle, the exact nature of the superior space often remains somewhat
vague, and the liquid element is more explicitly mixed up with the
conception of the Celestial Creator than it is elsewhere. Nevertheless, even in Polynesia, that Creator often resides in space, and is referred to as fishing up the islands from the bottom of the sea.

Among some peoples the Supreme Power *resides* in the sun. But
this notion may also be regarded as a special phase, and sun-worship,
properly speaking, may be said to belong to the agricultural stage—
that is, to an already advanced stage of human development.

* Most of the American tribes are said to possess a word to express
the divine or *super*-natural, which like the word we ourselves use,
conveys a sense of place, and means "*above*." According to Brinton
("Myths of the New World," pp. 47-48), those words are: Algon-
quin, "Manito" and "Oki;" Iroquois, "Oki" and "Okhor;"
Dakota, "Wakan;" Aztec, "Teotl;" Guichua, "Huaca;" Maya,
"Ku," etc.

Many other languages bear the trace of the importance that primitive religions granted to the Superior Space and to the Spirit governing it: "Deus, Zeus, Dyaus," are evidences of it among the Aryans,
as well as "Tien" among the Chinese. Among the Aztecs and
Guiches, such phrases as "Heart of Heaven," "Lord of Heaven,"
"Prince of the azure planisphere," are said to be frequent (Brinton,
loc. cit.). In W. Africa, acc. to Tyler (Prim. Cult, II, 233), and

The power governing space is recognized by them in its various activities as Creator, dispensing life, as well as master of the heavenly fire, and in a conception which is quasi-universal, and which must be a very primitive one, this heavenly spirit appears to them incarnate or manifesting itself under the shape of a bird.

Not only do numerous legends, collected from all parts of the world, show us this bird associated with the lightning, the sun, and all phenomena connected with fire; but they often represent it as casting down or as bringing down upon earth the heavenly fire under the shape of aeroliths or of flints containing a spark of the igneous element; and even at times as introducing directly or indirectly the heavenly spark into wood.

Among non-civilized races, as well as the nations of antiquity, the idea which derives fire from heaven, and which sees in the beneficent action of the sun and in the destructive power of the lightning, simple aspects of the same elementary force, is too well known to need dwelling upon. *

Even as late as the time of Pliny,† science confused

Waitz (Anthrop. der Naturvoelker, II, 168), the same word designates the Supreme Being, the visible sky, and rain and thunder.

Among the ancient Egyptians, "Her," the "Superior," the "Above," was synonymous with God.—See below, p. 229.

* A. Kuhn, "Herabkunst des Feuers," Goblet d' Alviella "Hist. du feu," p. 30. Max Müller, "Physical Religion," Lectures VII, VIII, IX, X, XI, and XII.

† Comp. Pliny, II, 4, where he treats of the elements and explains (II, 18-20) lightning as a spark detached from an incandescent star, and says that "this heavenly fire cast upon earth brings to it omens of events to come, the detached particle not having lost its divine virtues." And further, after having explained in detail how according to him the spark, detached from the stars and falling upon the clouds

the fire of the stars with that of the lightning, and
there is a striking sameness in the manner in which the
explanation found by human imagination in its primitive stages, has been formulated in different parts of the
world, by races separated not only by distance, but also
by vast periods of time. The inhabitants of southern
Africa—Zulus, Kafirs, etc.—regarded celestial fire as a
manifestation of the life which animated nature; and
according to them thunder was produced by the flapping
of the wings of the gigantic Heaven-Bird. Among
them, as formerly among the Etruskans and the Romans,* it was a sacrilege to touch objects and persons

can by agitating the air produce the tempest, he adds: "It is also
possible that the spirit, whatever it may be, is engendered by friction
when it is cast forth with so much strength. It is possible that from
the shock of the two clouds the lightning bursts forth, as happens
when from the shock of two stones there springs forth a spark . . .
. . but all these things are casual . . . . . Those that foretell the
future come from above, and according to established rules, come
from their special stars." (Comp. Aristotle, "de Meteor." "Nihil
ut aliud ventus άνεηος sit, nisi aër multus, fluctuus et compressus qui
etiam spiritus (πνευμα) appellatus."

Elsewhere (II, 111) Pliny says: "To these fires must be added
those innumerable stars and the great sun itself. There is also the fire
made by men and those which are innate in certain species of stones,
and those which are produced by the friction of wood, and those
which are in the clouds, and which give rise to lightning." Ancient
Physiology said: "Corpus est terra, auimus est ignis."

* Pliny II, 55. "It is improper to burn on a funeral pyre a man
killed in this manner. Our religion commands us to bury the
corpse." See upon the subject of the Etruskan Liturgy (of which the
idea preserved in this passage is obviously a survival) and upon the
manner in which the bodies and objects struck by lightning were
buried, as well as the "Lightning-stones," and for the ceremonies
and sacrifices by means of which every place struck by lightning was
consecrated—the article of Mr. Boucher-Leclercq, "Revue de l' Hre
des Religions," III, pp. 321–352.

struck by lightning. The eagle and vulture are worshiped in many parts of Africa.*

In New Zealand mythology, Tangaroa, the Creator,
inhabits the Heavens or the Sun which he has created.†
He is frequently represented in the form of an enormous
bird.‡ It is his son Maui, who in an often-quoted
legend introduced fire upon earth, and was the cause of
the presence of the fire-spark in stones and in wood.

Similar notions are found among the indigenous tribes
of the New World. The authors who have at various
times treated questions connected with the beliefs of
non-civilized races, have so often quoted the numerous
American legends in which the Heaven-Bird plays the
principal part, that it would be superfluous to do more
than recall them here. There is, however, one point
upon which attention should be drawn: that is, that
throughout the whole length of the American continent
those myths are very similar, and that taken collectively
they are as the welded links of a long chain of legendary
lore, in which the celestial bird pursues his evolution.

At first the incarnation, then the messenger of the

* Ellis, Travels, etc., I, p. 325.

† A. Réville, loc. cit., II, p. 46.

‡ Burton, "Dahomey," II, p. 142, also A. Réville, loc. cit. I, p. 65.
Mr. Tyler, "Researches into the Primitive History of Mankind," p.
222, mentions a certain West African god, Gimagong, who once a
year comes down into his temple with a loud rustling noise like that
of a "flock of geese in the spring," and to whom an ox is sacrificed,
not with a knife, but with a sharp stone. Among other tribes of
Africa, for instance among the Yoroubas, Thunder is a special divinity known as the "Stone-flinger," and it is from him, it is said, that
come the stone-axes found in the ground, and which are preserved as
fetishes. (See Smithsonian Contributions, I, XVI, Rev. J. T. Bowen,
"Grammar and Dictionary of the Yorouba Language.")

great spirit above, it plays according to the degree of civilization reached by its worshipers, the varied rôles of Creator, or of his celestial agent, the Storm-bird, who sometimes *inhabits* the Sun. But, under whatever aspect it may present itself, it is always the giver of celestial fire—sometimes destructive, sometimes beneficent—which it casts down upon earth under the shape of stones containing a spark of the igneous element and which often becomes its symbol.* Among the most civilized tribes of America, as well as among those who were still in the rudest stage of culture, the relation existing between the Heaven-Bird, the igneous phenomena, and the fire-flint thrown from heaven upon earth, is clear and often most explicit.

The Sioux,† who possess numerous legends upon the subject of the Creator-Bird—giver of fire to men—tell us‡ that lightning in striking the ground bursts and scatters on all sides the thunder-stones which are flints ; and they demonstrate this by the spark which these silicious stones contain. They regard as sacred the blaze kindled by the lightning.

* Brinton, "Myths of the New World," p. 143, etc., says that, in the American myths, the Sun is always regarded as a fire created or set in motion by a superior power, or by legendary beings. Among several tribes, for instance, among the Natchez, the Texuques (New Mexico), the Kolosch (Columbia), the words for "fire" and "sun" are derived from the same root. Among the Algonquins the words for "sky" and for "sun" are so derived, and the heaven was the wigwam of the Great Spirit. Among the Maya, "Kiu" also expressed the same idea. Among the Peruvians, Viracocha-pacha-camac was the Supreme God, whose son, or whose manifestation, was the Sun. In him may be recognized the ancient Aymara God, whose weapon was lightning. (Brinton, loc. cit., p. 155, also *ibid.*, 55.)

† Mrs. Eastman, "Legends of the Sioux," p. 71.

‡ E. B. Tyler, "Primitive Culture," II, p. 238.

Among the Northwestern tribes, the great creative spirit is the Crow, who is regarded as the source of life.*

There is in the Museum of Archæology of the University of Pennsylvania at Philadelphia,† a curious image of this legendary Crow, carved in stone and painted black, from Alaska, which represents him in his rôle of Creator, holding tightly pressed against his breast a human mask, which he is in the act of incubating.‡

In South America, we find in Brazil, among the Lupis, the eponymous bird Lupan, the flapping of whose wings produces the lightning; who is worshiped as supreme god, and who, incarnate in the first man, had introduced agriculture and the use of fire.‖

Among the American nations who, at the time of the landing of the Spaniards, were in possession of a civilization more or less advanced, the primitive myth, however refined and altered it may have been, had preserved traits that permit us to recognize it without trouble. The anthropomorphic legend of Quetzalcoatl presents

* Waitz, "Anthropology der Naturvoelker, III, p. 330. Bancroft, loc. cit. III, p. 102.

† No. 634 of the Catalogue of "Objects Used in Religious Ceremonies," etc. 1892. (See accompanying illustration.)

‡ The Thlinkeets have similar myths (E. B. Tyler, "Prim. Cult.," II, p. 237.) See also for the Haidahs of Queen Charlotte Island, and the Sticksen and Tongass of Southern Alaska, whose myths are almost identical, James Deans, in the "American Antiquarian," 1888, p. 273, etc. The Mandans heard in the the thunder and saw in the lightning the flapping of the wings and the shining eyes of the terrible bird "who belongs to the Great Manito, or is perhaps the Great Manito himself." (E. B. Tyler, "Prim. Cult.," II, p. 237.) In Oregon the Great Spirit inhabits the Sun; but when he is angry he sallies forth and produces the storm.

‖ Elsewhere (Cumana, South America), it is the sun itself whose wrath is manifested in the storm (Waitz, loc. cit., III, p. 421.)

one of the most interesting phases of the subject. The allegory of this "bird-serpent," * that white man, "author of light," who, coming from the East, pursues his civilizing journey, bringing with him plenty; and who, his task accomplished, goes away promising to return, is too transparent to need commentary.

He was the son of the spirit of the hurricane, Ixtac-Mixcoatl, the Serpent of the White-Cloud, and the precursor of Tlaloc, the rain-god. Wherever he went birds accompanied him. After he disappeared, he sent four young men,† his companions, "of incomparable swiftness and speed," who divided the earth between them awaiting his return. His decrees were promulgated with a voice so formidable that it was heard one hundred miles off; his bolts could pierce the largest trees ; and the stones thrown by him could sweep down forests. Wherever his hand rested upon a rock it left an ineffaceable mark, and by shaking his sandals he gave fire to his subjects.

We have here, therefore, the primitive myth completely developed, yet still simple in its form. That is to say that although anthropomorphic, its various features are still combined in the one personality of the Heaven-Spirit, incarnate and conceived as the benefactor of the human race. To complete the circle that links the abstract development of the legend to its pri-

* Brasseur de Bourbourg, "Histoire du Mexique," I, p. 302. Acc. to Kingsborough (Antiq. of Mexico, V, p. 109), he is son of Tonacateotl, god of the flesh or of subsistence. Brinton, loc. cit., p. 182.

† Among the Navajos these four, who here are anthropomorphized, are swans who swiftly fly from the four corners of the horizon, carrying bolts under their wings. They are the creators of men and of animals.

meval form, the symbols of Quetzalcoatl are the bird, the serpent, the cross, and the flint.*

In Peru, Apocatequil, Son of the Sky, but born of *an egg*,† represents the thunder who casts lightning from its sling in the shape of stones; and the thunder-stones which fall upon the earth are his children. It is said that few villages were without these precious talismans— round stones which were worshiped as gods of fire as well as of human ardor—and were supposed not only to insure the fertility of the fields and to protect against lightning, but to possess the property of kindling passion in the coldest, sternest breast.‡

In China, it is in the nest of the celestial bird that the tempest is brewed, and the lightning is the trace of its flight.‖ The Storm-spirit is still represented by the

---

* Brinton, loc. cit., p. 133. Tohil, the god of the quichés, which was represented under the shape of a silex, was, according to Brinton, identical with Quetzalcoatl. The legend relates that, in the beginning, a silex fell from heaven upon earth and broke into 1600 fragments, of which each became a god (loc. cit., p. 157).

† The legend says that the first man, Guamansuri, created by the Lord of Heaven, Ataguju, descended upon earth and seduced the sister of the "*dark*" beings who inhabited it, and who revenged themselves by killing him. The woman died in giving birth to *two eggs*, of which issued forth two brothers. The most powerful, Apocatequil, exterminated the "dark" beings and freed the Indians from the soil where they were buried, in upturning the earth with a golden spade. (Brinton, loc. cit., p. 153, quoting Montesinos, "Ancient Peru," II, xx.

‡ Ibid. Comp. Prescott, "Conquest of Peru," I, 96, quoting Herrera, "Histoire Générale," Dec. 5, lib. 4–4.
The god of the Incas, Viracocha Pachacamac, father of the Sun, had retained the attributes of the ancient heaven-god of the Amayras, and the latter's name under his stormy aspect. The Condor was the messenger of the storm, which was regarded as a huge bird. Brinton, loc. cit., p. 156.

‖ Tyler, Researches into the Early History of Mankind, p. 252.

Chinese as a human form, whose shoulders are supplied with powerful wings and whose visage is armed with a bird's long beak.   He flies through the heavens brandishing his mace.*

Similar legends and superstitions may be traced among the peoples of the great Mongolian stock, and all regard with reverence and as heaven-sent the flint implements, associating them, in their folk-lore, with the heavenly fire.

It may therefore broadly be stated that the association of the legendary Heaven-bird with igneous phenomena is quasi-universal, and that its relation not only to the lightning, the sun and the stars,† but also to the spark enclosed in the flint, seems to assign to it an early date in the intellectual evolution of man.

But it is not only among contemporary races in varying degrees of culture that we find these beliefs ; if such were the case, our researches would be of little value. These naïve products of the imagination of men whose minds have remained more or less unprogressive, are only interesting to us because they help us to understand a large number of poetic legends, religious rites, and, to us, singular customs observed among the ancients, and which were survivals of a primeval age already long left behind and almost forgotten, at the opening of the historical period.

Viewed in this light they afford valuable information

* It is represented upon sheets of yellow paper, which are used as talismans to ward off the lightning. One is classified under No. 356 of the Catalogue of Religious Objects Exhibited at the Museum of the University of Pennsylvania in 1892. See also the Chinese legend of the bird who struck fire from a tree. (A. Kuhn, "Herabkunst des Feuers," p. 28.)

† Comte Goblet d' Alviella, "H^{re} du feu," p. 64.

upon the evolution of the human intellect, and enable us to appreciate the conditions under which existed, in pre-historic times, the founders of ancient civilizations, of which they represent the religion and the science.

The mythical bird plays an important rôle in Aryan tradition. That of the eagle as messenger and lightning-bearer of Zeus need not be dwelt upon. Among the Iranians the raven, according to Mr. Darmesteter,* is the seventh incarnation of Verethragna ; and when Yima, having strayed from the straight path of truth, lost his "Glory," this flew away under the form of the bird Vâraghna,† and was seized first by Mithra, the Sun-god, then by Thraêtona, the Storm god, and finally by Keresâspa, the hero who, on the last day, is to anni-hilate the principle of evil and of darkness.‡ The XIVth Yast, of which each paragraph begins with a sacrifice offered to Verethrâghna and which is entirely consecrated to that god, assimilates him first to the raven, then to the great bird the Saêna,‖ that is, the eagle or the hawk who inhabits the sacred tree where germinate the seeds of all plants as well as the remedy for all evils ;§ and where resides truth.

* Zend Avesta, II, Yast, XIV, 19. (Max Müller's "Sacred Books of the East," Vol. XXIII.)

† Zend Avesta, II, Yast XIV, 18-21. Comp. *Ibid.*, 35. The raven is one of the incarnations of the genius of victory, and this "royal glory" is described as "flying in the shape of a raven."

‡ *Ibid.*, II, XIX, 34-39.

‖ *Ibid.*, II, XIV, 19 comp. 41.

§ Yast XII, 10. "And whether thou, O holy Rashnu (truth) art on "the tree of the eagle that stands in the middle of the Sea Vouru-"Kasha, that is called the tree of good remedies, the tree of all reme-"dies, and on which rest the seeds of all plants ; we invoke, we bless "Rashnu the strong," etc. The eagle, Saêna, in later mythology, is

We have here, therefore, the god—a type derived from Indra—represented by the raven or, according to others, by the hawk of light and the eagle of the fertilizing-storm; that is, by the heaven-bird now divided and appearing separately under his two principal aspects.

The feather and the bone of the bird Vârengana,* in the Iranian legend, are endowed with a magic power which assures to its happy possessor, not only a glorious victory over his enemies and a protection against an evil destiny, but also life and health.†

In order to guard against an evil spell, Ahura Mazda gives the following advice:‡ (35) "Take thou a feather "of that bird . . . the Vârengana—O Spitama Zara-"thustra! with that feather thou shalt curse back thine "enemies. (36) If a man holds a bone of that strong "bird, or a feather of that strong bird, no one can smite "or turn to flight that fortunate man. The feather of "that bird brings him help; it brings unto him the "homage of men; it maintains in him his glory . . . "(38) All tremble before him who holds the feather, "they tremble *therefore* before me; all my enemies

the Sînamrû or Sîmûrgh; his resting place is on the tree which is Yad-bêsh (opposed to harm) of all seeds; and always when he rises a thousand twigs will shoot forth from that tree; and when he alights he will break off a thousand twigs, and he sheds the seed therefrom. And the bird Châmnrôsh forever sits in that vicinity, and his work is to collect that seed which sheds from the tree of all seeds, which is Yad-bêsh, and conveys it where Tishtar seizes the water, so that Tish-tar may seize the water with the seed of all kinds, and may rain it on the world.

* Karl F. Geldner regards it as probably the hawk, like that which figures in the Odyssey, 13, 87.

† Comp. Pliny Nat. Hist. See below, page 222.

‡ Yast XIV, 35-36-38.

"tremble before me and fear my strength and victorious
"force and the fierceness established in my body."

In this last verse, the supreme heaven-god of the Persians seems to recall his origin, and the explanation of
the terror inspired by him might lead us to believe that
he had not quite forgotten the time when this terrible
feather described by him was his own.[*]

We find these miraculous properties of the feather of
the celestial bird attributed to those of the eagle not
only by other ancient peoples, but by the later Persians
themselves. In the Shâh-nâmeh,[†] the feather whose
magic power heals the wound made in the flank of Rû-
dâbah at the birth of Rustem was that of the eagle
Srgmûîh ; and Rustem, wounded to death by Isfendyâr,
was cured in the same manner.

In the Rig-Veda,[‡] Indra is the hawk of which the
flight cannot be impeded, and which carries in its talons
the Soma—that is, the essence that prolongs existence
and brings the dead to life.[||] There also,[§] the Sun is
spoken of as a beautiful bird, with golden wings, *who
flies* through the heavens as a messenger of Varuna—
who like Zeus wields the lightning.

The eagle Garuda, son of Vinâtâ, also plays a conspicuous part in Hindu mythology ; and in the Bhaga-
vad-gîtâ,[¶] in enumerating his forms, the god says : " I
"am Vishnu, among the Âdityas, and the beaming sun
"among shining bodies . . . I am thunder among

---

[*] In the Greek legend of the war of the Titans, it is the eagle that
brings Zeus the lightning.—Comp. Gubernatis, II, p. 194. London,
1892.

[†] J. Darmesteter, loc. cit., p. 241, note.

[‡] IV, 27, 1-4.   [||] X, 144-5.

[§] X, 123-6.   [¶] Ch. 10-30.

"weapons; I am the son of Vinatâ among the birds."
Now Garuda is the vehicle of Vishnu.

Elsewhere, the Chaldæan legend of Etana, such as it
has been handed down to us in the cuneiform texts of
El-Amarna,* shows the hero, guided by the advice of
the Sun-god Shamas, going to seek the eagle to obtain
from it the plant that produces birth ; and in this myth,
the bird plays the double rôle of healer and of sage. · He
is also the traditional enemy of serpents.

It is curious to find among the Babylonians the notion
of the vital principle associated with the Heaven-bird,
now become the shadow of his former self, and whose
fallen divinity having passed into the legendary stage,
seems to have preserved in their traditions a vague reminiscence of its ancient power as creator and wielder of
the heavenly heat.†

But it is more remarkable to be able to trace similar
survivals more or less well-preserved from primitive
times in the superstitions of nations intellectually nearer
to us.

Pliny,‡ in his Natural History, which brings us the
echo of the science and popular beliefs of his epoch,
tells us that the feathers of the eagle, if brought into
contact with those of other birds, consume them.§

* Winckler, "Thontafelfund aus Tel-el-Amarna," II, 166. E. T.
Harper, "Academy," May 30, 1891.

† Among the Finns the same healing power is attributed to the eagle,
and Mr. E. Beauvois (Rev. de l' H^{re} des Relig^s , VI, 270–1. "La
magie chez les Finnois") cites an exorcism in which that bird plays
the part of celestial healer.

‡ X, 5.

§ This superstition was, it is stated, shared by Albertus Magnus, who
is said to have made the experiment.

He adds that this bird, in order to construct its nest, uses eagle-stones, "aëtites," otherwise called "gangites," which are used as a remedy and are fire-proof. Further on,* he describes at length these aëtites, which probably were geodes of a siliceous nature ; and he gives numerous details as to the virtues that were attributed to them.   According to him they were regarded as male and female, and as animated with a principle of reproduction.   Not only was their presence in the nest intimately connected with the birth of the young eagles, but they exercised an occult influence upon the birth of man ; and wrapped in the skin of an animal offered up in sacrifice,† and worn by women approaching their term of confinement, they assured the safe birth of the child.

Here again we have a hazy reminiscence of the eagle's former elevated mythological position.

Pliny also attributes a magic power to the feather of the vulture, and states that it puts the serpents to flight.‡

The primeval Heaven-God seems therefore to have been closely associated in the minds of the ancestors of the civilized peoples of antiquity, as well as by those of non-civilized modern races, with a bird of prey ; and its attributes, in the secondary myths to which he gave rise, seem later to have become divided among the different

* XXXVI, 39.

† The association of the sacred stone with the animal skin must have been a common one in antiquity. (See Lenormant, "Les Betyles. Ber. de l' H^re des Religions," III, 45.) It may be remarked that in Savoy, stone axes, it is said, are still found wrapped up in a goat-skin and used as protective talismans.

‡ In Egypt, the ibis-feather put to flight the most voracious crocodile. (Maspero, Etudes Egyptiennes.) I. 43, 1879.

varieties which more and more diverged from the original type. Its evolution seems to have followed the
same road as that of other divine types, and in the same
manner as certain primitive deities. Such, for instance,
as the Nature-goddess, whose various aspects, whether
beneficent or terrible, gave birth to several distinct
mythological types under different names. So do we
find the Heaven-bird playing in turn the part of Solar-
bird, of bird of the fertilizing storm, and of the terrible
Storm-bird.

In the Aryan tradition, and without taking into account forms that became more and more highly special-
ized, we have seen the hawk or the crow Vârengana,
whose feather heals and protects, and the Saêna who
lives in the tree of life; we also find him in the shape
of the gigantic Ramâk, who obscures the earth and
"holds back rain until the rivers are dry," and who
struggles against the hero, benefactor of humanity.*

Likewise in the Chaldæan legend,† the bird of the
south wind, the terrible messenger of Anu, who struggles against Adapâ the Son of Ea, and breaks his wings,
does not exclude, as we have seen, the eagle-creator of
the legend of Etana, or the Akkadian Lugal-Tudda, or
others still.

In studying the confused multiplicity of legendary
types that characterizes the national literature of the
civilized races of antiquity, we should not however for-
get to take into consideration the local cults and the
special myths and mythological types of which these

---

* J. Darmesteter, "Zend-Avesta," II, pp. 296. (Sac. Books of the
East.)

† Texts of El-Amarna, pub. by Winckler, "Thontafelfund," etc.,
II, p. 166. Transl. by E. T. Harper, "Acad." May 30th, 1892.

became the source.   These local influences made themselves felt in the general literature of the people, when
with the political fusion of tribes or of petty states there
came about the religious syncretism which produced a
more or less national mythology.

The confusion of ornithological genera and even order which reigns in the legendary narratives cannot fail
to strike the observer, and at first sight tends to obscure
the link that united each to the primeval family tree;
but a more serious study of these ancient myths proves
that this confusion of the eagle, the hawk, the vulture,
the raven, and even of other birds, in no way affects the
fundamental idea, and that the myth-makers themselves
did not allow their imagination to be trammeled by such
considerations.

According to Mr. Houghton,* in Mesopotamia the
eagle and the vulture are mentioned on the monuments
by the expression: "Bird of Heaven," and the same
term serves to designate the two genera, although occasionally a special name is given to a particular bird.

The eagle which, in the Zend-Avesta, we have just
seen inhabiting the tree of life,† among the Germanic
peoples bore the hawk between its eyes.‡

The raven was sacred to Apollo, as he was among the
Persians to Verethraghna, and among the Germans to
Odin ; and according to Porphyry,|| the priests of the
Sun, in Persia, were called "ravens." §

---

* "On the Birds of the Assyrian Monuments," Proc. of the Soc. of
Biblical Arch., Feb. 7th, 1882.

† See below, p. 218.

‡ E. Hugo Meyer, "Germanische Mythol.," p. 82.

|| Cf. Georgida, I, 45.

§ J. Darmesteter, Z. A., Part II, p. 236, note.

The hawk, which with the eagle was by the Homeric Greeks consecrated to Zeus, was regarded as the messenger of Phœbus;[*] and for the Aryan peoples remained a luminous type. Ælien,[†] has collected numerous superstitions in which the hawk represents light and life.

The gods and goddesses of the Germanic pantheon metamorphose themselves in the forms of eagles and falcons;[‡] and although the raven seems to have been more especially consecrated to Odin,[||] that god none the less assumes the form of the eagle;[§] and upon his seal, it is the eagle which is said to be associated with the wolf.[¶] If the eagle is the symbol of the sun[**] as well as that of the storm, the raven plays the same rôles,[††] and the Valkyries, in their wild race through the air, are represented as accompanied by both species of birds.[‡‡]

The genealogy of several of the mythical birds as furnished us in the Ramayana[||||] may give some idea of the vagueness which existed in the ancient mind with regard to their ornithological classification. Tamra gives birth to Kraûnci (the mother of the herons) and to Çyeni—that is, the female Hawk of which Vinatâ was the offspring. Vinatâ laid the egg of which were

---

[*] Odyssey, 15, 525.

[†] Comp. Gubernatis, "Zoological Mythol." II, p. 194.

[‡] E. H. Meyer, loc. cit., p. 151.

[||] E. H. Meyer, loc. cit., p. 59.

[§] E. H. Meyer, loc. cit., p. 183.

[¶] Grimm "Deutsche Mythology," p. 10.

[**] E. H. Meyer, loc. cit., p. 94.

[††] E. H. Meyer, loc. cit., p. 112.

[‡‡] E. H. Meyer, loc. cit., p. 177.

[||] III, 20.

hatched Aruna and the famous eagle Garuda; and Garuda in his turn became the father of the two enormous vultures, Gatayâ and Sampati. Evidently nothing could be wilder than this mythical pedigree.

We have seen that the vestiges of a similar train of thought are found in the Valley of the Euphrates. There, however, as might have been expected in the presence of a civilization already old when it appears before us, the original type had already given birth to complex myths in which the ethical and abstract elements had been superadded to the naturalistic foundation; and where the principal theme is surcharged with details and abstractions which indicate the length of the road it had traveled since its first start.

The legend of Etana, which so nearly approaches the Iranian tradition, has already been alluded to, as well as that of Lugal-Tudda, the celestial bird of the Akkads, who was the tutelary god of Marad, near Sippara, the City of the Sun. Like Prometheus, the bird steals the sacred spark which he brings upon earth. In communicating it to men, he teaches them the art of foretelling the future in the lightning,* and, like Prometheus, he is proscribed and punished by the gods.†

This myth, like that of the Greeks, has already passed

---

* Divination by means of the lightning was an ancient practice which probably originated in the primitive notion that heard in the thunder the voice of the heavenly Power. As says the Psalmist (xxvii. 18), "The voice of thy thunder was in the whirlwind," "The voice of God breaks down the cedars." We have seen that the same belief was similarly expressed in the American Myths, notably that of guetzalcoatl. The Etruskans, as well as other ancient people, used the lightning to forecast future events.

† A. Sayce, "Hibbert Lectures," 1887, pp. 291-295; Chaldæan Genesis, p. 193, IV, pp. 23-1.

far beyond the primitive phase that is now occupying
us, but there is little doubt that these legends have each
been developed from indigenous local myths, the origins
of which belong to the inferior state of the Chaldæan
history.   One of the principal monuments, unfortunately much mutilated, which Mr. de Sarzec discovered
at Telloh, represents half an eagle with outstretched
wings, whose talons rest upon the back of a standing
lion.   It is evident that the kings of Telloh had made of
it the head-piece of their consecration tablet, and that
perhaps already at that epoch it represented, as has been
suggested by Mr. Léon Heuzey, "Victorious Royalty,"
that is, "the royal glory" of which, as we have seen, it
was the type later among the Persians of the Avesta,
and which with the development of Sun-worship in
Mesopotamia eventually was conventionalized into the
form of the winged sun-disk.

On the reverse side of the Stela of the Vultures (Telloh),
the eagle stands behind the head of a seated warlike
divinity.*   A Chaldæan cylinder, published by Mr. de
Sarzec,† shows us the eagle with stretched-out wings
carrying a human figure; by his side is the eight-rayed
star; below, two animals facing each other raise their
heads, and certain personages seem to invoke the eagle.
This is possibly an allusion to the Etana Myth.

The eagle is also associated with the god of Telloh,
Nin Ghirsu—the "god of shining light"—who is iden-
tified by Mr. Oppert with the Chaldæan Herakles
Ninip, on a cylinder of the de Sarzec collection.‡

* Léon Heuzey, "Description des Monuments de la Chaldée," p.
81; cf. with Mr. de Sarzec "Découvertes en Chaldée," pl. 4 B.

† De Sarzec, "Découvertes en Chaldée," pl. 30, bis fig. 13.

‡ P. 34. Léon Heuzey, loc. cit., pp. 41 and 91, also note by Heuzey
in de Sarzec's "Découvertes en Chaldée," p. 65.

The equivalent of the divine bird of the Akkads in
the Semitic Mythology of Mesopotamia is "Zu," whose
legend furnishes a frequent theme to the ancient en-
gravers,* who often represent episodes of his mishap
upon the cylinders.†

This variety of legendary types is evidently due to
local developments of the primeval myth and to the interchange of mythological lore that followed upon the
foundation of a national life.

The number of totemic eagles—double 'or single-
headed—that have been preserved to us by the art of
Western Asia is large.

One of the most interesting is that found upon a Hit-
tite monument at Euiku (Pteria), and reproduced by
Messrs. Perrot and Chipiez.‡ ' It is double-headed, and
stands like that of Telloh, but upon two hares instead of
a lion.

Mr. Goblet d' Alviella, in his work on the Migration
of Symbols,|| mentions a number of specimens found
upon ancient coins, ranging from the Mediterranean to
India where the bicephalic type seems to prevail.

We have seen that the belief in the Heaven-bird is
very wide-spread on the African Continent.   It is therefore not surprising to find it playing a conspicuous part

* Ménant, "Recherches sur la Glyptique Orientale; Cylindres de la
Chaldée," 1883, p. 42; p. 107, fig. 61; p. 109, fig. 63, etc.

† This bird is brought into mythological contact with the Sun by the
fact that the "divine bull," the "Bull of Light," which personifies
the Sun, is made the son of "Zu." (A. Sayce, "Hibbert Lectures,"
1887, p. 295.)

‡ Hre. de l'Art dans l'Anliq., IV, fig. 343.

|| La Migration des Symboles, p. 31, 1891.   Mr. d' Alviella correctly,
I think, traces this form to India through Persia from the older types
referred to.

in the faith of the ancient Egyptians. Indeed, with their characteristic conservatism, they at all times preserved to the primeval celestial bird a place in their religion and its symbolism. The animism of their forefathers, like that of other races, seems to have had for principal object in prehistoric times, the Power that ruled the Superior Space; and, like many others, they seem to have conceived it as embodied in the form of the high-flying hawk.* Although, at the opening of the historical period, the Egyptians had already reached a high stage of civilization, and although that Power, by a process common in mythology had already become confused with its chief manifestation, the Sun, with which it was almost identified, enough traces remain of the original conception to enable us to distinguish the primeval character of the elder Horos, the Heaven-god,† from the Solar Horos, in which latter form he typifies the rising sun. Not only does his name‡ mean the "Highest," the "Superior," but he is the brother of Osiris (the inferior space), and of Set (the earth-god, the determination of whose name is a stone). The four cardinal points are his forms, or his children, and he is

* "A hawk issued out of the Nun," (Heavenly Abyssus), Book of the Dead, lxxi, l. 1.
The texts are far too numerous even to select from in which the Hawk or Golden Hawk are mentioned. See lxxvii.

† Horos, "Avant de personnifier le Soleil levant, était la partie Supérieure de l'univers. Le firmament, le ciel, père des dieux, qui fut insensiblement transformé en dieu distinct vivant au ciel." (Maspero, "Rev. de l'Histoire des Relig.," 1889, Vol. xix, p. 5.)

‡ "Her" is the equivalent of the Greek γπερίων. (Le Page Renouf Proc. Bib. Arch., April, 1890.) "Her" was originally the part of the world situated above. The word means above, upon, superior, the most high.

frequently identified with "Shu," the "luminous air," who supports the heavenly vault, and "of whom the air was the soul."*

The antiquity of his worship in this form is shown not only by the fact that time out of mind was expressed by the Egyptians as "in the days of the followers of Horos," but by the immense proportion of his local forms in the Egyptian Pantheon. Even in later times, twenty-two out of the forty-nine nomes of Egypt worshiped Horos under some name or other, and this statement does not include doubtful forms.† Even Amen-Rê, whose following was next to that of Horos in point of numbers, was only worshiped in eight nomes. In early times, his hawk was the determinative used to indicate the divinity of the gods.‡

But the most important fact bearing upon this point, is that the early monumental kings, who were worshiped as the embodiment of the divine power, were termed the Horos ; and that, forever afterwards, whatever might be the personal predilection of a king for any other divine type in the pantheon—the frame enclosing the royal "Ka" name—that is, the name of the immortal. life which the royal person was supposed to derive directly from the god,—was surmounted by the crowned Hawk of Horos. It is only with the second reign of the IVth dynasty that the formula "Son of Rê" appears among the royal titles, and in the enumeration of titles, this was always placed after the older form and

---

* Brugsch, "Recueil de Monuments, etc., XXXIV, 4.

The four cardinal points, or the four winds, although their names change, are always the sons of Horos.

† J. de Rougé, Monnaies des Nomes, etc.

‡ See Pyramid Texts,·in "Recueil de Travaux pr. servir," etc., etc.

implied, as it were, a carnal descent from the Sun.   As
Mr. Maspero,* in a very suggestive treatise on the royal
titles has shown, the relative importance of these two
names is expressed in the thought that the king is the
"flesh of Rê," but that the *Spirit* of Horos is incarnate
in him.

It would therefore seem that Horos, whose primeval
rôle of Lord of the Upper Space is generally admitted,
and whose Spirit was supposed to be incarnate in the
Hawk, which in their graphic system stood as his ideogram, belongs to the pre-historic period of Egyptian
development.

In later times, when abstract speculation superseded
Sun-worship on the banks of the Nile, the original
character of Horos appears to have once more become
clear to the Egyptian mind, for his name is found written with the hieroglyph of the heavenly vault.†

In the Egyptian mythology Horos generally assumes
a warlike rôle.   He is represented as the Avenger, the
great Heavenly Striker, and it is perhaps worthy of remark that in the myths connected with the wrath of Rê,
and which belong to a period when sun-worship had
over-shadowed and, to a great extent, even absorbed
others, the Sun-god is not represented as striking himself, but always commissioning Horos or one of the
goddesses to strike for him.

Most of the Egyptian goddesses may broadly be said
to represent either luminous space or the activity of the
god with which they are associated.   And their common

* Études Égyptiennes, II, p. 276.   1890.

† Champollion, Notices publiées, p. 142–143.

Comp. Naville, Textes relatifs au Mythe d'Horus, and Lefébure Les
yeux d'Horus, Chap. VI, p. 95, etc.

attributes made it easy for the Egyptians to reduce them
to one type*—Sekhet, the "Striker"—Neith, who
"Shoots"—and "Hat-Hor,"† the mother of Horos, one
of whose designations is the "Mighty Striker, son of
Hat-Hor," and who, at Denderah, where she was especially worshipped as the "Only One," is expressly called
"Sekhet-Neith," are all called "Eye" of Rê.

This after all is but another way of expressing, in a
poetic metaphor, the idea symbolized in the winged sun
disk, especially in its Mesopotamian form, where the
god was represented in the center between the wings
and above the tail of the flying-disk, shooting his arrows
from his bow.   It is the warlike victorious strength of
the Heaven-spirit of old, now come to dwell in the sun,
and become what the Persians of the Avesta termed the
"Royal Glory." ‡

With the gradual development of the primitive
Egyptians into an agricultural people, and with the
coincident evolution of their primeval beliefs into a
religion in which the beneficent action of the sun was
glorified above all other, Horos, the primeval god of
the superior space, whose eye was the sun, came to be
regarded as dwelling in the sun,|| or as the sun itself,

* There are exceptions, such as Maat, who represented abstract
truth and justice, Safekh, etc., and in certain localities where the
goddess stood alone, like Neith at Saïs, she included all the attributes of divinity. But her place in the local Triad is as indicated above.

† Her name means the "House of Horos."

‡ This symbolism seems to have presented itself to the imagination
of other remote peoples; at least an Aztec prayer recorded by Sahagun
(Hist. Nueva España, lib. IV, cap. 4), and quoted by Dr. Brinton, Myths,
etc., p. 144, says that the ancient god, father or mother of all the gods,
is "the god of the fire who stands in the centre of the court with four
walls and who is covered with brilliant feathers like wings."

|| "I am he who resides in his eye. I come and I give truth to Rê,"

and the Hawk, in whose shape he was made visible to man, became more especially a solar-symbol. But although many were the solar types to which a hawk's head was given, the bird remained the special hieroglyph of Horos; for to the primeval Egyptians, as to other men in a primitive stage of culture, the Spirit of the Superior Space was incarnate in that bird. Once having taken up his abode in the sun, the Primeval Heaven-God seems to have retained his attributes. This is conspicuously brought forward in his local form of the Flying Sun-Disk of Edfu. In the Horos myth of this locality, where Rê orders Horos to strike his enemies, Horos flies to the sun as the great flying-disk and then strikes:* from that day forward he is known as the Horos of Edfu.

According to Mr. Lepage Renouf,[†] Behuted, the Egyptian name of the Flying Sun-disk, means "Seat." The form therefore would seem to be the Seat of Horos —the body in which he enters and dwells.

This myth is evidently not one of great antiquity (see Wiedemann, loc., p. 43), and it is not improbable that it was invented to account for the symbol.

says the B. of the D., XCVI, l. 1. That is the Heavenly Spirit manifested in the sun. According to many texts (for instance comp. Recueil de Trav., I, p. 121). "Hail to thee, O mighty lord, who raises the double feather. Thou art the lord of the numerous becomings (Kheperu), and of the appearances which hide him (the god) in the Solar-Eye (Utá) at his birth."—Pierret "Etudes Egyptolog., I, 66." Such expressions are common. The process is a common one. Compare with similar transitions among the American beliefs. For instance, in Oregon the Great Spirit inhabits the sun; when angry he issues forth and produces a storm. A Réville, "Relig. des Non-civilisés, I, p. 217.

* A. Wiedemann, "Religion des Alten Ægypter," p. 38, 1890.

† Proc. Soc. Biblical Arch., 1886, Vol. 8, p. 144.

Under the IVth dynasty the flying-hawk itself protects the victorious King Khufu.*

The winged sun-disk, as a symbol, makes its appearance for the first time on a monument of the Vth dynasty. Then it is a simple disk set between two wings slightly inclining downward. Under the VIth dynasty an inscription of Unas found at Elephantine by Mr. Flinders-Petrie,[†] shows us the Flying-disk conventionalized. The wings are straightened out and the sacred asps already have been added.

At Wadi-Magharah, Pepi I. appears protected on one side by the flying-hawk, on the other by the flying-disk, then evidently regarded as equivalent.[‡] (See accompanying illustration.)

Under the XIIth dynasty, like other forms of Egyptian art, the type became fixed, and other dual symbols were gradually added, such as the two ram's horns, etc.

Although the idea of the Heaven-bird belongs as we have seen to the dawn of mythology, and is quasi-universal among men in the stone-age of their evolution; it would seem somewhat perplexing to know how the flying sun-disk, as a symbolic object, originally suggested itself to the mind of the ancient artist, but we may perhaps furnish a clue to its pedigree.

Among the fine diorite statues of King Khafra which were found in the well of his sepulchral temple at Ghizeh, there is one which has not been so widely noticed as the more celebrated one, casts of which are in nearly all museums. It represents the monarch, the "living Horos," in the usual way ; but close behind his

* Lepsius, Denkmäler, III Bl., 2. c., Peninsula of Sinaï.

† Flinders-Petric. A Season in Egypt, 1887, p. 13, fig. 312.

‡ Denkmäler, IV Bl., 116.

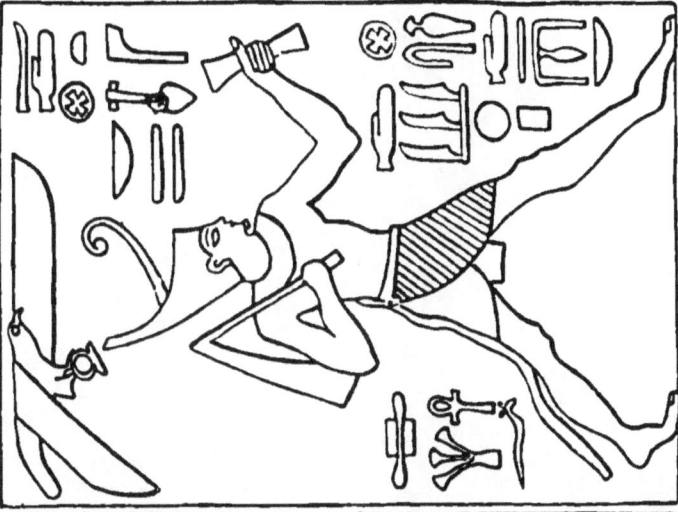

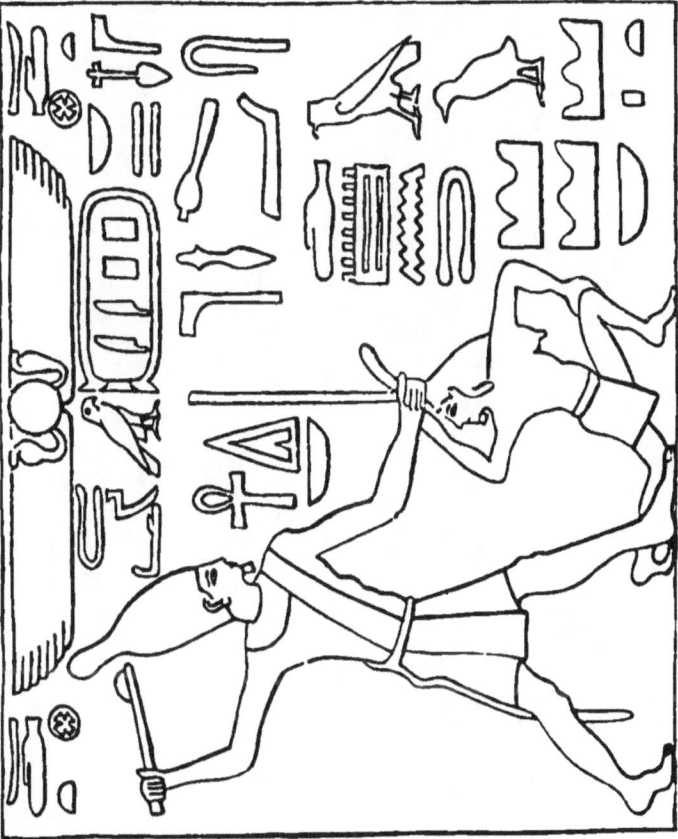

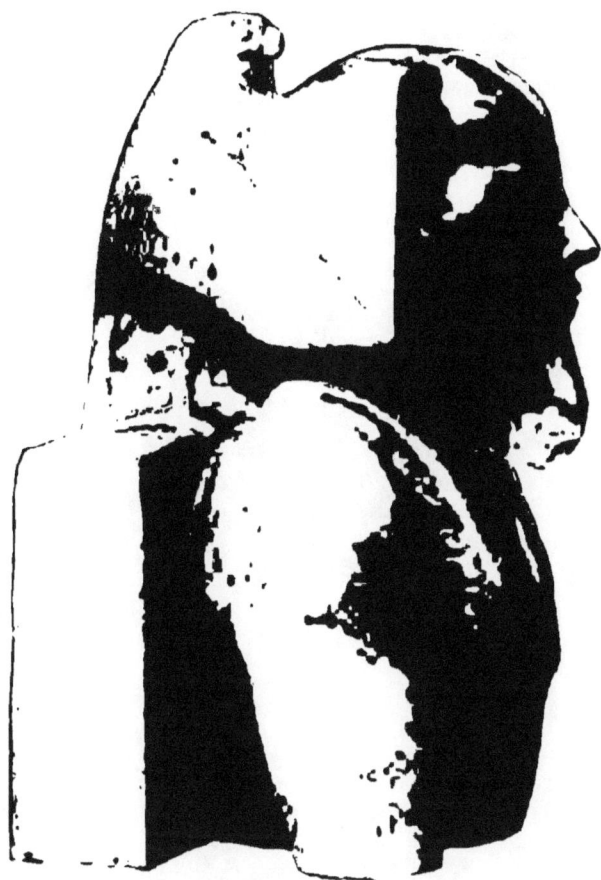

head stands the divine bird, enclosing it between its down-stretched wings. (See illustration.)

If we remember the peculiar ideas of the Egyptians concerning the seat of life and of vital heat in man, as indicated in their funeral ritual and customs, and the manner in which the life was called down into the mummy or into its substitute by means of the imposition of hands by the priest at the back of the head;* if we call to mind the way in which an idol, once animated by similar esoteric means, could communicate its "life" to another statue by touching it on the back of the head,† it will not be difficult to understand the intention of the artist or of those who ordered this statue. The god, or its incarnation, the Hawk, is in the very act of imparting his essence, his life, his divinity, to his living self upon earth—the King.‡

It is worthy of remark that Khafra is the king who for the first time added to the claim made by his predecessors to be the "living Horos," that of being "Son of Rê" the Sun-God.   He was obviously a devoted sun-worshiper; and it is to his reign that the Egyptians of the New Empire attributed the great Sphinx of Ghizeh, which represents Har-em-Khu (Horos-on-the-Horizon), the Horos of Heliopolis.   .

From these indications, it would seem as though Sun-worship proper had received great encouragement under his reign.   We have seen that an example of the flying sun-disk has been preserved to us, which dates from the

* Maspero, "Rituel du Sacrifice funéraire," 1887.

† E. de Rougé, Étude sur une Stèle de la Bibliothèque Nationale, p. 111–136.

‡ Compare above the representation of the Alaska Crow in his role of Creator, p. 214.

following dynasty—how much earlier than the reign of Ra-en-user the symbol was evolved is, of course, not known; but those who conceived and executed the statue of Khafra, evidently pointed the way to the artist who first represented the sun-disk set between the wings of the Divine-bird.   At least the same train of thought, the same symbolism, inspired both.

The idea of incubation, practiced by the gods as a life-imparting process, is a very common one in Egyptian myth; and it is constantly and clearly expressed in art, as well as in the religious literature of all periods, by the divinity or its symbol spreading out its wings over the body to be animated.

Isis and Nephthys are repeatedly called the two "Setters" or incubators;* and these goddesses spread their wings over the mummy to impart new life into it.   The mother-goddess, in the shape of a vulture, spreads her wings, and a text† makes her say: "I cover thy couch and give life to the back of thy neck."   This process of incubation is often expressly connected with the idea of heat.   The mother of the Sun-god, for instance, in a text,‡ is said at the moment of the birth of the god, to bring her own life "to the back of his neck in flame;" and in another it is said, "I light in you a spark to create (or produce) life in you."‖

A disk-amulet inscribed with magic devices was in later times placed under the head of the mummy to preserve this vital heat; and a chapter of the Book of the

---

* Book of the Dead, ch. XX, p. 6.   Pyr^d de Teti, "Rec. de Travaux," V, p. 32, p. 257 and p. 260.   The expression is used in many texts.

† Lepsius, Denkmäler, IV, 46.

‡ Lepsius, Denkmäler, IV, p. 11.

‖ De Rougé.   Etude sur une Stèle de la Bibliothèque National, p. 117.

Dead* gives the formula for "placing heat under the head of the defunct."

The idea of heat or fire as the source of life is widespread. The Egyptians conceived the Intellect (or Khut) as a divine spark clothed in the soul or Ba. This belief was shared by the Alexandrians who, according to the Hermes Trismegistus,† regarded this ligneous element as capable of resuming, "at death, its garment of flame which it could not wear upon earth."

But to return. It therefore seems probable that the artist or the priest who conceived the symbolism of this statue laid the egg from which the winged-disk was afterwards evolved. From the representation of the king, the son of the Sun, with his head held between the wings of the Divine Hawk—the primeval incarnation of strength, of life and of power, which thus were communicated to him,—to the same device applied to the sun disk which many texts call "the body" in which the soul dwells, and which is, therefore,—like the king himself,—but another embodiment of the great Heavenly Power, there was for the symbol-maker but a step which, as we have seen, was soon afterwards taken.

The winged-disk was the emblem of the Heavenly Power conceived in primeval times as a bird, and which, under the form of its embodiment, the hawk, had come to dwell in the sun. Of somewhat rare occurrence under the old Empire, when it appears only on royal commem-

* Ch. CLXII.

† Ed. Ménard, pp. 65–67. According to Heraklitus eternal fire was not only one of the four elements; it was the primordial essence, source of all things and superior to the gods. And as he says that the "lightning governs the world," it is evident that he means celestial fire as representing the vital principle. Comp. Max Müller, Physical Religion, 245-6.

orative inscriptions, its importance as a symbol increased
so much that from the XVIIIth dynasty it was set over the
entrance of monuments, which it was supposed to guard
and to protect.   It played in Egypt the rôle which the
great winged Bulls of the Assyrians played upon the
banks of the Euphrates.

It is likely that it is to the same order of ideas and to
a local variante of the same primitive myth that the
vulture, which typified Upper Egypt and was worshiped
at El-Kab, on its southern border, under the name of
Nekheb, owed its place in the Pantheon.

This was the embodiment of motherhood as well as its
hieroglyph in the graphic system.   The mother-goddess
of Thebes, Mut, wore it upon her head as a head dress,
and the Queens of Egypt adopted it as an insignium of
their royalty.*

That the notion which in primitive times lurked at
the base of the vulture symbolism of Upper Egypt was
similar in its general bearings to that of the Hawk symbolism of Horos, is indicated by many texts.   The goddess Nekheb is called, as are other goddesses, the "eye
of Rê."   She is a "light" goddess, and the eye of Horos
is likened unto "the light which appears in El-Kab."†

Nekheb sits upon the head of the gods,‡ and her vul-

---

* In this connection it is interesting to find the maternal relation of
the goddesses determined in the Egyptian graphic system by an egg.

† Comp. Rec. de Travaux, I, 112–131 : "Les deux yeux du disque
solaire," by Mr. Grébaut, who has collected many passages which
bring the attributes of Horos and of Nekheb in close relation.   The
two uræi added to the Flying Sun-Disk of Edfu represent Nekheb and
Uati, which stand for Upper and Lower Egypt, or for the Northern and
Southern Divisions of the Heavens.

‡ Mariette, Abydos, I, 43.   Nekheb appears in the text of the Pyr.
of Teti, I, 359, as wearing the white crown with the two feathers.

ture, soaring in space, replaces the solar "Eye," which
she personifies. Above an inscription * may be seen the
"ut'a" or "eye," which here is the equivalent of the
sun-disk, represented with the wings, the feet and the
head of the vulture.†

The texts are innumerable that speak of the god as
hidden in the disk, whilst a winged goddess makes light
with her feathers or with her wings.‡ The Solar-Eye is
constantly made the equivalent of the feathers,‖ and the
disk is frequently alluded to as the egg.¶ Even Rê is
spoken of§ as "in his egg which shines in his disk."
Other birds seem to be brought into relation with the
same symbolism ; for instance, in the text of the Pyramid of Teti ** the wing of Thoth is referred to as the
vehicle of the eye of Horos in its journey towards the
east of the Heavenly Abyssus. The goose, the swallow,
etc., as the embodiments of certain deities play rôles,
similar to those of the hawk, the vulture or the ibis.
This confusion is no doubt due to local cults at a time
preceding the political consolidation of the Empire, and
the tendency to mythological syncretism that followed
upon that event.

The feather and the wing in Egyptian myths are al-

* Denkmäler, III, 25–1; see also "Papyrus de Luynes," in Rec. de
Travaux, I, Plate. at the end of Fascicule 3.

† Hymne de la Bibliothèque Nationale, l. 5.

‡ Hymne de la Bibliothèque Nationale, l. 15.

‖ For instance (Ch. XVII, Book of the Dead, l. 14), and here the
feathers are made the equivalents of the goddesses Isis and Nephthys,
who give life by incubation.

§ As in Ch. XXII of the B. of the D., also Ch. XLII, l. 13.

¶ B. of D., XVII, l. 50.

** Recueil de Travaux, V, p. 22, l. 187–189.

ways and everywhere associated with the notion of heat and of light, and form endlessly varied themes. Not only are the goddesses, as we have seen, spoken of as making light with their feathers or with their wings, but "Shu," the god of the luminous air, who supports the heavenly vault, bears a feather upon his head, and "rising, he irradiates light with his double feather." * "Thou receivest thy double feather, thy double light," says a text.† "The sun, mighty king, divides the heaven with his two feathers," says another.‡

As already remarked, this feather of light, at the dawn of the monumental history, had already given birth to an abstract conception and was worn by Maat, the goddess of truth and justice, of which it was the symbol. In this connection, of course, the feather represented moral light, and in this the primeval idea had now reached its highest possible development.

It would be absolutely impossible to understand how a feather ever could have become the embodiment of Light and Life, of Power, Truth and Justice, unless we knew the part played by the Heaven-Bird in the beliefs of primeval days.

This inquiry is only interesting because it illustrates how, in the course of millenniums, a gradual uninterrupted development of the human intellect will, under favorable circumstances, from the crudest and most concrete beliefs common to primitive humanity, produce among certain nations the highest metaphysical conceptions, whilst other less-favored races remain stationary or perhaps even descend from the original starting-point.

* Hymne à Osiris de la Bibliothèque Nationale, 1. 12.

† Mariette, Abydos, I, p. 58.

‡ Pierret, Etudes Egyptologiques, II, 3.

One fact stands out plainly from the above study: that is, that one should be cautious in drawing conclusions as to ethnic affinities, or even contact and influence, from any similarity in the methods used by various races to express ideas that seem more or less common to mankind.

Beginning with our non-civilized contemporaries in all parts of the world, we have traced one primeval idea through nations of more or less rapid growth, and through those whose national existence was more or less prolonged. We have followed the thread through the labyrinth of time and of human evolution, through the Chinese, the Indo-Germanic races, the Iranians, the Romans, the Greeks, the Vedic Hindus, the Babylonians, etc., until we reached Egypt where, upon the very confines of the prehistoric, we found ourselves in the presence of a mode of expressing the divine relation to man, similar to that which on starting our inquiry, we saw in use to-day in Alaska. Who will contend that, between the tribes of the North Western coast of America in the 19th century A. D., and the Egyptian subjects of King Khafra in the IVth mill. B. C., any closer connection exists than that of a common humanity?

THE BOOK OF ECCLESIASTES.

BY PAUL HAUPT.

SCHOPENHAUER says that a man cannot fully appreciate the second verse of Ecclesiastes until he has reached the age of seventy.[1] If this remark of the great philosopher be true, it would seem as if the days of the years of all the commentators—whose number is legion—fell below the three-score years and ten, and that the rest of this strange, though fascinating book is as difficult to comprehend as the beginning.

The book is marked by an exceptional originality : it is unique in the whole range of Biblical literature. RENAN spoke of it as the only charming book that was ever written by a Jew. HEINRICH HEINE called it the *Canticles of Skepticism*, while FRANZ DELITZSCH thought it was entitled to the name of the *Canticles of the Fear of God.* Others say it appears to be the production of a melancholy misanthropist, the work of a patriarch of agnosticism ; we seem to hear the language of an Epicurean sensualist, and the disputations of a wavering skeptic. The first four chapters have been termed the *catechism of pessimism*, and HARTMANN styles the book the *breviary of modern materialism.*

From the earliest times down to the present age, Ecclesiastes has attracted the attention of thinkers. It was a favorite book of Frederick the Great, who referred to it as a *Mirror of Princes.* But Biblical students of all ages have experienced some difficulties about this remarkable production. Some in the Jewish Church denied the canonicity of the book : we read, the "wise men tried to hide (*ligènòz*) the book," *i. e.*, sought to declare it apocryphal. They said, the book ought to be regarded as inferior to the other books of the canon, being written not under the guidance of a higher than human inspiration, but as the outcome of Solomon's natural wisdom. So the Bishop Theodore of Mopsuestia († 428 A. D.) said : "*Salomonem proberbia sua et Ecclesiasten ex sua saltem persona ad aliarum utilitatem composuisse, non ex prophetiae accepta gratia, sed saltem prudentia humana.*"

In the first century after Christ the book was still an *Antilegomenon*, until the synod of Jabne, or Jamnia, (90 A. D.) decided in favor of the canonicity of the book. The rival schools of SHAMMAI and HILLEL were divided on the subject. ·The school of SHAMMAI objected to several passages which, apparently, were not only at variance with statements in the Mosaic law, and "David's'" teachings in certain psalms, but seemed also to contradict one another. They pointed out *e. g.*, that Ecclesiastes in **4**, 2, praises the dead more than the living, while he says in **9**, 4 : *Verily³ a living dog is better than a dead lion.*⁴ They called attention to the fact that we read in Eccl. **11**, 9 : *Walk in the ways of thy heart, and in the sight of thine eyes,* while we are taught in Num. **15**, 39 : *Seek not after your own heart and your own eyes.* They found in the book an alarming recommendation of sensual pleasures. HILLEL and his disciples, on the other hand, laid stress on the exhortation as contained in **5**, 6, and **12**, 13 : *Fear God and keep his commandments.* A careful examination, however, will reveal the fact that these and similar passages are later interpolations. One-half of the book consists of subsequent additions,[5] and it is solely on account of these secondary interpolations (which are on a par with the Deuteronomistic expansions in Judges and Kings) that Ecclesiastes has been admitted to the Canon. The genuine portions are out of place in it: they are anti-Biblical, though by no means irreligious or immoral. Their author is not a theologian, but a man of the world, probably a physician,[60] with keen observation, vast experience, and penetrating insight. A New Testament believer, however, could not have written Ecclesiastes or the Book of Job.

Both works must have stirred up a sensation when they first made their appearance: they must have had an effect somewhat like Count TOLSTOI's *Kreutzer-Sonata*, and it required no Jewish WANAMAKER[42] to advertise them. RENAN says: "Ecclesiastes, as well as the Song of Solomon, are a few profane pages which, by some curious accident, have found their way into that strange and admirable volume termed the Bible. The Jewish doctors understood neither the one nor the other, otherwise they would not have admitted such compositions to the collection of sacred writings. It was their stupidity that made them able to make out of a dialogue of lovers a book of edification, and out of a skeptical book a treatise of sacred philosophy. Solomon's Song and Ecclesiastes are just like a love ditty and a little essay of VOLTAIRE which have gone astray among the folios of a theological library."

I cannot agree with the famous French critic in this respect: I believe the theological contemporaries of Ecclesiastes were by no means too stupid to grasp the import of his anti-Biblical statements, but, as they were

unable to suppress the book,[6] they endeavored to darken
its real meaning for dogmatic purposes, saying, as GEO.
HOFFMANN[7] puts it in his striking translation of Job recently published : " Let us save the attractive book for
the congregation, but we will pour some water in the
author's strong wine."

As GRAETZ observes, a dislike seems to have prevailed
against the book in the Christian Church as well as in
the Jewish Synagogue. It is characteristic that Ecclesiastes is never cited in the New Testament, or in the
early Fathers. Some exegetes, to be sure, have pointed
out a number of passages which they say are based on
the book of the Old Testament philosopher, but it is
difficult to see any connection between the passages referred to.[8] There is a chapter in the Gospels, however,
which is evidently directed against Ecclesiastes, and it
is remarkable that the fact has never been noted.[9]

The chief maxim of Ecclesiastes is : *There is nothing
better than to eat and drink and be merry.* We find this
Epicurean teaching repeated five times (**2**, 24; **3**, 12,
22; **5**, 17; **8**, 15), and the *rejoice* of Ecclesiastes is different from the χαίρετε of Philippians. Now we read in Luke
12, 15–31,[10] a passage which contains several allusions to
the book of Ecclesiastes :[11] The ground of a certain rich
man brought forth plentifully. And he said, I will
pull down my barns and build greater. And I will say
to my soul : Soul, thou hast much goods laid up for many
years, ἀναπαίου, φάγε, πίε, εὐφραίνου,[12] take thine ease, eat, drink
and be merry. But God said unto him : Thou fool, this
night thy soul shall be required of thee. Seek ye first
the kingdom of God and his righteousness. Take no
thought for the morrow. Sufficient unto the day is the
evil thereof,[13] ἀρκετὸν τῇ ἡμέρα ἡ κακία αὐτῆς—κακία, *i. e.*, κακότης, or
as CHRYSOSTOM explains it : ταλαιπωρία.

There can be no stronger condemnation of the teachings of Ecclesiastes than these words of our Saviour; and it seems to me, this ought to settle the question whether Ecclesiastes has any claims to canonical authority.

The old dispensation digs its own grave in the book of Ecclesiastes. The Old Testament philosopher says: nothing is lasting, it is all transitoriness, the world alone abideth for ever. In the New Testament, on the other hand, we read (1 John **2**, 17): *The world passeth away and the lust thereof, but he that doeth the will of God abideth for ever;* and in 1 Cor. **13**, 13 : *Faith, hope, love abideth, and the greatest of these is love.*

It would be rash, however, to draw the conclusion that the New Testament was optimistic and the Old Testament pessimistic. SCHOPENHAUER[14] is right in saying that on the whole the spirit of the old dispensation is optimistic, and the spirit of the New Testament pessimistic—*i. e.*, of course, so far as this world is concerned, the πάντα καλὰ λίαν, *behold it was very good*, finds no echo in the New Testament. Righteousness is the ethical ideal of the old dispensation, love one another the καινὴ ἐντολὴ "the new commandment," in which are comprehended all Christian virtues.

Some people consider the appearance of the pessimistic school of philosophy as one of the saddest phenomena of the present age : they regard pessimism as the outcome of atheism leading to the denial of the existence of the Eternal ; they believe that the conclusions of the advocates of this philosophy are destructive not only of faith, but also of morality. We must remember, however, that we are told in the New Testament to overcome the world, to hate our life in this world, and the things that are in the world. Pessimism—*cum grano salis*—may be found among men not only outwardly reckoned as faithful, but really believers.

While SCHOPENHAUER is right in saying that the atmosphere of the old dispensation is anti-pessimistic, it is undoubtedly true that certain portions of Hebrew literature are decidedly not optimistic.[15] We read in *Bĕresh-îth rabbâ*, c. 9; that in the copy of Rabbi Meir the words *wĕhinnêh ṭôb mĕódh*, "behold it was very good," were altered into *wĕhinnêh ṭôbh môth*, "behold it was good to die," and in another passage we are told : *ṭôbh mĕódh zĕh mal'akh hammâwĕth = ṭôbh mĕódh* ("very good "), that is the angel of death.[16]

The most striking pessimistic *pendant* to Ecclesiastes is the great didactic poem known as the Book of Job. The chief subject of this remarkable composition (probably written about the time of Darius Hystaspis, B. C. 521–485) seems to be : The sufferings of man are greater than his sins; and why is it that so many villains are never punished? Wherefore do the wicked prosper, become old, yea are mighty in power? They die in their full strength, being wholly at ease and quiet, and the righteous passes away in the bitterness of his soul, having never tasted happiness. Man is born unto trouble. Our days are vanity, our life wind, our days upon earth are as a shadow ; we are but of yesterday, and know nothing. Man that is born of a woman is of few days and full of trouble; he cometh forth like a flower and is cut down ; he fleeth as a shadow and continueth not. Wherefore are we brought forth out of the womb? Why are we not carried from the womb to the grave though he that goeth down to the grave shall come up no more?[17]

So Ecclesiastes says: The righteous perish in spite of their righteousness, and the wicked prolong their life in spite of their wickedness. The wicked are buried in the place of the holy, and they that have done right must make room and are forgotten. The race belongs not to the swift, nor the battle to the heroes; everything depends on time and chance. Like fishes caught in the death-dealing net, like birds entrapped in the snare, so are the sons of men ensnared at the evil hour that falls upon them suddenly. Perhaps it has been thus arranged to show men that they, *ipsissimi*, are beasts. Certainly the same fate happens to man and beast, there is no superiority of man over the beast. All is transitoriness. Who can tell whether the spirit of the sons of men ascends upwards, and the spirit of the beasts descends downwards? Nevertheless I praise the dead more than the living, and better off are those who were never born, because they do not see the sufferings of this world. What is the use of living and raising children born to suffer? If a man beget a hundred and live a great many years, yea however numerous may be the days of his years, even if no grave waited for him— if his soul should not drink in happiness to the full, I say: better is an untimely birth!"[h]

It is not wonderful that the canonicity of the book was seriously contested. But while objections were brought against the inspired character of the work, no doubts were raised as to the Solomonic authorship of the book. Up to the period of the Reformation, Ecclesiastes was always regarded as a work of the great king of Israel. LUTHER was the first who ventured to deny the truth of the traditional view. He considered Ecclesiastes one of the latest books of the O. T., and thought it more probable that it was written by Ben Sira than by Solomon.   He remarked in his *Table Talk*, the book seemed to him to have been compiled like a Talmud from a number of books," perhaps from the library of King Ptolemy Euergetes in Egypt (*c.* B. C. 170). LUTHER's later opinion was that the book contained a collection of Solomonic sayings, but not compiled by Solomon.

A similar view was advanced by RENAN in his well-known work on the History of the Semitic Languages. He thought it impossible that a work of such daring skepticism should have originated during the post-exilic period of Judaism.   His argument is not formidable, but it is just as questionable to consider the pessimistic attitude of the book as evidence of a late period.   Pessimism is perhaps as old as mankind.

There is an old clay tablet published in the second volume of Sir HENRY RAWLINSON's *Cuneiform Inscriptions of Western Asia*, which may be called the oldest known specimen of *mashal*-poetry, *i. e.*, didactic poetry as represented by the Book of Proverbs, Ecclesiastes, and Ecclesiasticus.   This cuneiform text contains a remarkable passage which has been entirely misunderstood heretofore.[20]   SAYCE translates it in the eleventh volume of the *Records of the Past* (London, 1878), p. 155:

To the waters their god[21]
has returned :
to the house of bright things
he descended (as) an icicle :
(on) a seat of snow[22]
he grew not old in wisdom
. . . .[23]

The real meaning of the lines is: "When their God had turned away, misery[24] invaded the dwelling places. The wicked established himself,[25] but the righteous[26] waxed not old."[27] The religious and devout whose devotion his Lord disregarded,[28] and everything noble which his Lord forsook, their want set in, and their suffering[29] was heightened."

The pessimistic tendency of Ecclesiastes is no criterion for the date of the book. RENAN seems to have perceived the weakness of his argument, for in his essay on Ecclesiastes published in 1882, he abandoned his former view, and advanced the theory that the book was written about the time of John Hyrcanus (B. C. 135–106).

There is scarcely a scholar of eminence now who ventures to defend the Solomonic authorship. The most conservative critics believe that the book cannot have been written before the time of Ezra and Nehemiah (c. 450 B. C.). EWALD thought it was composed about the end of the Persian period (B. C. 331), HITZIG and NÖLDEKE during the Greek dominion, while GRAETZ tried to prove that the work was directed against Herod the Great, so that Ecclesiastes would have been a contemporary of Horace. This date is probably approximately correct. While I do not believe that the book is aimed at Herod, I am inclined to think that Ecclesiastes represents the latest book of the Old Testament, later even than the books of Daniel and Esther, a view which is shared by so conservative a scholar as Professor EDWARD KÖNIG, of Rostock (see his *Einleitung*, § 80). C. H. H. WRIGHT'S[30] statement that satisfactory evidence was afforded of the existence of the Book of Ecclesiastes at least two, if not three

centuries before the Christian era is untenable.   We are
told that the two apocryphal books of Ecclesiasticus and
the Wisdom of Solomon which were written, at the
latest, about B. C. 180 and 150 respectively, presuppose
the Book of Ecclesiastes.   It is true that the Wisdom of
Solomon seems to have been designed as an Anti-Eccle-
siastes.   Of course, that is conclusive only so far as the
genuine portions of Ecclesiastes alluded to in the Book
of Wisdom are concerned; the theological interpolations
in Ecclesiastes may be considerably later, and perhaps
partly based on the Book of Wisdom.   But it can not
be proved that the Book of Wisdom was written, at the
latest, about 150 B. C.   It may be considerably later
(see KÖNIG, *Einleit.*, § 107).   TYLER made an attempt
to prove that the author of Ecclesiastes was acquainted
with the writings of post-Aristotelian philosophers.   It is
evident that the work cannot have originated before the
Ptolemaic-Seleucidan era, but I fail to discover any real
trace of Greek influence.   The alleged Grecisms first
discovered by Canon ZIRKEL, of Würzburg (in 1792),
and recently defended by GRAETZ, are imaginary."

   To determine the exact date seems to me impossible.
There are several passages which appear to allude to
some particular historical event, but the facts related do
not agree with any well-known incidents in history."
Nor is this wonderful if we bear in mind that Jewish
history since the death of Nehemiah (about B. C. 415)
down to the accession of Antiochus Epiphanes (about
B. C. 175) is almost a complete blank.   The annals,
too, of the Persian Empire are very deficient from the
death of Xerxes (in 465) down to the appearance of Alexander the Great on the stage of history.

   The only sure criterion is the language.   The linguistic features of the book are incompatible with the traditional view of the Solomonic authorship. The idiom approximates in some respect to that of the Mishna, and is decidedly not Solomonic: it teems with Aramaisms. There are nearly a hundred words and forms characteristic of an era of the Hebrew language far later than Solomon[33]—a fact which was first pointed out by the famous Dutch scholar, HUGO GROTIUS,[34] in 1644. It is true that the book has undergone several changes, some words and passages may have been altered, and considerable interpolations[35] have been introduced into the original work, but if the genuine portions were Solomonic there would be no history of the Hebrew language.

Advocates of the traditional view have made various attempts to account for the Aramaisms. The Vienna theologian, ED. BÖHL,[36] thought that Solomon used the Aramaic language, so uncommon at his time, in order to show his erudition! An English divine believes that the great king tried to accommodate and approximate the style of the book to the dialect of the Eastern peoples under his sway. The book was a great *missionary manifesto* to the heathen inhabitants of these lands! Such naive ignorance can only do harm to the cause it endeavors to help. The Aramaisms in Ecclesiastes, just as in the Book of Job, are simply due to the late date of the book.

Most critics believe that the author of Ecclesiastes assumed the name of Solomon and stepped forward in this character, in the same way as the author of the Book of Job introduces into his magnificent dialogue that patriarch and his friends as speakers, or as Cicero in his treatise *De senectute* selects Cato Major as the exponent

of his views, or as Plato brings forward Socrates. This
would be, of course, a perfectly allowable literary device,
and not a *pia fraus*." It has always been considered
entirely justifiable for an author to portray the feelings
and sentiments of distinguished persons on remarkable
occasions. The references and allusions to Solomon,
however, in the Book of Ecclesiastes are so scanty that
it is hard to believe the original author meant to assume
the mask of the famous king of Israel. Nor does the
author of the epilogue " appear to know anything of
this assumption. After the second chapter there is no
allusion to Solomon whatever, so it is most likely that
the distinguished Catholic theologian, Professor GUS-
TAV BICKELL, of Vienna, is right in believing that the
superscription : *Words of Ecclesiastes who was a son of
David and king in Jerusalem*, as well as the few allusions to the great king, represent subsequent additions.

Just as the post-exilic psalms written by unknown
writers were ascribed to David, who was ever regarded
as the religious poet of the nation, so Solomon was
looked upon as the impersonation of wisdom, the representative of the largest practical experience and highest
intellectual knowledge. Most maxims and proverbs,
therefore, were attributed to him. But the legends concerning Solomon's wisdom and writings in 1 K. **3. 5.
10**, occur in late sections of the book and are probably
devoid of any real historical truth. It cannot be proved
that we have anything written by Solomon, nor is it
certain that there is a song of David in the Psalter."
The Psalter is a product of post-exilic Judaism; several
of its songs belong to the Maccabean " period (after the
death of Antiochus Epiphanes, B. C. 163).

I do not believe that to deviate as widely as possible

from tradition constitutes the chief criterion of an un-
prejudiced philologian, but it must be owned that no one
is less entitled to the halo which tradition has woven
around him than Solomon (*c.* B. C. 950).   He was nothing more than a ruler of the average Oriental type.[1]
His people groaned under heavy taxes and bond service.
He levied 30,000 men every year, and sent them to
Mount Hebron to break stones and cut trees.   He had
70,000 that bare burdens, and 80,000 hewers in the
mountains.   He loved many strange women, had 700
wives and 300 concubines.   He went after Ashtoreth,
the goddess of the Sidonians, and after Milcom, the
abomination of the Ammonites ; he built a high place
to Chemosh, the abomination of Moab, in the hill that
is east of Jerusalem, and burnt incense and sacrificed
unto the gods of his strange wives.   His yoke was
grievous and his burden heavy.   It was not wonderful
that the people came to Rehoboam (*c.* B. C. 925) saying :
Make the yoke which thy father put upon us lighter !
The actual Solomon of history was no philosopher, still
less was he the author of a pessimistic treatise like the
· Book of Ecclesiastes.

There is no author of the Book of Ecclesiastes, at any
rate not of the book in the form in which it has come
down to us.   If the book in its present shape should
have been written by one author, he must have been a
duplex personality of the HYDE-JEKYLL[2] type.   But the
book we have is not intact.   It reminds me of the remains of a daring explorer who has met with some terrible accident, leaving his shattered form exposed to the
encroachments of all sorts of foul vermin.   It is a mistake to suppose that the hypertrophic portions are the
work of one interpolator.   In some cases there are half

a dozen parallel strata of glosses." And not satisfied
with the obscuration of the original book, the theological revisers tried to cut up and dislocate the text as
much as possible, destroying the order and logical sequence. This accounts for the phenomenon, acknowledged by all commentators, that in the present form of
the book there is no proper arrangement, no intimate
connection between the individual verses : it seems like
a conglomeration of *disjecta membra*, or, as GRAETZ remarks, like hieroglyphics or cuneiform characters where
some words or clauses are intelligible, but the whole
without any sense whatever. I protest, of course, on
behalf of Assyriology, against this unfair comparison.

The fact that dislocations had taken place was first
recognized by J. G. VAN DER PALM" in 1784". Professor
BICKELL published a little book," in 1884, in which he
endeavored to show that the confusion was merely due to
a mistake of a book binder, who misplaced the quires"
of the manuscript, but the demonstration of the learned
Catholic critic is not convincing. The disarrangement
was certainly not accidental, but intentional. GRAETZ
tried to explain the hopelessly obscure character of the
book on the theory that the author did not dare to speak
freely ; that, as HENGSTENBERG conjectured, it was
dangerous for the author to give vent to his feelings.

The fact that there are two entirely different elements
in the book, is indirectly recognized by the exegetes, who
believe the work to be dialogical. DÖDERLEIN and
NACHTIGALL thought the book contained a dialogue
with questions and answers. HERDER and EICHHORN
found in it a disputation between student and teacher ;
HENGSTENBERG believed he heard the voice of the spirit
in opposition to the voice of the flesh. Some passages

have often been explained as ironical. SCHENKEL, in his *Bible Lexicon*, says we hear two voices, the voice of true wisdom (*hassékel*) and the voice of ψευδοσοφία (*haddimyôn*). SIEGFRIED sees in it a controversy between philosophy (*hokhmâ*) and religion (*yir'áth elohîm*). The English Hebraist TYLER believes that Stoicism and Epicurean maxims are contrasted in order to show that all philosophy is useless, and to inculcate the fear of God.

It will perhaps be never possible to find out how the present disarrangement took place, but I quite agree with GEO. HOFFMANN,[48] who, speaking of the Book of Job, says : "Any conjectures as to the course which the thoughts of the destroyer may have followed, are less important than the fact than the sons of twilight were unable to bear the clearness of the great author, and to hand it down in its pure form."

Many interesting questions present themselves which I cannot discuss here. Nor will time permit me to give a survey of the whole book restored in its original order and freed from the glosses that have clustered about it. I will confine myself to translation of the final section of the book, restored by combining 9, 7–10 ; 11, 1–3 ; 10, 8–11 ; 11, 4. 6. 9ᵃ. 10 ; 12, 1–5ᵃ. 6. 5ᵇ ; 11, 8ᶜ.

After having shown that everything is ceaselessly going on the same rounds, that there is nothing new under the sun, and nothing lasting, nothing that gives real satisfaction, neither wealth, nor knowledge, nor sensual pleasure ; that there is competition and oppression everywhere, and no justice ; that it is better not to be born, and that the best a man can do is to eat, drink and be merry, and try to enjoy his work—Ecclesiastes closes with the following apostrophe :

The Closing Section of Ecclesiastes."

9, 7 Come, eat thy bread with joy,
 And drink thy wine with a merry heart;
 For God hath long ago approved of (all) thy doings.⁵⁰

8 Let thy garments be always white,
 And let oil not be lacking upon thy head.   5

9 Enjoy life with a woman whom thou lovest*ᵃ*
 All the days of thy fleeting life;
 For this is thy share in life,
 And in the toil, wherein thou toilest under the sun.⁵¹

10 But whatsoever thy hand findeth to do within thy
 power—do it!   10
 For there is no work, nor planning, nor knowledge,
 nor experience
 In Sheol, whither thou art going.*ᵝ*

11, 1 Send forth thy bread-corn over the waters,
 Though many days may pass, thou wilt recover it.

2 But give a share to seven (ships), or even to eight, 15
 For thou knowest not what evil may happen upon
 the earth.⁵²

3 If the clouds are full of rain,
 They empty themselves upon the earth;
 And if a tree falleth in the south, or in the north,
 In the place where the tree falleth, there it will be.⁵³ 20

9, 9 (*a*) all the days of thy fleeting life which he hath given thee
under the sun.

* *
*

4 (*ᵝ*) because for him who is associated with all the living there
is some prospect, for indeed "a living dog is better than a
5 dead lion." Though the living know that they must die,
the dead do not know anything, and they have no more any
reward, except that the memory of them is forgotten—their
love as well as their hatred and their rivalry is passed long
ago, and for ever they have no longer any share in anything
that is done under the sun.

10, 8 He that diggeth a pit, may fall into it,
And whoso breaketh down a wall, a serpent may bite
him.

9 Whoso quarrieth stones may be hurt therewith,
And he that heweth trees may cut[54] himself thereby.

10 But if the iron be blunt,[γ] he must put forth more
strength,[55]   25

11 And if the serpent biteth before enchantment,
The charmer is of no use.[56]

11, 4 He that watcheth the wind will never sow,
And he that observeth the clouds will never reap.[δ]

6 In the morning sow thy seed,   .   30
And in the evening let thy hand not rest,[57]
For thou knowest not whether will thrive,
Either this or that, or whether both together will be
good.[58]

10, 10 (γ) that means : if he hath not sharpened the edge.

**

8, 8 (δ) there is no man that hath power over the wind (*to check the
wind*), neither hath he any power over the day of death; just as
there is no quarter in war, ‖ *nor will wickedness deliver those*

11, 5 *that are given to it* ‖. Just as little as thou knowest what will
be the course of the wind, or the bones in the womb of her that
is with child, so thou doest not know the doings of God that
doeth all this.

Now the finale of Ecclesiastes' pessimistic symphony
sets in : the Epicurean motive *Rejoice* is heard once
more, but after the opening bars the key is changed from
major to minor ; the music becomes gloomy, and ends
with a pathetic *morendo.*

The subject of the last strain is an allegorical description of the decay in old age of the various parts of the
human frame.

Time will not permit us to review in detail the various

conflicting interpretations of the closing passage proposed
by eminent scholars.   There are more individual opinions—to use the phrase of a Baltimore journalist*—than
a brown mule can pull.   The English Hebraist TAYLOR
regards the closing verses as a formal dirge of death.
Others thought the passage depicted the age of the un-
godly, or the last days of a worn-out sensualist.*   HAHN
believed that the inspired writer described the night of
death before man goes to his eternal home, the kingdom
of glory, attempting to ingraft ideas of the new dispensation on the book of the Old Testament philosopher.

According to UMBREIT, whose views have been
adopted by GINSBURG, Ecclesiastes depicts in these verses
the advance of death under the imagery of an approaching storm which darkens the heavens, startles even men
of power, and puts a stop to all work ; the bird raises its
voice to a shriek, flying low, and fluttering about un-
easily in dread of the coming storm which is gathering
overhead.

KAISER, in his curious little book entitled : *Koheleth,
the collectivum of the Davidic kings in Jerusalem, an historical didactic poem on the downfall of the Jewish state,*
(Erlangen, 1829), explains the twelfth chapter as referring to the downfall of the Jewish state.

A remarkable prophetic exposition is found in the introduction to the Midrash on the Book of Lamentations.
The days of youth are explained as the period of
Israel's prosperity, while the days of evil are referred to
the time of the Babylonian captivity.   The light is the
law, the moon the Sanhedrin, the stars are the Rabbis,
the clouds returning after the rain are the troubles pre-
dicted by Jeremiah, etc., etc.

Some modern commentators explain the clouds to

mean severe attacks of catarrh, or refer them *ad crassos illos ac pituosos senum vapores ex debili ventriculo in ascendentes continuo.* FRANZ DELITZSCH thought the clouds which return after the rain were attacks of sickness and bodily weakness ; the sun was explained by him to be the spirit, and the moon, he thought, represented the soul, while the stars were the five planets symbolizing the five senses.

VAIHINGER pointed out that the similes describing the winter of man's existence were drawn from the winter of Palestine, when heavy rain storms follow one another in rapid succession, darkening the whole face of nature.

C. H. H. WRIGHT (whose valuable commentary on Ecclesiastes I have followed here in sketching the various untenable explanations proposed for the closing section) remarks that the words of Ecclesiastes have been expounded by TENNYSON, when he says in *The Princess* :

> Ah sad and strange, as in dark summer dawns
> The earliest pipe of half-awakened birds
> To dying ears, when unto dying eyes
> The casement slowly grows a glimmering square ;
> So sad, so strange, the days that are no more.

WRIGHT thinks, Ecclesiastes presents two pictures : the one death in life, the other nature re-awakening from its temporary grave. The almond tree is in blossom, and the locusts are crawling out, but in yon chamber the old man is lying, and even the caperberry cannot arouse his failing appetite.

Several old Jewish commentators, as well as BÖTTCHER, GRAETZ, and KÖNIG, regard these three words : *almond*, *locust*, and *caperberry*, as having concealed references to the sexual organs. But FRANZ DELITZSCH was right in stating that Ecclesiastes was no Juvenal or Martial. RENAN said : "Ecclesiastes is a book *de scepticisme élégant.* We may find it bold, or even free, but it is never immoral or obscene. The author is *un galant homme,* but not a *professeur de libertinage.*" We must not, as FRANZ DELITZSCH remarked with reference to GRAETZ, allow our critical nose to degenerate into a hog's snout. BÖTTCHER and KÖNIG think that the almond is a euphemism for φάλλος, while HITZIG explained it to be an allegorical name for the youthful maiden who refuses to give her fruit to the aged man.

But there is no allusion to sexual intercourse, except in the beginning of the twelfth chapter. Instead of *Remember thy Creator in the days of thy youth,* we must translate : *Remember thy well, i. e.,* the mother of thy children; do not neglect your legitimate wife, while you are in possession of your manly vigor, as is shown by the passage in Proverbs 5, 15 and 18 : *Drink waters out of thine own cistern ;* i. e., *let them be only thine own and not strangers with thee, so shall thy fountain be blessed, and thou shalt have joy of the wife of thy youth.*

The word *zěkhór,* "remember," is a specimen of what the Arabs of Syria term *talḥin, i. e.,* the use of words with a concealed meaning. The Hebrew verb *zakár* means, as a rule, "to remember" (properly *to infix,* to impress on the memory), but it may, at the same time, have suggested a denominal verb derived from *zakár,* "male," which is still used in Arabic with the meaning of φάλλος.

I now proceed to give a translation of the final song of Ecclesiastes, adding, in the notes appended, some explanations of the imagery employed by the poet :

11, 9 Rejoice, O youth, in thy childhood,[61]
   And let thy heart cheer thee in the days of thy man-
      hood ;   35
   Walk in the ways of thy heart,
   And in the sight of thine eyes,ᵣ
  10 Banish moroseness from thy heart,
   But keep away evil from thy flesh,ː
   For childhood and manhood are fleeting,[62]   40
12, 1 Remember thy well[63] in the days of thy vigor,
   Ere there come the days of evil,
   And the years draw nigh
   In which thou wilt say I have no pleasure.
  2 Ere is darkened the sun, and the light of the day, 45
   And the moon, and the stars,
   And the clouds return after the rain ;[64]
  3 When the keepers of the house[65] tremble,
   And the men of power[66] bend themselves :
   The grinding maids[67] cease7   50
   And the ladies that look out through the lattices are
      darkened ;[68]
  4 The doors are shut toward the street,ᵛ[69]
   He riseth at the voice of the birds,[70]
   And all the daughters of song are brought low,[71]
  5 He is afraid of that which is high,   55
   And fears are in the way ;[72]
   The almond tree blossometh,[73]
   The locust[74] crawleth along with difficulty,
   The caper-berry breaketh up,[75]
  6 The silver cord[76] is snapped asunder,   60
   The golden bowl[77] crushed in,
   The bucket at the well smashed,[78]
   And the wheel breaketh down at the pit.[79]
  5ᵇ Man is going to his eternal house,
   And the[80] mourners go about in the street,ᵋ   .65
  8 Vanity of vanities,[81] saith Ecclesiastes,

11,8ᵇβ All is vanity, and all that is coming is vanity.ᵅ

11, 9ᵇ (ε) but know that for these things God will bring thee into judgment.

* * *

7, 26 (ζ) I find more bitter than death the woman who is (all) snares, her heart a net, her hands fetters. ‖ He who is good before God will escape her, but the sinner will be caught by her. ‖

27 Behold this have I found, saith Ecclesiastes, (counting) one by one to find out the result: I have found oneᵉⁿ man out of a thousand, but aᵉˡ woman whom my soul sought all the while without finding, I have not found among all those.ᵉ²

* * *

12, 3 (η) because they are few.

* * *

(ϑ) because the sound of the grinding mill is low.ᵉ⁴

* * *

12, 7 (ι) The dust shall return to the earth (to become) what it was, but the spirit will return to God who gave it (*cf*. 3. 20.)

* * *

9 (κ) It might be well to add that Ecclesiastes was a wise man who constantly taught the people knowledge, composing,ᵉ⁵ and thinking out, and arranging many proverbs. Ecclesiastes

10 tried to find pleasant words, but what is written is correct

11 (*words of truth*).ᵉ⁶ "Words of wise men are like the points of goads, but like nails firmly driven in are the verses of a

12 collection,ᵉ⁷ they are given out from one leader."ᵉ⁸ ‖ And it might be well to add: my son, be on your guard against these (sayings), there is no end of making books in great numbers,

13 too much reading wearieth the flesh. ‖ Let us hear the end of all this talk : Fear God and keep His commandments, that

14 is what every man ought to do. God will bring all doings into the judgment upon all that is hidden, whether they be good or evil.

You will admit that this is one of the most beautiful pieces of poetry that was ever written. Now let me add a word in conclusion. I think we may enjoy Ecclesiastes from a literary point of view, without adopting his teaching. In the light of the New Testament it is need-

less to darken the meaning of the Old Testament philosopher. Beware of the leaven of the Pharisees ! There
is nothing covered that will not be uncovered, nor
hidden that shall not be known. Whatsoever ye have
spoken in darkness shall be heard in the light !

(¹) See ARTHUR SCHOPENHAUER'S works, edited by JULIUS FRAUEN-
STÄDT, (Leipzig : Brockhaus) vol. V, p. 526 (= *Parerga and Paralipomena*, vol. I : *Aphorismen zur Lebensweisheit*, chap. VI : *Vom
Unterschiede der Lebensalter*): *Erst im 70. Jahre versteht man ganz
den ersten Vers des Koheleth ; cf. ibid.* p. 525 : *Während der Jüngling
meint, dass Wunder was in der Welt zu holen sei, wenn er nur erfahren
könnte, wo ; ist der Alte vom Kohelethischen "es ist Alles eitel"
durchdrungen und weiss, dass alle Nüsse hohl sind, wie sehr sie auch
vergoldet sein mögen.*

(²) See below, p. 273, n. 39.

(³) Heb. *lĕ-*, *i. e.* the Arabic emphatic *la-* ; *cf. panôh el-harbĕh
wehinnĕh lim'ât,* Haggai 1 , 9 (*contra* WELLHAUSEN, *Skizzen und
Vorarbeiten,* part 5 , Berlin, 1892, p. 168) ; also *lĕkol-'obĕr, 'alâ(i)w
iššôm,* 2 Chr. 7 , 21 ; *hēma lahĕm,* "ipsissimi," Eccl. 3 , 18, &c. See
the abstract of my paper, *A New Hebrew Particle,* in the *Johns Hopkins University Circulars,* May, 1894.

(⁴) Eccl. 9 , 4, is an interpolation, see p. 257, n. *β*.

(⁵) *Cf. e. g.* 2 , 24ᵇ. 26 ; 3 , 13 . 14ᵇ. 17 ; 5 , 6ᵇ. 8 . 18 ; 6 , 6 ; 7 , 13 .
14 . 18ᵇ. 20 . 26ᵇ. 29 ; 8 , 11–13 ; 9 , 3 &c. See also pp. 257 and 263
and compare F. SCHWALLY, *Das Leben nach dem Tode* (Giessen,
1892), p. 106.

(⁶) The same reason prompted the redactors of the Hexateuch to
combine JED with P, because JE could not be suppressed. See my
paper on *The Origin of the Pentateuch,* in the American Oriental Society Proceedings at New York, April, 1894.

(⁷) *Hiob,* nach GEO. HOFFMANN, Professor in Kiel (Kiel, 1891), p. 25.

(⁸) Eccl. 7 , 20 said to be quoted in Rom. 3 , 10 (see STRACK in
HERZOG-PLITT's *Realencyklopädie für protestantische Theologie und
Kirche,* Vol. VII, p. 427, n. *) is an interpolation. Professor PAUL
KLEINERT, of the University of Berlin, enumerates quite a number of
New Testament parallels to the Book of Ecclesiastes (see his paper,
Der Prediger Solomonis, printed in the Annual Report of the Fried-

rich-Wilhelms-Gymnasium, Berlin, 1864, p. 38). Professor KLEINERT compares Matth. 6 , 7 with Eccl. 5 , 1 ; Matth. 6 , 9 and Eccl. 5 , 1 ; M. 6 , 10 and E. 3 , 11 (!) ; M. 6 , 11 and E. 5 , 17 (ἄρτος ἐπιούσιος = hälte!); M. 6 , 12 and E. 7 , 22 ; Rom. 8 , 18 and E. 1 , 2-11 ; John 9 , 4 and E. 9 , 10 ; Matth. 5 , 45 and E. 2 , 14 f. ; Luke 10 , 42 and E. 7 , 18 ; Rom. 2 , 5 f. and E. 12 , 13 ; Eph. 5 , 16 and E. 8 . Most readers will not be able to discover any parallels in the passages cited.

(⁹) I may be allowed to state here that WELLHAUSEN, after having read my remarks on the subject printed in the *Johns Hopkins University Circulars*, No. 90 (June, 1891), p. 115, informed me that he had made the same observation.

(¹⁰) Luke 12 , 22-34 gives the section in its original form and connection ; the parallel in Matth. 6 , 19-34 is a later insertion.

(¹¹) *Cf. e. g.* Luke 12 , 18 and Eccl. 2 , 4 ; Luke 12 , 20ᵇ and Eccl. 2 , 18ᵇ ; and note especially Luke 12 , 27 (=Matth. 6 , 28. 29)—the familiar passage of the lilies of the field and Solomon in all his glory.

(¹²) *Cf.* the well-known ἐσθίε, πῖνε, παῖζε (or rather ὄχεVε; Arrian 2 , 5 : τὸ παῖζε ῥαδιουργότερον ἐγγεγράφθαι ἔφασαν τῷ Ἀσσυρίῳ ὀνόματι), often quoted as the "translation" of the Assyrian inscription on the monument of (Sardanapalus, or rather) Sennacherib at Anchialos ; see *e. g.* Strabo, § 672 (IΔ, 5 , 9) and ED. MEYER, *Geschichte des Alterthums*, vol. I (Stuttgart, 1884), p. 473, n. 1.

(¹³) Matth. 6 , 33 . 34.

(¹⁴) SCHOPENHAUER'S *Sämmtliche Werke*, ed. FRAUENSTÄDT, vol. III, p. 713 ; *cf.* FRAUENSTÄDT'S *Schopenhauer-Lexikon* (Leipzig, 1871) vol. I, p. 89.

(¹⁵) SCHOPENHAUER refers twice to the well-known passage, Eccl. 7 , 4, translated in our Authorized Version : *Sorrow is better than laughter ; for by the sadness of the countenance the heart is made better.* Vol. V, p. 78 (i. e. *Parerga*, Vol. I, *Fragmente zur Geschichte der Philosophie*, § 12) SCHOPENHAUER remarks : *Spinoza verwirft alle tristitia unbedingt, obschon sein Al. T. ihm sagte: "Es ist Trauern besser denn Lachen ; denn durch Trauern wird das Herz gebessert (Koh. 7, 4) ; and in vol. III, p. 731 (Die Welt als Wille und Vorstellung, Zweiter Band, Ergänzungen zum vierten Buch, Kaß. 49 : Die Heilsordnung) we read : Ja schon der noch jüdische aber so philosophische Koheleth sagt mit Recht : "Es ist Trauern besser, denn Lachen ; denn durch Trauern wird das Herz gebessert."* (7, 4). The words : *for by the sadness of the countenance the heart is made better*, are a theological interpolation, just as the second half of the preceding verse : *for that is the end of all men, and the living can lay it to his heart*. Two other passages in Ecclesiastes quoted by SCHOPENHAUER are 4 , 6, and 7 , 11. In his *Preisschrift über die Grundlage der Moral, I, Einleitung, § 1 ; Ueber das Problem* (vol. IV, p. 110) we read : *Da bleibt mir nichts übrig als an den Spruch von Koheleth (4 , 6) zu erinnern : "Es ist besser eine Hand voll mit Ruhe, denn beide Fäuste voll mit Mühe und Eitelkeit."* Eccl. 4 , 6 must be combined with 4 , 7 ; 5 , 9–11 ; 6 , 7–9 (4 , 5 as well as 10 , 8 . 15 are glosses to 4 , 6).—The second passage, Eccl. 7 , 11, is mentioned by SCHOPENHAUER, vol. VI, 462 (= *Parerga & Paralipomena*, Vol. II, c. xix : *Zur Metaphysik des Schönen und Aesthetik, § 221*) : *Ein Philosoph kann nicht wohl ein anderes Gewerbe daneben treiben ; da nun aber das Geldverdienen mit der Philosophie seine anderweitigen und bekannten grossen Nachtheile hat, wegen welcher die Alten dasselbe zum Merkmale des Sophisten, im Gegensatz des Philosophen, machten; so ist Salomo zu loben, wenn er sagt : " Weisheit ist gut mit einem Erbgute, und hilft, dass einer sich der Sonne freuen kann " (Koheleth 7, 12)*. The passage, however, means : *Wisdom is as good as (cf. 2 , 16) an inheritance, yea better, too, for them that see the sun, cf.* A. V. margin, and R. V.   Eccl. 7 , 11 . 12 must be combined with 7 , 19 ; 8 , 1 ; 9 , 17ª ; 10 , 2 . 3 . 12 . 13 (10 , 20ᵇ is a gloss to 7 , 12). V. 10 , 1ᵇ belongs to 7 , 16 (cf. 8 , 14 . 10 ; 7 , 15–18 ; 9 , 11–12 ;—8 , 11–13 is a theological gloss to 8 , 14 &c.), while 10 , 1ª must be combined with 9 , 18ᵇ.

([16]) *Cf.* FRANZ DELITZSCH, *Commentar über die Genesis*, fourth edition (Leipzig, 1872), p. 532, n. 16.   See also LEVY'S *Neuhebr. Wörterbuch*, vol. III (Leipzig, 1883), p. 3ᵇ below, and p. 60.   In his *Neuer Commentar über die Genesis* (Leipzig, 1887) p. 68, n. 1 (= p 104 of the English edition) DELITZSCH'S suggests that the words refer not to Rabbi Meir's copy of the Pentateuch, but to his recitation of the Thorah ; but this explanation is untenable.

([17]) *Cf.* Job (5 , 7ª) ; 7 , (7ª . 9ᵇ .) 16ᵇ ; 8 , 9 ; 10 . 18ª . 19ᵇ ; (14 , 1 . 2) ; 21 , 7 . 23 . 25 &c.   According to SIEGFRIED, in the new critical edition of the *Sacred Books of the Old Testament* (Baltimore, 1893), 5 , 6 . 7 is an interpolation belonging rather to the range of thought of c. 3, and 7 , 7ª . 9ᵇ as well as 14 , 1 . 2 represent *parallel compositions*, while the authenticity of the other passages is not questioned.

([18]) *Cf.* Eccl. 1 , 2 ; 3 , 18 . 21 , 4 , 2 . 3 ; 6 , 3 ; 7 , 15 ; 8 , 10 ; 9 , 11 . 12 &c.

(¹⁹) LUTHER seems to have been struck with the fact that the work (*e. g.* Eccl. 3, 9 ff.) exhibits the most divergent views side by side without any logical connection.

(²⁰) The text has since been translated, on the basis of my explanation, by Dr. MARTIN JÄGER, in his paper *Assyrische Räthsel und Sprüchwörter*, printed in the recent volume of our *Beitr. zur Assyriologie*, p. 281), as well as by BRÜNNOW in his review of the *Beiträge*, ZA VIII, 130. JÄGER translates: "*Seitdem ihr Gott sich hinausgewendet hat, ist eingezogen in die Niederlassung der Frevel, ist sesshaft geworden die Bosheit; nicht wird alt der Fromme; der Verständige, Weise, auf dessen Weisheit sein Herr nicht achtete, und der Edle, den sein Herr vergass, sein Mangel tritt ein, nicht erhebt sich wieder sein Haupt.*" BRÜNNOW proposes the following rendering: "*Wenn ihr Gott (Götterbild?) in Verfall gerathen ist, dann tritt ein in das bit nadî* (J. wohl richtig: *Niederlassung*) *der Frevler* (oder *Zerstörer*), *der böse aššab; nicht wird er alt werden lassen den Frommen, Verständigen, Weisen, dessen Weisheit sein Herr nicht (mehr) merkt; und jeder Gewaltthätige, den sein Herr verlassen hat, dessen Begehr wird erfüllt, und es erhebt sich sein Haupt.*"—HALÉVY (*Mélanges de critique et d'histoire relatifs au peuples sémitiques*, Paris, 1883, p. 328) divides the passage into two proverbs. The meaning of the first is said to be: *l'homme sensé évite le malheur par sa prévoyance* (p. 333 below), and according to p. 334 the second sentence *exhorte les supérieurs à se montrer reconnaisants envers leurs serviteurs fidèles.* HALÉVY's translation of these proverbs is often incorrect, but he has anticipated some of JÄGER's best interpretations; he also considers (*contra* BRÜNNOW, ZA VIII, 128 below) *mannu inamdin* the equivalent of Heb. *mi yitten* (BA II, 279 below), and for the first proverb translated by JÄGER: *ina lâ nâki mi erât ina lâ akâli mi kubrat*, he suggests substantially the same rendering as BRÜNNOW (ZA. VIII, 127). The interrogative pronoun does not indicate a riddle: it is a rhetorical question. HALÉVY's and BRÜNNOW's explanation is undoubtedly preferable to JÄGER's translation, DELITZSCH's approval (*Wörterb.* 382, 3) nothwithstanding.

(²¹) SAYCE adds in a footnote: "This seems to be quoted from a hymn describing the return of Oannes to the Persian Gulf." On p. 132 of his *Hibbert Lectures* for 1887 (*On the Origin and Growth of Religion as illustrated by the Religion of the Ancient Babylonians*, second edition, London, 1888) SAYCE remarks: "A native fragment of the legend has, it is probable, been accidentally preserved among a series of extracts from various Accadian works, in a bilinqual reading.

book compiled for the use of Semitic students of Accadian. It reads
thus : ' To the waters their god has returned ; into the house of (his)
repose the protector descended. The wicked weaves spells, but the
sentient one grows not old. A wise people repeated his wisdom. The
unwise and the slave (*literally* person) the most valued of his master
forgot him ; there was need of him and he restored (his) decrees (?) ' "
The mark of interrogation is added by SAYCE himself, but I approve
of it.

(²²) It is interesting to compare with this translation the views set
forth by SAYCE in his inaugural address, delivered before the Assyrio-
logical Section of the Ninth International Congress of Orientalists, held
in London, 5th to 12th Sept., 1892 (*cf. Transactions*, vol. II, London,
1893, p. 175) : "What is nonsense in English, or French, or German,
is equally nonsense in Assyrian. The old scribes who have bequeathed to us the literature of Babylonia and Assyria must have intended that the words they wrote should have a meaning. They
would never have wasted their time in writing nonsense, and we may
therefore feel quite sure that if the translations we make of their
works do not yield a clear sense, the fault lies not with the original
author, but with his modern translator." I have advocated this principle for years (*cf.* my remarks in *Johns Hopkins University Circulars*, Feb., '89, No. 69, p. 18*, 2), but, with all due respect for the wonderful versatility of our great modern polyhistor, I never expected
SAYCE to echo my feelings in this respect. He who sits in a glass
house ought not to throw stones! (*Cf.* ZIMMERN's note in ZA. V,
16, 1). Nor can I endorse SAYCE's statement made on p. 173 of his
presidential address, that the translation of an Assyrian text made by
a competent scholar twenty years ago is not far behind that which is
made to-day. I am inclined to believe with JENSEN (*Die Kosmologie
der Babylonier*, Strassburg, 1890, p. 368) that five years of Assyriolog-
ical research mean more than an ordinary lustrum. In view of this
fact BEZOLD's remark (ZA. VIII, 140) concerning my translation of
the Sumerian family laws, which I published more than thirteen years
since, is rather strange. My translation was the "only correct interpretation" compared with OPPERT's explanation (see HOMMEL's
Semiten, p. 499, n. 259). It was undoubtedly more correct than
BEZOLD's famous rendering of *ruppi ši zeri-m šundili nannabi*, published in 1886 (*cf.* ZA. I, 42 ; *Beitr. z. Ass.* I, 132, n. *). Minor im-
provements in the explanation of certain terms (*e. g.* ZK. II, 272, 1 ;
cf. ZA. VII, 215 ;—ZIMMERN. *Busspsalmen* 59, 5 ; DELITZSCH, *Assyr.
Wörterbuch* 76 ; 215, 5 ; *Beitr. z. Assyriol.* I, 16. 124. 315) have not

affected my views regarding the general sense of the collection of
laws. Dr. MEISSNER's *Beiträge zum altbabylonischen Privatrecht,* is
undoubtedly a book of uncommon value, and full of new information,
but his translation of the first four family laws contains nothing new.
BEZOLD's remark in ZA. VIII, 130, is, therefore, just as gratuitous as
his note 2 on p. xxv of his *Oriental Diplomacy.* I am sorry that I
have no time to reply to BEZOLD's allusions at the conclusion of his
review of Dr. MEISSNER's work (ZA. VIII, 142), or his note on p. 185
of ZA. VI. I will add, however, that most of BEZOLD's remarks directed against DELITZSCH and myself seem to be due rather to some
personal feeling than to an earnest desire to promote the interests of
cuneiform research. It will be well to compare in this connection
the statement prefixed to the second part of my edition of the *Nimrod
Epic* (Leipzig, 1891).

(²³) SAYCE adds in the footnotes: *lacunæ,* but the text is complete,
at least in the Assyrian column. We must read, however, in the last
two lines: *ib-ba-ai-ii xi-ii.x-ta-iu-ma in-na-ii ri-is-su.* The character
after *ib-ba-* in the last but one line cannot be *li* (II R.); STRASS-
MAIER, No. 3371, reads *ib-ba-ii* instead of *ib-ba-ai-ii;* the *ii* after *in-
na* in the last line is quite clear, besides we have in the Sumerian
column traces of the ideogram for *naiŭ :* GA + TU-*la* (i. e. *il-la*), TU-*la*
is certain, and of the preceding GA we have at least the upper slanting wedge. I collated the text (K. 4347; *cf.* BEZOLD's *Catalogue,* vol.
II, p. 621) in 1891. It is a large tablet of light yellow clay, the obverse consists of 5 fragments, and the reverse of 7. In the right-hand
lower corner of the convex side, we find the proverb quoted by
STRASSMAIER in his *Alphabetisches Verzeichniss,* No. 6896: *âlu ia
kakkaĭu lâ dannu, nakru ina pân abulliĭu ul ippaṭṭar,* "the enemy will
not be scattered in front of the gate of a city whose weapons are not
strong." For *nakru ippaṭar* compare *ta.xazaĭunu raksu taptur* in col.
I, l. 24 of the broken Esarhaddon prism (III R. 15) = SCHRADER's
Keilinschriftliche Bibliothek, vol. II (Berlin, 1890), p. 142 Dr.
WINCKLER states there (p. 140, n. 3): "the text was published for the
first time III R. 15. 16," although III R. 15 expressly refers to LAY-
ARD's *Inscriptions,* pl. 54-58. *Cf.* also *Hebraica,* IV, 149, and my re-
marks in *Beitr. zur Assyriologie,* I, 167, n. †. For *patâru* "to
desert" in the Amarna texts from Jerusalem, see JENSEN-ZIMMERN,
ZA. VI, 247, n. 7. II R. 16 , 16 f., we must read *ta-pa-ak-ka,* not *ip-pa-
ak-ka,* as I suggested in SCHRADER's KAT⁴ 76 , 11 (*cf.* my *Beitr. zur
Assyr. Lautlehre,* Göttingen, 1883, p. 103, and *Beitr. zur Assyriologie,*
I, 2).

(²⁴) Literally : *darkness ; cf.* Eccl. 5 , 16 ; Psalm 18 , 29 ; Is. 15 , 10, &c.

(²⁵) BRÜNNOW (ZA. VIII, 129) seems to think it impossible that *aššab* represents a permansive form ; but *aššab* is a form like *kabbar* "he is long," or *qattan* "he is short " (MEISSNER, *Altbabyl. Privatrecht*, Leipzig, 1893, p. 152, n. 1), 3 f. pl. *qattanû* (quoted by BEZOLD, ZA. VIII, 142, n. 1) ; cf. *allakâ birkâ'a, lâ ânixâ šepâ'a*, &c., translated by JÄGER, *Beitr. z. Assyr.* II, 285 ; *cf.* JÄGER'S thesis, p. 21 = BA. I, 463, n. *. JÄGER quotes there the permansive forms *raggam* (ASKT. 87, 61) and *gammar (ibid.* 128, 62), but for *raggam* we must read *raksat*, and *gamrat* instead of *gammar ; cf.* JENSEN'S remarks in his review of the *Beiträge : Deutsche Literatur Zeitung* (Berlin) Oct. 3, '91, col. 1451 below.

(²⁶) Literally : *wise, understanding*, Assyr. *xassu ;* see *e. g.* Job 28, 28 (a polemical interpolation) : *Behold the fear of the Lord, that is wisdom ; and to depart from evil is understanding.* Cf. also Deut. 4, 6; Sir. 24 (NÖLDEKE, *Alttestamentliche Literatur*, p. 167), &c., and Heb. *nabâl* "fool," *i. e.* "irreligious," Psalm 14 , 1, &c. In the same way *holiness* and *devotion* is expressed in Assyrian by the words for *skill* and *wisdom (ummânu, nîmêqu, emqu).* The epithet of the Babylonian Noah, *Atra-xasis* (or *Xasis-atra =* Ξίσουθρος) must, therefore, be interpreted to mean *most holy*, or *most religious*, a *just and perfect* man (Heb. *iš ṣaddîq tamîm*, Gen. 6 , 9 ; *cf.* KAT² 66 , 4), not *eximie sollers* (DELITZSCH in BAER'S *Daniel*, p. vi ; *Assyr. Wörterb.* 167 , 91 ; 168 , n. 2 ; JENSEN, *Kosmol.*, 385 below ; JEREMIAS, *Izdubar-Nimrod*, 36 ; MUSS-ARNOLT in *The Biblical World*, Chicago, 1894, p. 112, n. 10. *Cf. Beitr. z. Assyr.* II, 401, and Am. Or. Soc. Proc., April, 1893, p. ix below. See also the conclusion of my paper, *On two passages of the Chaldean Flood Tablet*, Am. Or. Soc. Proc., April, 1894. The well-known phrase *mâr ummâni* in l. 86 of the Deluge text (*cf.* ZA. I, 34 ; ASKT. 209 = IV R.² 12, 18, etc.) must, of course, be interpreted in the same way.

(²⁷) It is true that Assyrian *ulabbar* is causative and means properly *he causes to grow old* (ZA. VIII, 129, no. 3) but we must supply : *his days, cf.* Heb. *ma'rîkh* Eccl. 7 , 15 ; 8 , 12 and Assyr. *urrikû ûme* in the first fragment of the Creation series ; *urrik* is causative like *ubbit*, "I destroyed," or *uddiš*, "I renewed," &c., but *urrikû ûme* means "a long time elapsed," *cf.* Heb. *lêmâ'an ya'rîkhûn yamêkha* in the fifth commandment, Ex. 20 , 12 ; Deut. 5 , 16 *(cf.* also 25 , 15). See GE-SENIUS-KAUTZSCH²⁵, § 53 . 3, remark.

(²⁸) Assyr. *lâ xassu.* The use of *xassu* here after the *xassu* in the line above : *ul nlabbar xassu*, is, of course, intentional paronomasia ; *cf.* Dr. I. M. CASANOWICZ's *Notes on Paronomasia in the Old Testament*, printed in No. 98 of the *Johns Hopkins University Circulars* (May, 1892), p. 96 and his article on the same subject in the *Journal of Biblical Literature*, vol. XII, Part 2 (Boston, 1894). See also my *Note on the Protevangelium* in the *Johns Hopkins Univ. Circ.* No. 106 (June, 1893) p. 107[b].

([29]) I read *innaïl ressu* = *reï-iu, i. e.* Heb, *reï* "poverty," *cf. roï* "bitterness," Lam. 3 , 5, &c., and for *innaïl* 2 Chr. 32 , 23 (*uuyinnassê* "he was magnified ") and 2 S. 5 , 12 (*nissê mamlakhtô* "he exalted his kingdom "). *Reïu* or *resu* (*cf.* BEZOLD's inaugural dissertation, p. 29) appears V R 18 , 15 ff. as a synonym of *xuïâxu*, "famine" (II, 7 , 5 ; V, 39 , 7) and *uïrtu* "oppression" (ZIMMERN, *Busspsalmen* 83 , 1).—For *naïû ïa reïi* "to lift up the head," see II R 26 , 57. *naïû ïa reïi* may, of course, have a double meaning, as in Gen. 40 , 13 . 19 . 20. The common Assyrian expression is *ullû ïa reïi* (*cf.* DELITZSCH, *Prolegomena*, 155 ; *Wörterbuch* 425). *naïû ïa reïi* (*cf.* ZA. V, 15 . 139, n. 7) and *ullû ïa reïi* are synonymous with *ïaqû ïa reïi* (II, 30, 1 ; IV[2], 60[a], B 5). but *ïakânu ïa reïi* (or *qaqqadi*) has a different meaning ; it means (like the English *to make head*) : to resist, *e. g.* NE. 51 , 17 : *Istar ana nakrïsu ul isâkan qaqqadsa* "Istar could not make head against its (the city's) enemy." See my paper *On some passages of the Chaldean Flood tablet*, in the American Oriental Society's Proceedings at New York, April, 1894.

([30]) See C. II. H. WRIGHT, *The Book of Koheleth, commonly called Ecclesiastes* (London, 1883), pp. 31, 56, &c. It gives me much pleasure to state here that I consider WRIGHT'S work the most useful commentary on the book of Ecclesiastes. His exegesis is based throughout on the valuable commentary of FRANZ DELITZSCH, but it is an intelligent reproduction of DELITZSCH'S views ; The remarks of my late venerable teacher are not sadly misrepresented as they appear in nearly all the English editions of DELITZSCH'S works. I am indebted to WRIGHT'S book for much useful information, in certain cases, if I remember correctly,—I have not read the book since 1891—I have been able to quote several of his statements *verbatim*, as I am always glad to follow a conservative theologian as far as possible, especially so excellent a scholar as C. H. H. WRIGHT. I regret that my time does not permit me at present, three years after the preparation of my popular lecture, to indicate in detail what statements I have been able to borrow from WRIGHT'S book *cf.*

my remarks in the programme of our new translation of the Bible, printed in No. 98 of the *Johns Hopkins University Circulars*, May, 1892, p. 87^b, § 15). I need hardly say, however, that my critical views are totally different from WRIGHT'S attitude towards the book.

(³¹) *Cf.* the abstract of Dr. CHRISTOPHER JOHNSTON'S paper on *The Alleged Grecisms of Ecclesiastes*, printed in No. 90 of the *Johns Hopkins University Circulars* (June, 1891), p. 118^b. For *the Berlin theologian ibid.* p. 119^a, l. 3, read *the Tübingen philosopher*, (ED-MUND PFLEIDERER, *Die Philosophie des Heraklit von Ephesus*, Berlin, 1886, pp. 255-258; not his elder brother, OTTO PFLEIDERER).

(³²) *Cf. e. g.* 4 , 13-16; 9 , 13-16, &c. D. HEIMDÖRFER (*Der "Prediger Salomonis" in historischer Beleuchtung*, 2d ed., Hamburg, 1892), p. 16, refers the passage 4 , 13-16 to Alexander Jannæus (B. C. 104-78); *cf.* KÖNIG, *Einleit.*, 433, n. 1. I would translate the four verses as follows: A poor but wise (*cf. supra* n. 26) youth is preferable to an old and doting king [*who will no longer take advice*], even if he (the youth) should have come to the throne from a family of outcasts, [*even if he should have been born poor in his kingdom*] (*i. e.* in the land that subsequently became his kingdom). I saw all that walk under the sun (*i. e.*) [*the living*] on the side of the youth (*i. e.*) [*the other one who stepped in his* (the old ruler's) *place*] (stealing the hearts of the people as Absalom stole the hearts of the people of Israel, *cf.* 2 S. 15 , 6). There was no end of all the people, [*of all of them before whom he stood*] (who accepted him as their leader), but the (people of a) younger generation will not be so enthusiastic about him. For this also (the popular enthusiasm for a new ruler) is temporary and transitory. The bracketed passages in *italics*, [*who will no longer take advice*] &c., represent explanatory glosses on the Hebrew text, the comments in parentheses *e. g.* (the youth) have been added by myself. The idea that everything in this world is temporary and transitory, is the keynote of the so-called catalogue of times and seasons, c. 3 , v. 1 ff. *Lakkōl zēmān we'êth lĕkhōl hēphêç tăhath hassamaiim* does not mean *everything has its proper time and season*, but *everything lasts but a certain time*.

(³³) See DRIVER, *Introduction to the Literature of the Old Testament*, New York, 1891, p. 445, and compare the glossary in DE-LITZSCH'S commentary, or in WRIGHT'S *Ecclesiastes.*

(³⁴) Cf. HUGONIS GROTII *Annotationes in Vetus Testamentum* (ed. VOGEL., Halae, 1775), p. 434 (*Ad Ecclesiasten*, Caput I): *Cum et initium et finis satis monstrent quod sit scriptoris propositum, ob eas*

*causas (Et aiunt Hebraei) merito in canonem receplus est. Ego tamen
Salomonis esse non puto, sed scriptum serins sub illius Regis, lanquam
poenitentia ducti, nomine. Argumentum eius rei habeo multa vocab-
ula, quae non alibi quam in Daniele, Esdra et Chaldaeis interpretibus
reperias.*

(⁸⁵) See above note (5).

(⁸⁶) In his dissertation *De Aramaismis libri Coheleth*, (1860).

(⁸⁷) Nor can the author of the Book of Deuteronomy, who introduces Moses as having spoken the discourses contained in the book,
be held to be guilty of literary fraud or dishonesty; *cf.* DRIVER, *Introduction*, &c., p. 85, and W. ROBERTSON SMITH's *The Old Testament in the Jewish Church*, second edition, London, 1892, p. 395.

(⁸⁸) See above, p. 263, footnote κ.

(⁸⁹) *Cf.* T. K. CHEYNE, *The Origin and Religious Contents of the
Psalter*, London, 1891, p. 193 : From the point of view of the history
of art, not less than from that of the history of religion, the supposition that we have Davidic psalms presents insuperable difficulties.

(⁴⁰) According to CORNILL, *Einleitung*, p. 316, psalms 44; 74; 79;
83 are certainly Maccabean ; *cf. ibid.* p. 221 ; CHEYNE, *l. c.* 99; and,
on the other hand, W. ROBERTSON SMITH, *l. c.*, p. 437, and KÖNIG,
Einl., p. 403.

(⁴¹) See ED. MEYER's *Geschichte des Alterthums*, vol. I (Stuttgart,
1884), p. 308; STADE's *Geschichte des Volkes Israel*, vol. I (Berlin,
1887), pp. 305 . 311, &c. (printed in 1884); WELLHAUSEN, *Sketch of
the History of Israel and Judah*, third edition (London, 1891), p. 54
=*Skizzen und Vorarbeiten, Heft 1* (Berlin, 1884), p. 28.

(⁴²) It is possible that even a man like WELLHAUSEN may know as
little about the duplex hero of ROBERT LOUIS STEVENSON's romance
of that name as he knew about the two distinguished French poli-
ticians, CARREL & GIRARDIN, with whom RENAN, in his *Histoire
du peuple Israel*, compared the prophet Isaiah (see WELLHAUSEN's
most interesting review of RENAN's *History of Israel* in the *Deutsche
Literatur-Zeitung*, April 6, 1889, p. 512), but my lecture was, of
course, intended for an American audience, just as RENAN wrote his
history principally for French readers. *Cf.* below the remarks at the
end of note (60). Wellhausen says (*l. c.*): *Jesaias haben wir uns
(nach Renan) vorzustellen wie Carrell oder Girardin ; ein wahres
Glück für den heferenten, dass er sich von diesen beiden gewiss hoch
bedeutenden Männern durchaus keine Vorstellung machen kann.*

(⁴³) *Cf. e. g.* 3 , 9–15, and see above p. 258, n. (δ) ; 12 , 9, n. (κ) and n. (ζ).

(⁴⁴) *Ecclesiastes philologice et critice illustratus*, Leyden, 1784.

(⁴⁵) A clear case is *e. g.* 2 , 11–23. Here we must evidently arrange the verses in the following order: 11 . 12ᵇ . 19 . 18 . 20–23 . 12ᵃ . 13–17. 24–26. The first hemistich of v. 12 (note the same beginning of vv. 11 and 12: *u-panthi ānt*) interrupts the connection and is out of place in its present position ; v. 12ᵇ *ki mi ha'adhām keyyabhô aharâi*) connects immediately with v. 11, and is continued in v. 19 (*u-mt*, &c.). The last five words of v. 12: *hammelckh eth asher kebâr 'asûhû*, i. e., "the king, he means the one whom they had appointed long before" (as his successor) are a gloss, also v. 19ᵇ (*weyîslât—haïïemeï*), 16ᵇ (*beïekkebhâr—hakkesîl*), and 18ᵇ (*ïc'annthennû—aharâi*), as well as 21. The latter verse belongs to 6 , 1 ff. *Cf.* the remark at the conclusion of note (15) on p. 265.

(⁴⁶) Der Prediger über den Wert des Daseins. Wiederherstellung des bisher zerstückelten Textes, Uebersetzung und Erklärung. Innsbruck, 1884, p. 3.

(⁴⁷) For the quires of ancient manuscript compare C. R. Gregory's instructive paper, *The Quires in Greek Manuscripts*, printed in *The American Journal of Philology*, vol. VII (Baltimore, 1886), p. 27 (*cf.* the *Comptes-Rendus* of the Paris *Académie des Inscriptions et Belles-Lettres*, July–August, 1885, pp. 261–8.

(⁴⁸) *Hiob nach* Geo. Hoffmann, Kiel, 1891, p. 29.

(⁴⁹) Parentheses, *e. g.* (all) l. 3, or (ships) l. 15, indicate supplementary words necessary for the English translation, but not expressed in the Hebrew original. The lines printed in the footnotes under the text contain the various interpolations, the parallels (‖) marking different strata of glosses. See *Johns Hopkins University Circulars*, No. 90 (June, 1891), p. 115ᵇ; *cf. ibid.*, No. 98 (May, 1992), p. 88ᵇ § 34.

(⁵⁰) It is all fate and predestination, so you need not have any scruples about it. Do not mourn and live in seclusion.

(⁵¹) This is all we can expect in this world, but this knowledge ought not to make us despondent or inactive.

(⁵²) Do not be too anxious about the future. You must run some risk if you want to succeed in this world. Act like a merchant who sends his grain to distant lands across the sea. Do not be timid, but cautious. Do not put all your eggs in one basket, do not ship all your goods in one vessel. Be prepared for all contingencies, for we cannot control the future.

(^{33}) Unforeseen occurrences out of the range of ordinary calculation are liable to happen at any time, but if you do not dare to run any risk you cannot accomplish anything. The simplest thing we undertake is attended with risk.

(^{34}) It is the same verb from which the word for "knife" *sakkîn* is derived. The word *miskên* "poor" (French *mesquin*) has no connection with this stem; it is an Assyrian loan-word derived from *muškînu* "humble, miserable, beggar," the participle of the Shaphel of the intensive stem *škînu* (ZA. VII, 354), *i. e.* Heb. *hithpallêl bekawwânâh*.

(^{35}) The risk is not so great, but then it requires a greater effort.

(^{36}) Do not lock the stable door after the steed is stolen. All your precautions help you nothing if you miss the proper time. You must watch the right moment. At the same time you must not be over-cautious, otherwise you will never accomplish anything.

(^{37}) Work whenever you can: constant occupation is a blessing in this world.

(^{38}) The two verses 7 and 8 belong to 6, 6. *Cf.* the conclusion of note (15).

(^{39}) See the Baltimore *American* of March 31, 1890 (article on the ARCHER defalcation.)

(^{40}) If the passage does not depict the last days of a worn-out sensualist, it is evident at least that the contemporaries of the author must have been quite degenerated: the old age of real healthy individuals (*e. g.* members of an uncivilized tribe) is not marred by the symptoms enumerated. Nervous degeneration is, of course, not a new *fin de siècle* phenomenon: it has existed at all ages; see Prof. ERB's academic address *Ueber die wachsende Nervosität unserer Zeit* (Heidelberg, 1894), p. 12, and *cf. ibid.*, p. 19, the remarks of the great specialist on the neuropathic diathesis of the Semites, especially the Jews. The allegoric description of the last days of a degenerated individual could not have been written unless degeneration existed for several generations before the time of Ecclesiastes, nor could the author have composed the passage unless he combined great literary talent with comprehensive medical knowledge: he must have been a physician, a Jewish WEIR MITCHELL (*cf. supra*, p. 273, n. 42).

(^{41}) The following verses form the basis of the well known German students' song, *Gaudeamus igitur*, which was originally a penitential song of two stanzas.

(⁶²) Amuse yourself while you are young, and try to be in good spirits. Do what you feel inclined to, and enjoy what pleases your eye. Be no hermit or ascetic, but do not ruin your health! Try to build up a family while you are in the full possession of your manly vigor! Do not neglect your legitimate wife!

(⁶³) See above p. 261. Prof. GILDERSLEEVE called my attention to the fact that Herondas employed the same metaphor. Prof. GILDER-SLEEVE writes me (March 17, 1894) : "The lines to which I referred when Herondas was first discovered run (Mim. I, 24 . 25) :

δέκ' εἰσὶ μῆνες οὐδὲ γράμμα σοι πέμπει
'αλλ' ἐκλέλησται καὶ πέπωκεν ἐκ καινῆς

The ellipsis to καινῆς is uncertain, and the marginal note is variously read. Is the ellipsis κρήνης, or κύλικος, or simply γυναικός, or something worse? At all events the hydraulic figure remains. *Das weib als* ῎Ερωτος κύπελλον *ist ein Bild, das der griechischen Erotik ganz geläufig war* (Crusius, *Untersuchungen zu den Mimiamben des Herondas*, p. 7.). In his recently published translation Crusius renders : *Neue Becher wirken ihm* and the ellipsis of κύλικος is perhaps the more natural. Still the appositeness of the parallel is hardly diminished. The main thing is the πέπωκεν. See Crusius, *l. c.*"

(⁶⁴) The sun is the sunshine of childhood when everything seems bright and happy ; the moon is symbolical of the more tempered light of boyhood and early manhood, while the stars indicate the sporadic moments of happiness in mature age. More and more the number of rainy days increases, but seldom interrupted by bright moments. And when we are going down the hill there is no sunshine after the rain, but the clouds return, and everything seems painted gray on gray.

(⁶⁵) The hands.

(⁶⁶) The bones, especially the backbone.

(⁶⁷) He loses his teeth.

(⁶⁸) The eyes begin to lose their luster, and sight becomes dim.

(⁶⁹) Te exits are barred, *i. e.*, secretions are insufficient, or vitiated, or cease ; he begins to suffer from constipation and retention (*ischuria*). In the morning prayer of the Jews there is a passage : "Blessed be thou, O Lord, who hast wisely formed man and created in him many openings and orifices."

(⁷⁰) His sleep is short, he awakens when the birds begin to chirp at daybreak, at cock-crowing.

(⁷¹) He is unable to perceive sounds distinctly.

(⁷²) He hates to climb a hill, or to go upstairs, and dreads a walk.

(⁷³) His hair turns hoary. It is true that the almond blossoms are pink at first, but before they fall off they become white as snow. BODENSTEDT in his *1001 Days in the East* (II, 237,) speaks of the white blossoms of the almond tree as falling down like snowflakes.

(⁷⁴) We would say *chrysalis; cf.* Nah 3 , 15: the cankerworm casteth off its skin and flieth away.

(⁷⁵) The soul is freed from the body as the butterfly emerges from the chrysalis.

(⁷⁶) The spinal cord.

(⁷⁷) The brain.

(⁷⁸) The heart loses its power to propel the blood through the body.

(⁷⁹) The water wheel, *i. e.*, the whole machinery comes to a stop, and this stoppage means dissolution.

(⁸⁰) The hired mourners (*qui conducti plorant in funere,* Hor. Ars Poet. 431).

(⁸¹) Prop. *transitoriness.* How utterly transitory is everything!

(⁸²) *ideal.*

(⁸³) Quoted by SCHOPENHAUER, vol. IV, p. 32 (*Ueber den Willen in der Natur : Physiologie und Pathologie*) : *Der geniale Koheleth sagt :* "*unter Tausend habe ich e i n e n Menschen gefunden, aber kein Weib unter allen diesen*" Eccl. 7 , 29 is an interpolation : the author of the original book was no misogynist, *cf.* 9 , 9 (see above p. 257, l. 6), also 12 , 1 (p. 262, l. 41).

(⁸⁴) The digestive apparatus does not work.

(⁸⁵) In metrical form, *cf.* Arabic *wazn* and *mîzân* "meter." The first verb refers to the poetic form of the book, the second to the contents, the third to the arrangement of the whole.

(⁸⁶) He never sacrificed the matter to the form.

(⁸⁷) Lit. *the lords of the assembly,* i. e. *members of an association* (*cf.* HALÉVY, *Recherches bibliques,* pp. 344-350).

(⁸⁸) An isolated maxim, a single proverb, is like the point of an ox-goad ; it pricks one particular spot for a moment, urging on and stimulating, but has no lasting effect. Sayings, however, which are systematically arranged in a special collection forming a connected whole are as impressive as nails firmly driven in. They infix themselves for ever in your memory, just as firmly as nails driven into a board or the like : they have a firm hold on you. This is also said with reference to the relative difficulty of memorizing isolated sayings as contained in the book of Proverbs, on the one hand, and the systematic treatise of Ecclesiastes, on the other. It is much harder to learn the book of Proverbs by heart (owing to the lack of connection between the individual verses) than the book of Ecclesiastes which is written by one shepherd or teacher, on a definite plan and with a definite object in view.

ERRATA

TO PP. 202 TO 241.

[Owing to an unforseen mishap certain corrections to be made for these sheets were omitted. The kind indulgence of the reader is solicited.]

Page 205, Note ‡—Read : Rev. instead of Rer.

Page 208, Note, l. 3—Read : Pend d'Oreilles instead of send d'Oreilles.

Page 209, Note *, l. 6—Read : Quichua instead of Guichua.

   "   "   "   l. 11—*Ibid.*

Page 220, Note, l. 2—Read : Gubernatis instead of Gubematis.

   "   " l. 14—Read : Sîmûrgh instead of Srgmuîh.

Page 222, Note †, l. 3—Read : Rev. instead of Ber.

Page 224, l. 7—Read : orders instead of order.

Page 227, l. 4—Read : stage instead of state.

Page 237, l. 8—Read : igneous instead of ligneous.

www.ingramcontent.com/pod-product-compliance
Lightning Source LLC
Chambersburg PA
CBHW020509270326
41926CB00008B/796